TRAVELS IN TIME

Colin M. Barron

Other Books by
Colin M. Barron

TRAVELS IN TIME

The Story of
Time Travel Cinema

Colin M. Barron

Travels in Time: The Story of Time Travel Cinema by Colin M. Barron.

First published in Great Britain in 2019 by Extremis Publishing Ltd.,
Suite 218, Castle House, 1 Baker Street, Stirling, FK8 1AL, United Kingdom.
www.extremispublishing.com

Extremis Publishing is a Private Limited Company registered in Scotland (SC509983) whose Registered Office is Suite 218, Castle House, 1 Baker Street, Stirling, FK8 1AL, United Kingdom.

A CIP catalogue record for this book is available from the British Library.

ISBN: 978-0-9955897-7-3

Typeset in Goudy Bookletter 1911, designed by The League of Moveable Type.

Printed and bound in Great Britain by IngramSpark, Chapter House, Pitfield, Kiln Farm, Milton Keynes, MK11 3LW, United Kingdom.

Cover artwork by Genty at Pixabay.
Incidental interior illustrations from Pixabay.
Book design is Copyright © Thomas A. Christie.
Author image is Copyright © Thomas A. Christie.

Contents

TRAVELS IN TIME

The Story of
Time Travel Cinema

Colin M. Barron

Time Travel Films
An Introduction

I T is fitting that these words should be written in 2019, because in two years we will be celebrating the 100th anniversary of the very first time travel movie: the 1921 version of *A Connecticut Yankee in King Arthur's Court*. Since the release of this ground-breaking film there has been a steady increase in the number of such movies, as can be seen in the table below:

Decade	Number of time travel movies released in cinemas
1920-29	1
1930-39	5
1940-49	3
1950-59	3
1960-69	8
1970-79	7
1980-89	25
1990-99	27
2000-09	46
2000-18	33

To clarify these figures, to qualify for inclusion in the above table (and this book) the film in question must have been shown to a cinema audience at some point, even if it was released on a home entertainment format soon afterwards. So TV movies and straight-to-video/DVD/BluRay films have not been included in the count. I have also excluded productions which have been made purely for Netflix and other online streaming services.

The table shows that the most popular decade for time travel movies was the noughties, with a staggering forty-six films released. At the time of writing it is unclear how many time travel films will be released in 2019 but, at the very least, there will be new *Terminator* and *Bill and Ted* movies.

But just why are time travel films so popular with the general public? My own theory is that they appeal to our needs and desires at a very deep level. A very common plot point in time travel movies involves the hero travelling back in time to correct a mistake they have made in their lives. This is something we can all identify with.

A few months ago, British newspapers carried a story – based upon academic research – about how the average person makes four major mistakes in their life. For example, we may marry the wrong person and get divorced, with all the emotional pain and expense this involves. Or we may miss an opportunity to date someone when we are young and never get married at all. Or we may make the wrong career choices, resulting in us not enjoying our job. Sometimes even the choice of the property we live in, or the town or city in which we reside, can have a great impact on the rest of our lives. I myself have made many mistakes in my life, and recently I calculated that I had made twenty-four serious errors between 1970 and 2018.

My own parents (who were both doctors) were highly intelligent, well-educated and usually quite wise, yet in 1969 (when they were both about fifty) they made a crass decision which affected the rest of their lives, and those of their family. They sold their large house in Greenock (which was the bottom half of a huge Edwardian villa and on a single level) and moved into a cramped, semi-detached house which had been built in 1958. Their idea was that this would be a smaller house suitable for their retirement. It was one of the worst decisions of their lives, as the new house was on three levels with many of the facilities (such as the washing machine, tumble dryer and freezer) being in a basement level accessible only by a rickety staircase. The garden was vast, with many flower beds, and parts of it were wild. There was a huge gully in the centre of the garden, which was very dangerous. The house was several blocks from the nearest bus stop.

In later years, the house proved to be wholly unsuitable for a frail elderly couple, and almost became a death trap. When it was eventually marketed after their deaths, it proved hard to sell and failed to attract a good price, which in turn meant that my parents' estate was not as large as it could have been. I often wish I could go back to 1969 in a time machine and persuade my parents to stay where they were and modernise their house, instead of moving to an unsuitable property.

My parents' experiences are not unique. We all make mistakes, sometimes every day. So a film in which the hero goes back in time to change things can have great emotional appeal, and this is indeed a common theme in such movies. Sometimes the hero uses this ability to help with their own personal life, as in 'time travel romances' like *Groundhog Day* and *About Time*. On other occasions, the protagonist is more intent on changing history by interfering with historical events. For example, they may attempt to prevent the assassination of President Kennedy or stop the Vietnam War from happening.

Another thing that is remarkable about time travel films is that they employ a huge number of ways of travelling through time. Sometimes a technological apparatus or craft is used, as in *The Time Machine*. But other methods can be employed, such as a time portal (whether man-made or naturally occurring), a 'time storm', a drug, a magic potion, a hypnotic trance, a bang on the head, an acute illness, magic crystals, travelling through a 'time tunnel', having a dream, reading a book or journal about the past, or having a genetically-determined ability to travel in time. The possibilities are endless.

A number of themes often occur in these movies. The hero journeys to the future and discovers that humanity has been divided into two species as a result of nuclear war. The normal people live outdoors while the mutants live underground or in a city. Or it is the other way round, with the mutants occupying a wasteland and the human survivors barricaded into a city.

The hero travels to the past to change a certain event, but this has unforeseen consequences and he has to put things back to the way they were. The hero travels just 10-20 years into the future and discovers that everyone is driving around in futuristic cars which can fly. This is an interesting point, because one thing that movies and TV series usually get wrong are the cars of the future which are always far too advanced, with features like motors which sound like jet engines, spaceship-like styling and gull wing doors. A good example would be the film *Freejack*, which was made in 1991 but largely set in 2009. Yet the motor vehicles which are depicted in the film look far too advanced for 2009. In reality, the cars which were around in 2009 didn't look that much different from those that existed in 1991.

Another common technical error in time travel films concerns the concept of 'mutations'. According to such films, when humans and animals are exposed to radiation from a nuclear blast they 'mutate' and turn into monsters. This is best seen in the series of Japanese *Godzilla* films, in which various monsters are created by exposure to radiation.

In fact, this is scientific nonsense. When humans or animals are exposed to radiation they may develop acute radiation sickness and burns. In the long-term there is an increased risk of cancer, including leukaemia. Damage to DNA may result in the *offspring* of such individuals, having an increased risk of birth defects, but the idea that the world will be taken over by 'mutants' created by nuclear blasts is a scientific impossibility. Yet it has become a common trope in science fiction films.

Another common error in time travel films is that many writers seem to think that it is possible to journey backwards in time by travelling very fast. What they are referring to is what Einstein described as 'time dilation' in his Special Theory of Relativity. Einstein theorised that time passes more slowly as your velocity increases. This is best illustrated by the hypothetical case of a pair of identical twin brothers. One stays on Earth while the other goes on a long space journey for ten years, travelling at close to the speed of light. When he returns to Earth, he will have aged less than his identical twin, as his personal time will have passed more slowly.

That does not mean, though, that people can travel backwards in time by moving faster than light. For one thing, it is not possible to travel faster than light. Einstein said that if a person's velocity was to reach the speed of light, their mass would increase to the point where it was greater than that of the entire universe. Furthermore, all the spacecraft that have been created to date travel relatively slowly – usually no more than 25,000 miles per hour (and often considerably less fast) – and travel at near-light speeds is currently impossible.

At present, time travel remains a scientific impossibility. Yet who knows what might be feasible in the future? If nothing else, the concept of travelling through time has provided inspiration to thousands of writers and film-makers, and I would predict that in the next hundred years there will be many more such films.

Colin M. Barron
January 2019

1
Early Days
1920 to 1959

TIME travel has fascinated filmmakers for a hundred years. The first movie about the subject was *A Connecticut Yankee in King Arthur's Court* (1921), which was directed by Emmett J. Flynn, produced by William Fox and scripted by Bernard Conville. The screenplay was based on Mark Twain's 1889 book *A Connecticut Yankee in King Arthur's Court*, and is distinctly odd.

The film begins with Martin Cavendish (Harry Myers) reading Twain's novel (thus coming dangerously close to 'breaking the fourth wall'). Cavendish then falls asleep and dreams that he has been transported back to the time of King Arthur (Charles Clary), just like Twain's protagonist Henry Morgan. The hero then uses his modern knowledge to defeat the king's foes, including Merlin (William V. Mong) and Morgan Le Fay (Rosemary Theby).

The script features many modern references including the Volstead Act, the Battle of the Argonne Forest and Ford

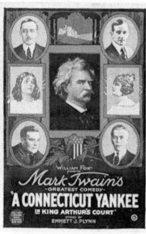

A Connecticut Yankee in
King Arthur's Court (1921):
Fox Film

Model T cars, and the film's success encouraged Fox Studios to produce a new version with sound in 1931, this time called just *A Connecticut Yankee* and directed by David Butler, which this time more closely followed the novel. More about this version shortly.

The previous year (1930), another time travel film – *Just Imagine* – premiered, also directed by David Butler, who made a total of three time travel pictures. The movie begins in 1980. J-21 (John Garrick) is at the controls of a futuristic aircraft and lands in New York so that he can speak to LN-18 (Maureen O' Sullivan). As you will have noticed, in this movie everyone has numbers rather than names – rather like the titular robots in the *Doctor Who* story *Robots of Death* (1977). This decision by the writers makes the film rather hard to follow.

After landing, J-21 explains to LN-18 how the marriage tribunal had refused to consider his wedding application. As a result LN-18 is going to have to get hitched to MT-3, a man she does not like. RT-42 (Frank Albertson) tries to buck up J-21 by taking him on a trip. They visit a group of doctors who revive a man from the year 1930 who was killed by a lightning bolt while playing golf. The man – formerly known as Peterson – has now been re-named Single-O (El Brendel). RT-42 and J-21 take responsibility for Single-O. He is surprised to learn what has changed in the world. Aircraft have replaced cars, numbers have supplanted names, pills are consumed instead of food and drink, and babies come from vending machines.

Later that evening, LN-18 pretends to have a headache so that her father and MT-3 go out without her. As soon as they have left, RT-42 and J-21 arrive and woo B-27 and LN-18. Then MT-3 and LN-18's father return earlier than expected. RT-42 and J-21, hide but their plan is inadvertently foiled by Single-O who has become addicted to 'highball' pills and tries to get some more from J-21.

J-21 feels down, but is contacted by the scientist Z-4 (Hobart Bosworth). J-21 learns that Z-4 has built a rocket plane that can carry three men to Mars. The *Pegasus*, a form of dirigible airliner, blasts off for Mars carrying J-21, RT-42 and Single-O, who has stowed away.

After landing on the Red Planet they meet the Queen, Looloo (Joyzelle Joyner), and the King, Loko (Ivan Linow). The two Royals take the visitors from Earth to see a Martian opera, which involves a number of trained apes dancing on stage. The Earth visitors are attacked by Booboo and Boko, evil twins of the King and Queen. Fortunately they escape and make their way back to Earth, where J-21 is now allowed to marry LN-18 as a reward for exploring another planet, while Single-O is reunited with his son Axel (uncredited).

The film is best remembered for its massive, Art Deco cityscape which was built in a former US Army balloon hangar. This structure employed 205 technicians and took five months to build, at a cost of $168,000. The miniature used 15,000 small lightbulbs, and 74 additional arc lights were required to illuminate the structure.

The special effects were also memorable, as was the scene in which El Brendel is revived using the same electrical equipment (created by Kenneth Strickfaden) which was later employed in James Whale's *Frankenstein* (1931). Extensive use was also made of rear projection, miniatures and glass paintings.

The film was expensive and did not recoup its production costs, but clips from the movie and many props were reused in the *Flash Gordon* and *Buck Rogers* serials in the midthirties. *Just Imagine* was also nominated for an Academy Award for best Art Direction. It did not win, but has a place in film history as the first science fiction film to be nominated for an Oscar.

In 1931 – one year after the release of *Just Imagine* – another time travel film directed by David Butler was released, *A Connecticut Yankee*, which was again based on the book by Mark Twain. This new production was inspired by the success of the earlier silent production a decade earlier. It was produced by the Fox Film Corporation (later to be known as 20th Century Fox), and was written for the screen by William M. Conselman, Owen Davis and Jack Moffitt.

The plot was similar to the previous production. The hero, radio salesman Hank Martin (Will Rogers), falls asleep and dreams about going back to the Middle Ages during the time of Camelot and King Arthur. Once he arrives in this previous time, he has to use his modernday knowledge to battle Morgana Le Fay and Merlin.

The hero's name was changed from Hank Morgan to Hank Martin to avoid confusion with the reallife actor Frank Morgan who appeared in *The Wizard From Oz*. Incidentally 'Frank Morgan' was one of the character names in the BBC TV time travel series *Life on Mars* (200607), which starred John Simm, and this was thought to be one of many deliberate references to *The Wizard From Oz* in that production.

As in *The Wizard of Oz*, all the characters in this version of *A Connecticut Yankee* play one character in the 'real' world and another in the dream world. In this imagining, King Arthur was played by William Farnum, with Myrna Loy as Morgan Le Fay and Brandon Hurst as Merlin. Maureen O'Sullivan was Alisande. The film was released on 6th April 1931 and made $1.2 million at the box office. It was not the last version of this film, as the final (and probably best-known) remake of this story was released in 1949 with Bing Crosby in the title role.

Turn Back the Clock (1933) was an MGM fantasy film which was directed by Edgar Selwyn, scripted by Selwyn and Ben Hecht, and featured Lee Tracy as Joe Gimlet and Mae Clark as Mary Gimlet/Mary Clark. The comedy trio 'The Three Stooges' also appear in the film as wedding singers, although they are uncredited.

The film begins on 23rd March 1933. A cigar store owner, Joe Gimlet (Lee Tracy), meets his old childhood friend, banker Ted Wright (Otto Kruger). Joe has dinner with Ted and his wife Mary, and suggests that they invest $4000 in his company.

Joe is keen on the idea, but Mary refuses to have anything to do with it. Annoyed at her decision, Joe has a lot to drink and foolishly tells Mary that he wishes he had married the rich Elvina (Peggy Shannon) instead. He leaves their apartment and is promptly struck by a car and taken to hospital.

When Joe wakes up, he finds he is a young man again, as he has travelled back in time. He tries to talk to his mother (Clara Blandick) about the future but this scares her, so he chooses to remain quiet about what he knows. Later, on his way to his job as a soda fountain operator, he meets Elvina and they eventually become engaged. This revelation devastates Joe's former girlfriend Mary.

The couple get married and Joe makes a lot of money because of his knowledge of the future. Mary decides to get married to Ted while Joe pledges a million dollars to American servicemen returning from the First World War. The current US President, Woodrow Wilson, declares that Joe is a hero and gives him an appointment as head of the War Industry. Elvina is upset at these developments, but they decide to avoid a divorce because of all the scandal it would cause.

Many years later (in 1929), Joe sees Ted working in a cigar store. He has dinner with him and Mary and he offers the couple the chance to invest $4000 in a business venture. They both agree.

Unfortunately things go wrong due to the stock market crash of 1929. Joe loses most of his money because Elvina had invested it in shares. Joe is so angry that the couple get divorced, and his employees plunder the bank.

By now it is 6th March 1933, the date of the car accident. This means that Joe must live the rest of his life with no further knowledge of the future. He tries to run away and meets Mary, begging her to go with him, but she is reticent to leave her husband. Joe is then arrested by the police and taken into custody. When he wakes up he is back in the hospital room, with things as they were originally. In modern parlance he has jumped timelines, and he tells Mary he doesn't want to change a thing about their lives.

Berkeley Square (1933) was probably the best-known time travel film of the pre-war period, and starred Leslie Howard and Frank Angel. Rather like Cary Grant, Leslie Howard was born in England but moved to Hollywood where he made a number of highly successful films including *Gone with the*

Wind (1939), regarded as one of the most successful movies of all time and one of the first films to be made in three-colour Technicolor. A deeply patriotic man, Howard returned to Britain during the war and made *The First of the Few* (1942), a biopic about the life and death of R.J. Mitchell, who designed the Supermarine Spitfire fighter plane. Howard was killed in 1943 when a Douglas DC-3 Dakota flying him back from Lisbon was shot down by German Junkers Ju-88 long-range fighters. Ever since that event, there has been speculation that the Germans thought the plane was carrying Churchill. Although Howard looked nothing like Churchill, he did resemble the Prime Minister's bodyguard, Walter Thomson, who may have been seen boarding the aircraft. On the other hand it is possible that Howard himself may have been targeted because of contributions to the Allied propaganda cause. However, the most recent published review of this incident concluded that the shoot-down was simply an error by the Luftwaffe, who were patrolling the Bay of Biscay at the time in an attempt to destroy Allied anti-submarine aircraft.

Berkeley Square starred Howard as Peter Standish, a young American who is transported back to London just before the War of Independence, where he meets his ancestors. The film was based on a play by John L. Balderston, which in turn was based on an incomplete novel by Henry James called *The Sense of the Past*. Howard had previously played Standish in the Broadway play.

The film begins in 1784, eight years after the American Declaration of Independence in 1776. Peter Standish travels by boat from New York to England to marry his cousin and learns that a Frenchman has flown across the English Channel in a balloon.

In 1933 his descendant – Peter Standish – inherits a house in Berkeley Square, London, and becomes obsessed with his ancestor's diary; something which upsets his fiancée Marjorie Frant (Betty Lawford). Later, when they are both having tea with the American ambassador (Samuel S. Hinds), Peter reveals that he is certain that he will be transported back to 1784 at 5.30p.m. that same day. All he has to do to make this happen is to keep reading the diary.

He makes his way home, but when he opens the door he finds himself back in 1784. Furthermore, he has replaced the original Peter from 1784, and the house is owned by his relatives – Lady Ann Pettigrew (Irene Browne) and her children Kate (Valerie Taylor), Tom (Colin Keith-Johnston) and Helen (Heather Angel). For financial reasons, the Pettigrews want Kate to marry Peter.

Things get complicated from then on. Peter doesn't want to alter history, but finds himself attracted to Helen, not Kate. Unfortunately Lady Ann wants Helen to marry Mr Throstle (Ferdinard Gottschalk), but the young English girl is not happy with this arrangement and is attracted to Peter.

Helen asks Peter to explain how he knows about the future, but he is reluctant to disclose his secret. However, she guesses the truth. She also realises that Peter is unhappy about some aspects of 18th century life such as the lack of plumbing and hygiene, and she urges him to return to 1933. Eventually he does go back to his original time, despite his strong feelings for her.

After returning to 1933, Peter visits Helen's grave and discovers that she died on 15th June 1787, when she was just 23. Marjorie visits him, worried about his sanity as he has been claiming that he is from the 18th century. In an interesting plot twist, it appears that Peter's ancestor from 1784 had swapped places with him but has now returned to his original time. He tells Marjorie that he cannot marry her and points to an epitaph on Helen's grave which suggests that the two of them will be reunited one day, 'not in my time, not in yours, but in God's'. He is actually suggesting that the couple will be reunited after death, an ending which is similar to that in *Somewhere in Time* (1980).

The film was a box office disappointment, but received favourable reviews from critics. In 1951 it was remade as *The House in the Square* (aka *I'll Never Forget You*), starring Tyrone Power and Ann Blyth. Irene Browne reprised her role as Lady Ann Pettigrew in the remake. The original film was lost, but was later rediscovered in the 1970s and a restored 35mm print has since been made.

Ali Baba Goes to Town (1937) is an 80-minute film directed by David Butler which starred Tony Martin, Eddie Cantor and Roland Young. Cantor portrays a tramp called Aloysius 'Al' Babson, who walks into the camp of a movie company that is making the *Arabian Nights*. He takes a nap, and dreams that he is in Baghdad as an assistant to the Sultan (Roland Young). He then dreams that he has created a scheme in which he develops work programmes, taxes the rich and abolishes the army. This is all intended to be a spoof of US President Franklin D. Roosevelt's 'New Deal'.

The cast includes the well-known stripper Gypsy Rose Lee, who on this occasion used the stage name Louise Hovick to portray the Sultana. The song from the movie *Twilight in Turkey* was performed by the Raymond Scott Quintette. Several Hollywood stars made uncredited appearances in the film, including Douglas Fairbanks, Victor McLaglen, Cesar Romero, Tyrone Power and Shirley Temple.

An excerpt from the film appears in *The Day of The Locust* (1975), in which Karen Black plays an up-and-coming 1930s actress. A brief clip from the film was edited into the movie to give the impression that Black's character had worked as an extra on the earlier movie.

Where Do We Go From Here? (1945) holds the distinction of being the first time travel movie to be made in Technicolor. It is officially described as a romantic musical comedy-fantasy film which was directed by Gregory Ratoff and produced by William Perlberg. The screenplay was by Morrie Ryskind and Sig Herzig.

The film music was composed by Kurt Weill, with lyrics by Ira Gershwin. The movie was Weill's only musical to be written directly for the screen, with all his others being adaptations of stage shows which featured an anachronistic blend of history and 1940s slang. Weill was best-known for several Broadway shows including *Knickerbocker Holiday*, *Lady in the Dark* and *One Touch of Venus*.

Joan Leslie's singing voice was dubbed by Sally Sweetland, while the mock-opera sequence *The Nina, the Pinta, the Santa Maria* was one of the longest musical sequences ever created for the screen.

The plot of the film is quite simple. Bill Morgan (Fred MacMurray) is a young American who is keen to enlist in the Armed Forces during WW2, but he is unable to do so as he is classified as a 4F (unfit for duty). However, he tries to help the war effort by collecting scrap metal. One day he finds a strange brass bottle. He polishes it and a genie, Ali (Gene Sheldon), appears and grants him three wishes. Bill's first wish is that he wants to be in the US Army. There is a puff of smoke and Bill finds himself as an ordinary infantryman in George Washington's army during the American War of Independence in 1776. After a brief scrap with some Hessian soldiers, Bill escapes his predicament by wishing he was in the Navy, and now Bill finds himself on Christopher Columbus's ship during its maiden voyage to North America. Eventually he gets ashore and buys Manhattan Island from a local native (Anthony Quinn).

Bill then moves forwards in time and is transported to New Amsterdam (which later became New York) in the mid-17th Century. When he claims to own the island he is imprisoned. Ali the Genie finally comes through, and he ends up in the arms of Katrina (Joan Leslie).

Repeat Performance (1947) was an American crime film which incorporated some science fiction and time travel elements. It was produced by Aubrey Schenck, directed by Alfred L. Werker, and distributed by Eagle-Lion films.

The film opens on New Year's Eve 1946. Sheila Page (Joan Leslie) is standing over her dead husband Barney (Louis Hayward) with a gun in her hand, having shot him. She doesn't know what she should do, so she goes to two New Year parties to get help from her friends. In a state of great distress as the clock chimes, she wishes she could live 1946 all over again. Much to her surprise, her wish is granted, and she is transported back to the start of year and finds her husband alive and well.

She then lives the entire year again, determined not to repeat her mistakes, but certain events recur just as they had the first time. Sheila begins to wonder if she is paddling against the tide and that she is fated to kill her husband. Sheila and Barney argue and, on New Year's Eve, he dies – but this time it is their friend William (Richard Basehart) who fires the fatal shot.

The film was moderately successful, making $1.3 million at the box office set against a budget of $600,000. It was remade as the TV movie *Turn Back the Clock* (1989), which again starred original cast member Joan Leslie, plus Jere Burns and Wendy Kilbourne.

The next time travel film was the 1949 version of *A Connecticut Yankee in King Arthur's Court*, which starred Bing Crosby, Rhonda Fleming, Sir Cedric Hardwicke and William Bendix. This was the first film version of Mark Twain's 1889 novel to be made in Technicolor, and was produced by Robert Fellows and directed by Tay Garnett. The screenplay was by Edward Beloin.

The plot was obviously similar to the previous versions of the classic story. American mechanic Hank Martin (Bing Crosby) is knocked out and wakes up in medieval times. He is in the land of King Arthur, where he falls in love with Alisande la Carteloise (Rhonda Fleming). He also develops a friendship with Sir Sagramore (William Bendix), but incurs the wrath of Merlin (Murvyn Vye) and Morgan Le Fay (Virginia Field) who are plotting to usurp the throne. When Hank attempts to intervene he is catapulted back to his own time.

Distraught about losing the woman he loves, he visits a British castle and meets the owner, Lord Pendragon (Cedric Hardwicke). He introduces him to his niece, who looks just like Alisande.

Star Bing Crosby was perhaps better known at the time as a singer than an actor, and the film showcases his vocal skills as it features six songs, four of which include vocals from Crosby. The film soundtrack was composed by Jimmy Van Heusen, with lyrics by Johnny Burke, while the orchestral score was by Victor Young. One of the highlights of the film is a scene in which Hank Martin teaches contemporary musicians how to modernise their medieval music.

The film was only reasonably successful at the box office, making just $3.4 million against a budget of $3 million. It received generally favourable reviews from critics, and is the only film version of Mark Twain's tale which is regularly shown on television.

I'll Never Forget You (1951) was a remake of the 1934 Leslie Howard picture *Berkeley Square*, which has already been discussed earlier in this chapter. This second version was originally scheduled for production in 1945 with Gregory Peck and Maureen Hara in the starring roles, but was postponed until 1951 by which time some re-casting was necessary.

The film was also known as *The House on the Square* and *Man of Two Worlds*. It concerns an American nuclear scientist, Peter Standish (Tyrone Power), who is transported back to the 18th century where he falls in love with a woman, Helen (Ann Blyth). Later, when he returns to the 20th century, he meets a woman called Martha (also played by Ann Blyth) who looks just like Helen. Film and TV historians may notice how similar the plot is to John Wyndham's 1956 short story *Random Quest*, which was made into an episode of the BBC2 science fiction anthology series *Out of the Unknown* in 1969. In that production, physicist Colin Trafford (Keith Barron) is transported into a parallel universe as a result of a laboratory accident.

He awakens in this new world to discover he is married to a beautiful woman called Ottilie Harsham (Tracey Reed). The marriage is in trouble due to Colin's negligence and infidelity. Colin manages to repair the relationship, but is then catapulted back to his original world. He is convinced that Ottilie must exist in this universe and vows to track her down. Eventually he succeeds. In 1971, *Random Quest* was itself made into a feature film, *Quest for Love*, which starred Colin Bell and Joan Collins. But this movie was a flop, and is generally considered inferior to the 1969 teleplay.

I'll Never Forget You, though, has a similar opening to *Random Quest*. In this version of *Berkeley Square*, Peter Standish is an American nuclear scientist who is working in an atomic laboratory in London. His colleague, Roger Forsyth (Michael Rennie), is concerned that Peter is not having much of a social life, so he takes him to a house in Berkeley Square which he has inherited.

Peter senses that the house has a connection with the past, and expresses a desire to live in that building in the 18th century. His wish comes true when the house is struck by a lightning bolt and he is transported back to 1784, where he is mistaken for the very first Peter Standish, the American cousin of the Petigrews who is due to marry Kate Petigrew (Beatrice Campbell).

Peter is attracted to Kate, but is more interested in her sister Helen (Ann Blyth). The two fall, in love but Peter becomes disenchanted with life in the 18th century. He is particularly bothered about the poverty, the dirt and the lack of hygiene.

Eventually he confides in Helen and admits he is from the future. He even shows her his basement laboratory which is filled with modern inventions. Peter knows he has to marry Kate to avoid changing history, but he falls out with her and is increasingly drawn to Helen.

Unfortunately Peter's secret laboratory is discovered and he is committed to a mental hospital. As he is being taken away, he is struck by another bolt of lightning and is returned to the present (1951). He discovers that while he was away in the 18th century, his original self was behaving like a madman in 1951 (this again is a similarity with *Random Quest*, in which the two Colin Traffords effectively changed places). He then meets Forsyth's sister Martha, who looks just like Helen. He then finds Helen's grave, and discovers that she died of grief soon after he was taken away to a lunatic asylum.

World Without End (1956) was a science fiction film which was made in both Technicolor and Cinemascope. It was produced by Richard Heermance and directed by Edward Bernds from his own screenplay. In some countries the film was known as *Flight to the Future*.

The movie featured an early screen appearance by Australian actor Rod Taylor, who later starred in the definitive time travel movie – *The Time Machine* (1960) – which is discussed in detail elsewhere in this book.

The film opens in March 1957. A spaceship is returning from a mission to orbit Mars. The crew consists of the commander, Dr Eldon Galbraithe (Nelson Leigh), engineer Henry Jaffe (Christopher Dark), radio operator Herbert Ellis (Rod Taylor), and scientist John Borden (Hugh Marlowe). As the spaceship is on its journey home, it suddenly accelerates to an incredible speed. The crew are all knocked out, and their craft crashes on a snow-topped peak. When they exit the vehicle, they discover that they have somehow been transported into the future.

Their instruments show increased levels of radiation, so they deduce that they have arrived in the aftermath of a nuclear war which started in 2188, with the current date being approximately 2500. Later, they learn that the exact date is 2508. Jaffe is stunned when he realises that his wife and children have long since died.

The crew are attacked by giant spiders (a staple of science fiction), and are also ambushed by different remnants of human society. There are two distinct species. The 'mutates' are aggressive primitives who live on the surface. They have changed physically due to long-term exposure to radiation, which has now dropped to safe levels. As a result, the 'mutates' sometimes give birth to normal children, but these then become slaves.

While fleeing from the mutates, the spaceship crew take shelter in a cave and find the entrance to an underground city which is populated by the descendants of refugees from the nuclear war. Their society is very technologically advanced, and is led by Timmek (Everett Glass) who is the president of the ruling council.

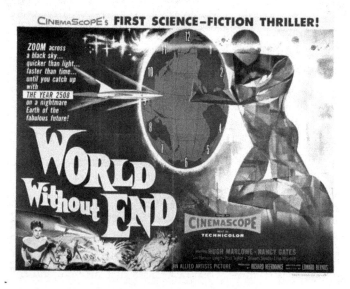

World Without End (1956): Allied Artists Pictures Corporation

Unfortunately, living underground has taken its toll on the natives and the men are becoming less virile. Birth rates are falling. The native women are attracted to Herbert Ellis (who has conveniently lost his shirt!), and one of their number, Deena (Lisa Montell), falls in love with him. The spaceship crew try to persuade the city's inhabitants to take up arms and reclaim the surface, but they are too apathetic and content with their current existence to do anything.

Timmek's daughter, Garnet (Nancy Gates), becomes attracted to John Borden. This causes Mories (Booth Colman) to become jealous. He arms himself with the astronaut's confiscated weapons, but is caught red-handed and has to kill a man. Mories then puts the guns in the astronauts' quarters, hoping this will be incriminating evidence against them. Timmek demands that the astronauts leave, but Deena has seen Mories plant the guns and is willing to speak up in the space travellers' defence. Mories escapes and makes it to the surface, but is killed by the mutates.

Timmek helps the astronauts to build a shoulder-launched rocket launcher, which is used on the surface to great effect against the mutates who are forced to take shelter in the caves. Borden then fights Naga (Mickey Simpson) in order to become the leader of the mutates. He eventually wins the battle, and orders the remaining deformed mutates to leave. The astronauts then set up a new colony which includes people from both species.

World Without End achieved moderate success when it was released in 1956. However, it was deemed sufficiently similar to *The Time Machine* to attract a threatened lawsuit from the estate of H. G. Wells. You will notice that there are indeed a number of plot similarities – a nuclear war in the future and humanity divided up into two species, one of which lives underground. One race is gentle and passive, the other is aggressive. *World Without End* has a female character called Deena who falls in love with Rod Taylor's character. *The Time Machine* features a character called Weena who falls in love with Rod Taylor's character (in the later film version). There are many other resemblances.

Elements of the plot of *World Without End* subsequently featured in other science fiction films of the fifties and sixties, including *The Mole People* (1956), *The Time Travelers* (1964) and *Planet of the Apes* (1968).

The Undead (1957) was a horror film directed and produced by by Roger Corman in which a prostitute, Diana Love (Pamela Duncan), travels back in time to the Middle Ages as a result of a hypnotic trance induced by psychic Quintis (Val Dufour). Corman was well-known for producing low-budget horror films which were often surprisingly effective.

In the film, Diana finds herself back in the Middle Ages, where her mind occupies the body of her past self – Helene – who is due to be executed at dawn for being a witch. Under the influence of Diana, Helene manages to break out of prison. This action comes to the attention of Livia, a witch who has carried out the crimes for which Helene is being wrongly blamed. Satan also discovers what is going on.

Quintus then travels back in time to change history by preventing Helene's death. The only problem is that this will prevent all her future selves – including Diana – from ever existing. Helene is thus forced to accept her death, but this results in Quintus becoming stranded in the past. Satan is amused.

The film was inspired by the real-life case of Bridey Murphy, which is generally considered to be the most convincing past-life regression case in history and was documented in

Morey Bernstein's book *The Search for Bridey Murphy* (1956). The original title of the movie was *The Trance of Diana Love.*

As with all Roger Corman pictures, it was made on a low budget – in this case, of $70,000. Filming took just ten days, and the whole production was filmed in the Sunset Stage, which was a converted supermarket in Sunset Boulevard. The fake bats which appear in the film were re-used from another Corman movie, *It Conquered the World* (1956).

2

The Time Machine

ERBERT George Wells (1866-1946) was a prolific English writer who wrote under the name H.G. Wells. He wrote novels, short stories and articles plus numerous non-fiction works, and is rightly regarded as the father of British science fiction. Three of his books – *The Time Machine* (1895), *The Invisible Man* (1897) and *The War of the Worlds* (1897) – have had a huge influence on popular culture, as they have inspired numerous films, TV series and spin-off books. *The War of The Worlds* even spawned a best-selling album.

The Time Machine was first published in 1895, but had previously existed in various formats, and was based on his earlier work *The Chronic Argonauts* (1888), which was printed in his college newspaper. Even by modern standards it is short, and would now be classed as a 'novella'. The version which the author possesses runs to just 104 pages in length, including many additional notes, essays and introductions.

The importance of the ideas in this book cannot be over-stated. It was the first tome which suggested that time travel might be achieved using some kind of machine or apparatus, using principles which were on the fringe of known science. The book and subsequent film and TV adaptations have therefore influenced a huge number of movies and TV productions including *Doctor Who*, the *Back to the Future* trilogy, the *Terminator* franchise, and many others.

Bearing in mind the revolutionary concepts found in the book, it is surprising that it took the film industry so long to make a film adaptation. Although *The Time Machine* was first adapted for BBC television in 1949, it wasn't until 1960 that a feature film was made. This was the brainchild of George Pal (originally Gyorgy Pal Marczincsak), a Hungarian-American animator, film director and producer who had made a number of fantasy and science fiction films including *Destination Moon* (1950), *When Worlds Collide* (1951) and *The War of the Worlds* (1953), in which he had served as a producer and special effects designer. *The Time Machine* was the first film he directed.

Pal's specialty was miniature effects involving stop-frame animation, and in the 1940s he produced a number of animated films featuring the *Puppetoons*. The word 'Puppetoon' suggests a cross between a puppet and a cartoon, and that is exactly what they were – small wooden figures which were moved slightly between each frame of film. This is the same method that has been used in recent years in childrens' TV productions such as *Wallace and Grommit*, *Thomas the Tank Engine*, *The Magic Roundabout*, and many others.

This method of animation gave Pal's films a certain 'look', and it played a key part in the special effects in *The Time Machine*. Originally, extensive stop-frame animation was to have been used in Pal's earlier epic *The War of The Worlds*, particularly in sequences involving the Martian war machines which Wells had described as giant tripods with a control cabin at the top. Unfortunately, it proved too difficult to create convincing footage of tripod machines walking using stop-frame animation, so an alternative, simpler design was created. This used the now-familiar saucer craft with mantra ray-shaped bodies, each fitted with a snake-like appendage which unleashed a death ray. These miniatures were made of solid copper and suspended on wires.

The protagonist in Wells' 1895 book was not given a name, and was simply called the 'Time Traveller'. In the 1960 film he is referred to simply as 'George'. A brass plate on the time machine stated that it had been built by 'H. George Wells'. So was this implying that the hero was actually H.G. Wells himself, or was 'George' a reference to director and producer George Pal? It is one of the questions posed by the 1960 film that has never been answered.

For the lead role of George, the Time Traveller, the producers originally considered using a middle-aged English actor such as David Niven or James Mason.

The Time Machine (1960): Metro-Goldwyn-Mayer/Galaxy Films

In the end they cast 29-year-old Australian actor Rod Taylor, who had appeared in minor roles in a few feature films and TV series. With his square-jawed good looks and muscular physique, Taylor excelled in the fight scenes in *The Time Machine* and was subsequently offered the title role in the first James Bond film, *Dr No*, in 1961. Taylor rejected the offer, stating that the role of James Bond was 'beneath him'.

In later years, Taylor regarded this decision as one of the greatest mistakes of his professional career, and said that he felt 'like tearing his hair out' every time he read about the success of the Bond films. A few years later, Taylor starred as a Bond-like character – Boysie Oakes – in *The Liquidator* (1966), which was written by John Gardner who had penned fourteen original Bond novels in the eighties and nineties, and also novelized the Eon productions *Licence to Kill* (1989) and *Goldeneye* (1995). *The Liquidator* had other connections with the Bond series, as it also starred Jill St John (who played Tiffany Case in *Diamonds are Forever* in 1971) and its title song was sung by Shirley Bassey, who provided the vocals for *Goldfinger* (1964), *Diamonds are Forever* and *Moonraker* (1979).

It was hoped that this would be the first of a series of such films, but by 1966 cinemagoers' appetite for cheap imitations of James Bond films had started to wane and no more Boysie Oakes adventures were made. In this respect, *The Liquidator* can be compared with *When Eight Bells Toll* (1971) – a low-budget Alastair MacLean-penned thriller starring Anthony Hopkins as agent Philip Calvert – which might have developed into a franchise if it had not been competing with the Bond series of films.

After a brief title sequence, *The Time Machine* opens with a scene set in the London home of inventor George (his surname is never mentioned in the film, though – as discussed earlier – the nameplate on his machine implies that it may be Wells). Four of George's friends – David Philby (Alan Young), Dr Phillip Hillyer (Sebastian Cabot), Anthony Bridewell (Tom Helmore) and Walter Kemp (Whit Bissel) – have been invited for dinner, but the inventor is not there. Suddenly, a door opens and George arrives, looking dirty, tired and bedraggled. He explains that he has just been through a terrible ordeal, and starts to explain more.

Five days earlier – on New Year's Eve, 1899 – the five men had met for dinner, and George had explained his theories about time and how it might be possible to build a machine which would enable man to travel in what he described as 'the fourth dimension'. George then showed them a small working model of his proposed craft, and invited one guest to press a lever. The machine promptly vanished, but all his guests had some difficulty believing that it had travelled forward in time. As far as they were concerned, it was just a conjuring trick. George, though, was quite adamant that the craft was still occupying the same space as before but had simply moved forwards in time. This is a very important plot point in the film, because other fictional time machines – such as Doctor Who's TARDIS – have travelled in time *and* space, while the craft in the 1960 film does not move during time journeys.

After his guests have left, George goes downstairs to his workshop, which contains his full-size time machine. It looks exactly the same as the model craft we saw a little earlier, and is a masterpiece of design. The Time Machine prop was created by MGM art director Bill Ferrari, and was based on suggestions made by George Pal himself. Pal's original concept was that it should be based on a wooden sledge with a Victorian barber's chair mounted on top. A large curved, rotating disc (looking a bit like a modern satellite dish, but with added painted hieroglyphics) was fitted at the rear, and powered by an electric barbecue spit motor via a worm gear. Pal had wanted the dish to rotate clockwise when the machine was going forwards in time and anti-clockwise when going backwards to the past, but this concept never made it past the drawing board as it was too expensive to create.

A cylindrical control panel with a moving time and date display and three coloured electric lights on top was fitted in front of the seat, and the machine was operated by a removable, jewelled lever. Brass metal bars were fitted around the machine, and the result looked like complex Victoriana, a type of design which later became known as 'steampunk'.

George sits in the comfortable, padded seat of the craft and pushes the jewelled lever forward, sending the craft into the future. The time journey is depicted by changes in George's surroundings, which are all created by stop-frame animation. The sun and moon move across the sky, flowers grow and then wilt, and fruit ripens on trees. The moving sun was nothing more than a studio light which was moved slightly between frames, while the shot of fruit ripening was a highly realistic painting by artist Bill Brace which was altered slightly between each frame. The passage of time is also depicted by the hands of a carriage clock whizzing round and a candle burning down, while long-term changes in time are represented by the changing womens' fashions displayed on a shop window mannequin in Filby's Department Store opposite.

George stops on 15th September 1916, and leaves the craft to meet Filby's son James (Alan Young again) who tells him that his father David has died in the Great War. Upset at this revelation, George returns to his machine and moves forward in time once more, this time stopping on 19th June 1940 to find that London is being bombed by the Germans. (This is actually inaccurate, as at this point in the war the Battle of France had still not concluded, the Battle of Britain had not begun, and the Germans didn't start full-scale raids against the capital until September 1940.) Both Filbys are played by Alan Young, who adopted dyed red hair and a Scottish accent for the roles as he was then very well-known on American television for playing Wilbur Post, the owner of *Mister Ed* – who was a talking horse!

George resumes his temporal journey and sees his house hit by a bomb, but his speed of travel through time protects him and he is unharmed. He stops on 20th August 1966 and discovers that all the bomb-damaged buildings in his neighbourhood have been replaced by modern buildings. Scenes of the landscape around the Time Machine changing and new buildings being constructed were achieved with miniatures and Pal's favoured stop-motion animation technique.

Once more, George leaves his machine and tries to speak to the local population. He meets a now-elderly James Filby, who urges him to take cover as a nuclear attack is imminent. Air-raid sirens are blaring, and people are rushing to the nearest air-raid shelter. These scenes look rather unconvincing. Although they were supposed to be set in London, they were actually shot on the back lot at MGM Studios in Culver City, California, to save money. A few cars can be seen in the background, but – apart from a couple of British sports cars – they are all big 1950s American automobiles .

Soon after George's encounter with Filby, a nuclear explosion destroys London, causing a volcanic eruption (something that is scientifically unlikely and never explained in the film). The area is swamped with molten lava, but once more George escapes in his time machine – although his craft is completely buried in lava, which then solidifies. Once more, the temporal bubble around the machine protects George from injury, although he is completely encased in the solidified lava. George realises the only way to escape is to travel forward in time as rapidly as possible in the hope that the mountain of solidified lava will eventually erode, freeing him.

George travels to the far future and eventually the lava wears away, revealing a lush landscape. The display on the control panel of his craft shows the date is 12th October 802,701, and he is near a building which looks like an Egyptian Sphinx. A group of beautiful young people, all with blonde hair and skimpy, simple clothes, are gathered round a stream. One of them, a young woman called Weena (Yvette Mimieux), falls into the water and appears to be drowning as she cannot swim. George dives into the water to rescue her and cannot understand why no-one else seems to be bothered. After she has been rescued, she walks off without saying a word. Yvette Mimieux turned eighteen during filming, and had little previous acting experience. She worked with Rod Taylor again in *Dark Side of the Sun* (1968).

George discovers that the blonde people, known as the Eloi, are completely lacking in aggression and initiative, and eat nothing but fruit. They also do not read books or work machinery, and know nothing about mankind's history. One of the Eloi shows him a bookcase, but when George tries to read one of the books it turns to dust.

That night George attempts to return to his machine but finds it is gone. Two skid marks prove that it has been dragged into the sphinx. The building has a pair of doors, but they have been locked shut. Weena tells George that his craft must have been taken by the Morlocks: frightening creatures

34

who only come out at night. One of them jumps out from behind a bush and attempts to abduct Weena, but George repels the creature by brandishing a blazing torch in its face. The Morlocks fear fire, as they live in the dark. They have an alarming appearance – pale skin, white hair, large sharp teeth and glowing eyes.

The following day, Weena shows George several well-like structures which are dotted around the landscape. The time traveller realises that these are ventilation ducts serving the Morlocks' underground complex. If he could climb down one of them, he might reach his time machine and escape! Before he does this, Weena takes him to a museum where there are 'talking rings' which give details of a war which lasted 326 years. Following this, mankind had evolved into two distinct species – the pacifist Eloi, who live on the surface, and the savage Morlocks who reside underground. The perspex dome which appears in the background in this scene is a re-used prop from *Forbidden Planet* (1956). In that movie, it was part of the C-57D cruiser's navigation system.

George then carries out his plan and starts to climb down one of the shafts, but has only gone a few yards when he hears a klaxon blaring. It sounds like a WW2 air-raid siren, and originates from the sphinx. George returns to the surface and sees scores of hypnotised Eloi walking towards the building, which now has its doors open. After a few moments, the sirens stop and the doors close. But a quota of Eloi has been taken underground... including Weena!

George returns to the well and climbs down the shaft. After a few minutes, he reaches the Morlocks' underground lair and discovers skeletons lying on the ground. The truth dawns on him – the Morlocks are cannibals, and are using the Eloi for food! George locates Weena and fights the Morlocks using his fists and a blazing torch. As he discovered earlier, the Morlocks fear fire and bright light as they live underground and only come to the surface at night.

After seeing the dramatic effects of George's actions, some of the other young male Eloi overcome their inhibitions and fight the Morlocks. George sets fire to the Morlocks' complex, and he and the Eloi escape to the surface where they throw large quantities of dead, dried branches down all the wells to feed the flames. The Morlocks' lair is destroyed by fire and the roof collapses, burying many of the evil creatures.

The next morning George returns to the sphinx, which has been damaged by the fire. The doors at the base are open, and the Time Traveller can see his machine inside. As he enters the building the doors close suddenly, plunging the room into darkness, and he is attacked by Morlocks. George fights them off and starts up his machine, sending it into the future. The stunned Morlocks lying beside the machine decay and turn into skeletons (an effect achieved by stop-frame animation). George then takes the machine back in time to 1900, and it materializes on the lawn outside his house.

George has now returned to the point in time which we saw near the beginning of the film. His friends are sceptical about his story, but the time traveller produces a flower which Weena had given to him in the far future and David Filby – who is an amateur botanist – admits that it is a species he has never seen before. As it is winter, where did he get it? George sees his friends out the door, but – when Filby returns a few minutes later – he discovers that both the machine and George are gone. There are skid marks on the floor, which suggest that the time traveller has moved the machine so that it will materialize outside the sphinx when it returns to the far future. George's housekeeper also confirms that three books are missing from his personal library, but she does not know which ones. She also wonders if he will ever return, and Filby remarks that he has 'all the time in the world' (a phrase which James Bond fans always associate with the film and book *On Her Majesty's Secret Service*).

The Time Machine was released on 22nd July 1960, and received generally favourable reviews. There was much praise for the stop-frame animation sequences, though some critics felt a number of the miniature effects were below-par. Despite this, the film won an Academy Award for Best Special Effects in 1961. Made on a relatively low budget of just $750,000, the film grossed $5.7 million worldwide.

The most memorable aspect of the film was the Time Machine prop itself, and this remained in storage at MGM for many years afterwards. On 3rd May 1970, David Weisz & Co. (acting for MGM) held a public auction of film props and memorabilia, including a pair of ruby slippers from *The Wizard of Oz*, costumes from *Gone with the Wind*, two chariots from *Ben Hur* and the Time Machine from the 1960 film. The control panel was missing from the Time Machine as it had been cut off in 1960 to make insert shots of the date display, employing stop-motion animation and rear projection. Special effects man Tom Scherman built a new one in just 24 hours using wood, pie tins and three Christmas tree lights.

Film historian and collector Bob Burns attended the event in the hope of purchasing the Time Machine, but only had a budget of $1000. When the bidding exceeded $4000, Bob and his wife Kathy left the auction. The prop was eventually sold to the owner of a travelling show for $10,000. Bob Burns phoned George Pal, who told him what had happened but predicted that Burns would eventually own the prop.

A few years later, effects artist Tom Scherman phoned Bob Burns to tell him that he had spotted what he believed was the original Time Machine prop in a thrift shop in Orange, California. Two hours later, the two men arrived at the store and – after some haggling – Bob bought the old movie prop for $1000.

Unfortunately the prop was in poor shape, as the barber's chair was gone, the pods were smashed, and other parts were missing or damaged. Fortunately Bob owned the original drawings which had been given to him by George Pal, and a restoration crew was assembled to rebuild the machine. The team comprised Tom Scherman, Dennis Muren, Mike Minor, Lynn Barker, Dorothy Fontana, Marc Richards, Grace Richards, Lee Richards, Val Richards and Wanda Kendal.

The restoration work only took four weeks, and the prop was ready for Bob Burns' Halloween show in 1976. One of the guests at this event was George Pal, who sat in the machine's chair for the very first time. Effects expert Joe Viskocil took a photograph of Pal sitting in the chair, and it became the director's official photograph for the rest of his life.

Many visitors to Bob Burn's home museum of movie props wanted to sit in the time machine, so – to prevent the chair from wearing out – Bob eventually commissioned a full-size mannequin of Rod Taylor in costume sitting in the machine.

Rather like the Robby the Robot prop from *Forbidden Planet* (1956), the Time Machine has since been used in a large number of film and TV productions including Carl Sagan's *Cosmos* (1981), *Time Tripper* (1978), *The Wizard of Speed and Time* (1989) and the documentary *Time Machine: The Journey Back* (1993), which I will discuss shortly. Bob Burns also owns a replica of the miniature Time Machine that is seen near the beginning of the film. The original, which was built by effects designer Wah Chang in 1959, was destroyed in a house fire at George Pal's home in Bel-Air, California, in November 1961.

George Pal always intended to make a sequel to *The Time Machine*, but died in 1980 at the age of 72 before he could achieve this goal. However, in 1993 a short sequel to *The Time Machine* – entitled *Time Machine: The Journey Back* – aired on American television. Produced and directed by Clyde Lucas, the 48-minute film was hosted by Rod Taylor and was partly a documentary about the history of the Time Machine prop and how it had been rescued and restored to original condition as described above. There were also extracts from some *Back to the Future* promotional films which featured the Time Machine prop, the DeLorean car used in that movie, and actor Michael J. Fox.

Probably the most interesting part of the production, though, was a brief sequel to *The Time Machine* which starred some of the original cast: namely Rod Taylor, Whit Bissel and Alan Young. This was scripted by the original writer of the 1960 film, David Duncan, and produced and directed by Clyde Lucas.

As Bob Burns was reluctant to allow his priceless original Time Machine prop to be moved to a soundstage, a replica was created by photographing the prop, blowing up the photos to nearly full size, pasting them on foam-core board, and then cutting them out. This resulted in a two-dimensional replica which could only be photographed from one angle.

The sequel begins in 1932 with an elderly Walter Kemp (Whit Bissel) remembering George while sitting in an armchair. There are some further scenes (with a voice over by Rod Taylor) which show the Time Machine being built.

These scenes employed a young stand-in, whose face is never seen.

The next scene is set in George's workshop in the lower ground floor of his London house in 1916 during the First World War. David Filby (Alan Young) is standing in the room, remembering how he last saw George in 1900 and wondering where he is now. Then he hears a familiar noise, and the Time Machine reappears with George sitting at the controls. For these shots Rod Taylor wore the same smoking jacket he had donned in the original film.

George has returned from the far future, where he has spent more than thirty years with Weena. He greets David, who is now an officer in the British Army and about to leave for France in an aircraft. George already knows (from his previous journeys in time) that Filby is due to die in a plane crash on 15th May 1916, and tries to persuade him to join him in a journey to the far future. But Filby refuses, as he feels his duty is to obey orders. At one point he picks up a jemmy with the intention of wrecking the machine, but then changes his mind. But he still will not leave with George and departs after the time traveller assures him that they *will* meet again. After David has left, George decides that he will make another journey in time to 14th May 1916 in the hope that he can persuade Filby to come with him.

The short film maintained perfect continuity with the 1960 original, as the set looked like the original basement workshop and also used some of composer Russell Garcia's film music. Although Rod Taylor looked his true age (62 at the time of filming), Alan Young looks much the same as he did in the original film.

In 2002, a remake of T*he Time Machine* was released which was directed by Simon Wells, who happened to be

H.G. Wells' great grandson. Wells' background was mainly in animated films, but had served as a 'future consultant' on the second and third *Back to the Future* films. The screenplay was by John Logan, and was based on H.G. Wells' original 1895 novel and the 1960 screen treatment by David Duncan.

As Wells' original story was now considered too simple for modern audiences, additional plot elements were added. In addition, the special effects were largely created using CGI rather than miniatures and stop-motion animation. The film starred Guy Pearce as Dr Alexander Hartdegen, an inventor teaching at Columbia University in New York City in 1899.

At the start of the film, Alexander and his fiancée Emma (Sienna Guillory) go for a walk in a snowbound New York park, but they are attacked by a mugger (Max Baker) who shoots Emma dead. Distraught, Alexander spends the next four years building a time machine so that he can go back in time to prevent Emma's death. By 1903 he has succeeded in constructing a suitable apparatus. He returns to 1899 and prevents Emma's death by ensuring that the couple do not venture into the park but, as he is buying some flowers from a shop, his fiancé is run over by a horseless carriage. Alexander concludes that it is impossible to prevent Emma's death as it is pre-destined, and further attempts to do so will only result in her dying in a different way.

Upset at his fiancee's demise, Alexander uses his time machine to travel forward to the year 2030 to find out if science has solved this apparent paradox. He visits New York public library, where he consults a holographic sentient librarian called Vox 114 (Orlando Jones) who insists that it is impossible to change the past. Alexander then journeys to the year 2037 and discovers that lunar colonists have destroyed the Moon, making the Earth uninhabitable. He is forced to restart his time machine, but is knocked unconscious and travels to the year 802,701 where he awakens.

He discovers that the Earth has survived, but everything is different. The human race has now evolved into two distinct species, the peace-loving Eloi and the savage Morlocks. Alexander is nursed back to health by an Eloi woman called Mara (Samantha Mumba), who is one of the few of her race who still speak English.

One night, Alexander and Mara's young brother Kalen (Omero Mumba) both dream about a horrifying creature with jagged teeth which calls their name. After waking, Alexander tells Mara about the dream and she explains that all their people have had the same vision. The next day, savage creatures – the Morlocks – attack the Eloi, and Mara is dragged underground. Unlike the Eloi, the Morlocks are carnivorous and use the Eloi for food.

Alexander wants to rescue Mara, but first he lets Kalen take him to Vox 114 – which is still working after 800,000 years. Vox tells Alexander how to find the Morlocks, and he enters their underground lair through an aperture which looks like the face he had seen in his nightmare. Unfortunately he is captured, and soon learns that Mara is imprisoned in a cage. He meets an intelligent, humanoid Morlock (Jeremy Irons), who is described in the script as the 'Uber Morlock'. This chief Morlock has white hair, skin and eyes, and a large exposed brain which extends over his dorsal spine. He is obviously more advanced than the other ape-like Morlocks, which come in two sub-species – the scout and the warrior – and is part of a caste with telepathic abilities who control the other two variants of the species.

The Chief Morlock knows of Emma's death, and explains to Alexander that she cannot be saved as it was her death which drove him to create the time machine in the first place. Saving her would therefore create a temporal paradox. He suggests that Alexander simply takes his machine (which is now within the Morlocks' underground complex) and return home. Alexander gets into the machine but starts to fight the Uber-Morlock, who is clinging on. Alexander moves the control lever to send the machine into the far future and then pushes the Morlock beyond the machine's temporal bubble, causing him to die through accelerated ageing. The time traveller stops in the year 635,427,810, where the sky is a reddish-brown and the landscape is a wasteland.

Realising that he cannot save Emma, Alexander goes back in time to rescue Mara. After freeing her, he sabotages the mechanism of the time machine, causing a derangement in time. Chased by the Morlocks, Mara and Alexander flee to the surface just as there is a huge explosion which kills all the Morlocks and destroys their caves. The time machine is also wrecked beyond repair. Alexander becomes resigned to a new life with Mara and the Eloi, while Vox 114 becomes the Eloi children's teacher.

The film was originally scheduled for release in December 2001 in time for the Christmas holidays, but had to be postponed till 8th March 2002 in order that a section of the movie – which depicted pieces of the damaged Moon falling on New York – could be removed, as it was thought to be too upsetting and inappropriate following the terrorist attacks of 11th September 2001.

The film received mixed reviews from critics, with many preferring the earlier George Pal version which relied on traditional miniature effects. It also did poorly at the box office, making only $123.7 million set against a budget of $80 million, and is probably a good example of the old rule that a success-ful classic film should never be remade.

A more successful attempt to make a spin-off of *The Time Machine* came some decades earlier in 1979 with the release of *Time After Time*, a romantic science fiction thriller with a brilliant premise. The movie was directed and written by Nicholas Meyer, based on an unpublished novel of the same name by Steve Hayes.

The film opens in London in 1893. Successful writer Herbert George Wells (Malcolm McDowell) shows his dinner guests a time machine which he has created. The apparatus is fitted with a removable 'non-return key' that keeps the craft at the traveller's destination, plus a 'vapourizing equaliser'. In reality, H.G. Wells only wrote a book about a time machine; he did not build one. The 1960 George Pal film implies that Wells himself was the time traveller (given that, as mentioned, the manufacturer's plate states that the machine was built by 'H. George Wells'). The 1979 film goes one step further, as the plot is based on the assumption that Wells really did build a working time machine.

Wells' dinner guests are sceptical about the machine's claimed capabilities, but they soon have other things to worry about as the police arrive at the door. They are looking for the famous murderer Jack the Ripper, and have recovered a bag containing bloodstained gloves which – they believe – belong to one of Herbert's friends, the surgeon John Leslie Stevenson (David Warner). But Stevenson is one step ahead of them and has already fled to the basement, where he escapes to the future using Wells' time machine. Wells races downstairs but finds only an empty laboratory.

Although Stevenson manages to escape to the future he does not have the return key – which is still in Wells' possession – so the machine soon returns to the inventor's basement workshop in 1893. Wells realises that there is only one thing he can do: follow Stevenson, wherever he has gone in time and space. Wells ends up in a museum in San Francisco on 5th November 1979, where the machine is part of an exhibition of H.G. Wells' life and achievements. This is where this movie departs from Wells' novel and the 1960 film, as this time craft can apparently travel in *both* time and space. It also has a transparent cabin rather like the bubble canopies of early helicopters like the Bell 47.

Wells is rather perturbed by what he sees of the future. Instead of the socialist utopia he had predicted in his own writings, he finds a chaotic society. He even has a burger and tea breakfast in McDonald's (which he later refers to as 'McDougalls'), and is unimpressed by late 20th century food.

Knowing that Stevenson will have to change his British currency to US dollars, Wells visits a number of banks to enquire if anyone resembling Stevenson's description has attempted to change some money. At the Chartered Bank of London, he meets liberated employee Amy Robbins (Mary Steenburgen), who remembers serving Stevenson. She also recalls that he had asked about nearby hotels, and she had directed him to the Hyatt Regency hotel.

Wells makes his way to the Hyatt Regency and confronts his former friend in his room. He demands that Stevenson comes back with him to 1893 to face justice, but the former surgeon is unrepentant and instead asks Wells for the return key so that he can make full use of his machine to travel forwards and backwards in time. Stevenson also admits that he rather likes the violent society of California in 1979.

Time After Time (1979):
Warner Bros./Orion Pictures

The two men struggle, and Stevenson attempts to steal the key. Their fight is interrupted by a chamber-maid, and Stevenson flees the hotel when he is hit by a car. He is taken to San Francisco General Hospital, where Wells wrongly believes he has died from his injuries. In fact, Stevenson has escaped unharmed.

Later, Wells goes back to the Chartered Bank of London and Amy asks him out on a date. Wells tells her about Stevenson and his wicked deeds. The next day, the murderer returns to Amy's desk at the bank to change more money, but her facial expression reveals that she now knows all about him. She leaves her desk on the pretence of checking the exchange rate and phones Wells who is staying in her apartment. The Englishman tells her to keep Stevenson at the bank until he arrives. Unfortunately Stevenson sees through the deception and leaves after threatening Amy. He then goes to a phone booth and finds Amy's address from the telephone directory.

Amy is still sceptical about time travel, so Wells takes her to the museum and shows her photos of H.G. Wells when he was a young man. Amy admits that there is a resemblance but is not totally convinced, so Wells takes her on a journey in his time machine. They go just three days into the future and Amy now believes that the machine is genuine when she picks up a newspaper and sees the date. Unfortunately the paper also mentions that she has been killed by the Ripper, making her his fifth victim.

Wells tells Amy that they must go back in time three days to prevent the murder of the Ripper's fourth victim and then save her as well. Unfortunately things go wrong, and Stevenson still manages to kill his fourth victim. Wells is arrested, while Amy is left in her apartment at the mercy of the Ripper. Wells begs the police to send a patrol car round to Amy's apartment, but they refuse. Eventually he says he will admit to any crime, sign any confession they want, if they will only do as he asks and send some policemen to Amy's flat. The police agree to this deal, but they are apparently too late as they arrive at the flat and find the body of a young woman who can only be Amy.

The police realise they have been holding the wrong man and release a broken-hearted Wells. Then he is contacted by Stevenson, who reveals that he had actually killed Amy's co-worker and is now holding Amy hostage. He offers Wells a deal – he will spare Amy's life if Wells will hand over the key, which will enable the Ripper to travel freely in time.

Wells agrees to this offer but Stevenson breaks his word and, after obtaining the key, attempts to escape in the time machine while holding onto Amy. But the American woman manages to break free, and Wells removes the crucial 'vapourizing equaliser'. As he had explained at the beginning of the film, this affects the function of the machine in such a way that the craft stays where it is and the passenger travels endlessly in time, effectively destroying him.

With the Ripper dead, Wells declares that he is now going to return to 1893 and then destroy the machine, as it has obviously caused a lot of trouble. Amy insists on returning with him and says she is going to change her name to Susan B. Anthony. The film ends with a caption explaining that Wells subsequently married Amy Catherine Robbins, who died in 1927.

The film was released on 7th September 1979 and garnered many positive reviews. It also received several Saturn Awards. There was much praise for director and screenwriter Nicholas Meyer, who then went on to write and direct *The Wrath of Khan* (1982), which is generally regarded by *Star Trek* fans as being superior to the first *Star Trek* movie, even though it had a far lower budget.

Two of the stars of *Time after Time*, Malcolm McDowell and Mary Steenburgen, fell in love during the making of the film and were married between 1980 and 1990. In 2016, *Time After Time* was made into an ABC TV series, although it was cancelled after just five episodes due to poor ratings. The 1979 film is rightly regarded as one of the great time travel movies, and a worthy successor to the 1960 film.

On 8th November 2018, the *Guardian* newspaper reported that a third cinema version of *The Time Machine* was to be made – directed by Andy Muschietti – so it seems we have not seen the last of H.G. Wells' classic tale.

3

The Classic Era
1960 to 1979

THE most significant time travel film released in 1960 was *The Time Machine*, and I have devoted an entire chapter to this very important movie in an earlier section of this book. The only other time travel film to premiere this same year was *Beyond the Time Barrier*, a low-budget movie filmed in Texas in just ten days on a budget of $125,000.

The plot involved US Air Force test pilot Major Bill Allison (Robert Clarke) accidentally travelling into the future during trials of an X-80 experimental aircraft. After completing his mission, Allison lands at his base and finds it looking forlorn. He heads towards a futuristic city, but is knocked out and captured.

When he recovers consciousness, he finds himself in an underground city known as the Citadel, where he meets his captor's leaders: the Supreme (Vladimir Sokoloff) and their second-in-command, known as the Captain (Boyd 'Red' Morgan). Apart from these two, the rest of the inhabitants are deaf-mute.

The Supreme's granddaughter, Trirene (Darlene Tomkins), reads Allison's thoughts and discovers he is not a spy. However, the American airman is still imprisoned with some bald, homicidal mutants. Eventually the Captain releases Allison, who discovers that he has travelled to the year 2024. A nuclear war has led many survivors to live underground with mutants remaining on the surface, but their race is now sterile. (Notice the plot similarity with many other sci-fi films and TV series of this period.)

Trirene and Allison fall in love, but the woman is killed by a stray bullet fired by General Kruse who had arrived from a colony on another planet in 1994. Allison takes Trirene's body to the Supreme. Distraught at his granddaughter's death, the Supreme shows Allison a secret passage which will return him to his own time zone.

Safely back in 1960, Allison recounts his fantastic adventure from his hospital bed. He warns officials about the dangers of nuclear war, but he himself has paid a stiff price for his journey into the future as he has aged dramatically.

La Jetee (1962) was a French film just twenty-eight minutes long, which mainly consisted of a series of still monochrome photos. Only one very brief shot was taken with a movie camera. This rather odd technique was used purely to save money and was actually quite common in TV productions of the sixties and early seventies, in which a scene might be depicted as a series of still pictures as a cost-cutting or time-saving device. For example, the famous 'cheese shop' sketch from a 1972 edition of the BBC comedy series *Monty Python's Flying Circus* (1969-74) opens with several still photos taken on location showing John Cleese's character arriving at the shop's exterior before the action begins in a studio set.

The plot of *La Jetee* is relatively simple. A man (Davos Hanich), who is in a prisoner in a post-World War III Paris, is sent back in time by scientists who hope that he may find information that will help them solve their present dilemma. They need someone who can mentally survive the shock of time travel. However, the prisoner is tormented by a recurrent childhood memory in which he sees a woman (Helene Chatelain) standing on an observation gallery at Orly Airport (the 'Jetee' of the title). Immediately after this, a man dies.

The prisoner participates in a series of journeys to the past in which he meets the woman and they fall in love. He also travels to the future, and is given a power unit which will enable him to regenerate his devastated society.

When he returns to his original time zone, he learns that he is to be executed by his jailers. But he is contacted by people from the future who offer to rescue him. He chooses instead to go back to Orly Airport before the nuclear war so he can be reunited with the woman. Once there, he realises he is being pursued by one of his jailers who has followed him back in time. The prisoner makes contact with the woman but is then killed by the jailer and, as his life ebbs away, he realises that the person he saw dying in his recurrent memory was actually himself – with the incident being seen through the eyes of his much younger self, who was also present at the scene. In effect, he is trapped in a time loop.

The film was highly praised by critics and, in 2010, *Time* magazine rated it one of the 'Top 10 Time Travel Movies'. It was also the inspiration behind *12 Monkeys* (1995), which starred Bruce Willis and was directed by Terry Gilliam.

The Time Travelers (1964) is a cult science fiction film which starred a cast of largely unknown actors and was made on a relatively small budget ($250,000). It was directed by Ib Melchior, with a screenplay by the director and David L. Hewitt. The film was very influential, as it inspired the Irwin Allen TV series *The Time Tunnel* (1968) and was also remade as *Journey to the Center of Time* (1967).

The film begins with the testing of a new viewing device, effectively a flatscreen television which can display images from the future. As it is drawing a huge amount of power, a technician – Danny McKee (Steve Franken) – is sent to shut it down. But strange shadows are flitting across the room and the screen shows an odd, desert landscape. Danny discovers the device has become a portal to another time and steps through it.

The other members of the scientific team follow Danny in the hope of bringing him back, but then the portal vanishes. They are stranded in the year 2071, and discover an underground city populated by people who have survived a nuclear war.

The city leader, Dr Varno (John Hoyt), explains that Earth is doomed and they are building a rocket that will take everyone to a planet orbiting Alpha Centauri. The following year, Hoyt played ship's doctor Philip Boyce in the first *Star Trek* pilot, *The Cage*. In fact, *The Time Travelers* has a very similar look to the classic *Star Trek* series, particularly in the areas of special effects and set and costume design.

Because of the vast distance involved in space travel, and the time the journey will take, the entire crew will be kept in suspended animation. But the four time travellers cannot board the rocket as there is insufficient room and supplies, so they must repair the time portal. Before the spaceship can lift

The Time Travelers (1964): American International Pictures/
Dobil Productions Inc.

off, the city is invaded by mutants and the space vehicle is
destroyed on its launch pad.

Dr Varno realises that the only way of escape now is via
the time portal, and he commits his people to repairing the
device. The four time travellers manage to escape to the present along with a few people from the future. One of them
throws an object through the portal. It travels forward in
time, damaging the equipment in the laboratory and shutting
down the time gate.

When the survivors return to the laboratory they find
their previous selves there, apparently frozen in time. It appears that the survivors are moving at an accelerated rate and
are ageing rapidly. (Incidentally, this same idea was re-used in
the *Star Trek* episode *Wink of An Eye* as well as *Timelash*, a

1970 segment of the *UFO* TV series, and the 2002 film *Clock-stoppers*).

The survivors' only option is to travel to the far future – 100,000 AD. The screen is dark and, as they move across the room, they cast their shadows – the same ones that were seen in the laboratory scenes near the beginning of the film.

The travellers step through the portal and, as they do so, the screen lights up again to show a scene of a future green and habitable Earth. Then their selves in the lab come to life and repeat the actions seen at the start of the film. The entire movie then repeats several times as a series of brief clips which get faster and shorter until the film ends without ex-planation. It is implied that the travellers are caught in a time loop, an idea that has featured in many other films.

The Time Travelers never won any awards but is regard-ed as a cult classic, particularly as it features a cameo appear-ance by Forrest J. Ackerman – editor of *Spacemen* magazine – who appears as a technician on a future Earth. It also influ-enced many other time travel movies and TV series.

The next time travel movie to hit the cinema screens was *Dr. Who and the Daleks* [[sic]], which was released on 23rd August 1965. It should be noted that the original BBC TV series has always been known as *Doctor Who* and not *Dr. Who*. (You will also see that here is a full stop after 'Dr', something that was a feature of sixties grammar but is now usually ignored.) It also fascinating that this relatively low-budget production and its follow-up, *Daleks' Invasion Earth 2150AD*, have been the only big-screen adaptations of the popular TV series, which has been running since 23rd No-vember 1963. Another *Doctor Who* cinema film was planned in 1976 during the Tom Baker era, but ultimately never hap-pened.

Doctor Who, the TARDIS and the Daleks are so well-known, and so much a part of popular culture, that I don't think any further explanation is required. The very first *Doctor Who* story – *100,000 BC* – was set in the Stone Age but it was the second adventure, *The Daleks*, which really made an impact, with the machine creatures (containing a mutant organism) proving very popular. Further Dalek adventures – written by their creator Terry Nation – were commissioned, and by early 1965 plans were afoot to adapt the first two Dalek stories for the big screen. These films were both produced by Milton Subotsky and Max J. Rosenberg and were made by AARU Productions.

The plot of the first film is similar to the original television production, but with some changes to make the story more understandable to people who had never seen the TV series. *Dr. Who* [sic] – played by Peter Cushing – his granddaughters Susan (Roberta Tovey) and Barbara (Jennie Linden), plus Barbara's boyfriend Ian (Roy Castle), are transported to an alien planet in the Doctor's TARDIS time machine. This is actually Skaro, but is not referred to as such in the film.

When they arrive at their destination, they see a futuristic city in the distance and discover a package of drugs which they take on board the TARDIS. The Doctor pretends they have a leak in the mercury fluid links – an essential part of the time machine – giving them a reason to investigate the settlement. Unfortunately the time travellers are captured by pepperpot-shaped cyborg creatures known as the Daleks. Each Dalek casing contains a mutant alien, the result of a nuclear war.

However, the Daleks are trapped inside the city by the radiation. They discover that the time travellers are now affected by radiation sickness and offer them a deal. If Susan will travel outside the city to obtain further supplies of anti-radiation drugs and bring them back, they will let them use some of the medication to treat themselves.

Susan meets Alydon (Barrie Ingham), leader of the Thals – a race of humanoid beings who also populate Skaro – and is given a supply of anti-radiation drugs to take back to the city. The Daleks offer the Thals a deal – they will provide food in exchange for more drugs. But the Daleks plan to double-cross the Thals and explode a neutron bomb which will destroy all life on the planet.

Meanwhile, the TARDIS crew have managed to immobilise a Dalek by insulating its base, preventing it from drawing electricity from the floor. Back at the Thal settlement, Dr. Who realises they will have to attack the Dalek base to recover the essential fluid link. Unfortunately the Thals are passive, but Ian spurs them into action by threatening to take a Thal woman to the Daleks. (You will notice the plot similarity here with *The Time Machine* which features the pacifist, blonde Eloi.)

Eventually the TARDIS crew and the Thals attack the Dalek base and trick the Daleks into destroying their main control console. This action kills them by cutting off their power, and also stops the countdown for the detonation of the neutron bomb. The TARDIS crew return to their craft with the refilled fluid link and go home.

The film was very successful in the UK but did not fare well in the USA, largely because both the Daleks and *Doctor Who* were unknown in that country at that time. Eight new Dalek props, plus some unmanned fibreglass dummies, were constructed for the film by Shawcraft Models of Uxbridge, who had made the original four Dalek casings for the TV series. These new models had much larger fibreglass fenders than the BBC originals, making them taller, and some had metal claws instead of the familiar bathroom plunger. Additionally, the electronic 'extermination' effect in the original BBC serial could not be easily reproduced on film, so CO_2 fire extinguishers were used to produce a puff of white gas.

The following year, a second AARU Dalek film was made. Entitled *Daleks Invasion Earth 2150AD*, it again starred Peter Cushing as 'Dr. Who' with Gordon Flemyng directing. The screenplay by Milton Subotsky was based on the 1964 Doctor Who TV serial *The Dalek Invasion Of Earth*, which again had been scripted by Terry Nation. The TV original was perhaps too ambitious for its limited budget and suffered from poor production values, although it is still regarded as a classic serial.

The plot of the film was again based on the original teleplay, but with some alterations to make the story understandable to moviegoers who had never seen the TV series. The film opens with a scene in which policeman Tom Campbell (Bernard Cribbins) surprises several men who are breaking into a jewellers. Realising he is outnumbered, he runs to the nearest police box to call for assistance and unwittingly stumbles into the TARDIS and its occupants, consisting of 'Dr. Who' (Peter Cushing), his niece Louise (Jill Curzon) and granddaughter Susan (Roberta Tovey) as they are about to leave for the future. Soon afterwards, the TARDIS arrives in London in the year 2150.

The TARDIS crew find a devastated landscape. The Dalek creatures, which they previously encountered in the first film, have now invaded Earth. Some surviving humans have formed a resistance movement, while others have been turned into Robomen to serve the Daleks. Others are being used as forced labour at a mine in Bedfordshire.

Dr. Who and Tom become separated from Louise and Susan, and are soon captured by Robomen and taken on board a Dalek spaceship where they are thrown into a cell. Dr. Who soon picks the lock, but it is a trick to test his suitability for conversion to a Roboman.

Meanwhile, Wyler (Andrew Keir) takes Louise and Susan to a resistance base where they meet David (Ray Brooks) and a wheelchair-bound scientist called Dortmun (Godfrey Quigley), who has developed special bombs to destroy the Daleks as conventional munitions have proved ineffective.

Dr. Who and Tom are recaptured and taken back on board the spaceship to be converted to Robomen. Suddenly, the resistance attack, with some of their number disguised as Robomen. The attack is only partially successful. Dr. Who and David escape, but Tom and Louise are trapped on the spaceship.

Susan leaves a written message for Dr. Who on a door and then departs with Wyler in an old red Post Office van. Wyler bashes his way through some Daleks in the vehicle, but the machine creatures are tracking the van from their flying saucer and destroy it with an energy beam just after Susan and Wyler abandon it.

The flying saucer used in the film was a triumph of design and was a large, highly-detailed miniature which incorporated lighting effects and a motor which rotated the mid-section of the craft. The only snag was that the model was suspended from highly visible wires. It survived the filming, and was later used in *The Body Stealers* (1969). It is still extant and owned by a collector.

Dr. Who and David escape from the Dalek spaceship and travel to the deserted underground station, but fail to see Susan's message and make their way to the mine in Bedfordshire. Meanwhile, Tom and Louise are still hiding in the Dalek spaceship, which takes them to the mine complex. They escape via a waste chute and then hide.

Wyler and Susan attempt to go to the mine but are captured by the Daleks after they are betrayed by a local. Dr. Who and Susan have almost reached the mine when they encounter Brockley (Philip Madoc), a black marketeer who has agreed to smuggle them into the complex. He takes them to a tool shed where Tom and Louise are hiding and they are joined by a prisoner, Conway (Keith Marsh). He tells them the Daleks' plan: the aliens are going to drop a bomb into the mineshaft to destroy the Earth's core. Then they will plant a device inside the planet so they can pilot it like a spaceship.

Dr. Who studies old plans of the mine and realises that if the location of the bomb's explosion was changed it would cause a powerful magnetic field which would draw the metal Daleks into the shaft, destroying them. Dr. Who asks Tom and Conway to carry out the sabotage while Louise and David lead the prisoners away from the mine. Brockley then proves to be a traitor as he brings the Daleks to the shed, but is then killed by them himself.

Tom and Conway enter the shaft to deflect the bomb, but Conway is killed in a fight with a Roboman. However, Tom manages to build a ramp out of old timber, which will divert the bomb down a different shaft.

Dr. Who is taken to the control room, but he manages to gain control of the radio link and orders the Robomen to attack the Daleks. Wyler, Susan and Dr. Who then escape while the slave workers flee. The Daleks soon defeat the insurgency but then their bomb explodes, causing a gigantic magnetic attraction which sucks them all into the mine shaft. Their flying saucer also crashes.

Dr. Who takes Tom back to his original time zone in the TARDIS, but at his request he arrives a few minutes early so he can foil the burglary and arrest the thieves.

Daleks' Invasion Earth 2150AD was released on 5th August 1966, but received lukewarm reviews from critics. It also performed only moderately at the box office, and made no impression in the USA where no-one had heard of *Doctor Who*. For this reason, a film version of the third Dalek story – *The Chase* (also written by Terry Nation) – was cancelled. This is a pity, because the original six-part TV version of *The Chase* – screened in the summer of 1965 – had one of the most interesting stories in the series' history and would have benefitted from a larger budget and colour filming.

The Chase started with the Doctor (William Hartnell) demonstrating a 'Time Space Visualiser' to his companions and learning that the Daleks have developed their own time machine with which they intend to pursue the Doctor.

Over the next six episodes the TARDIS crew are repeatedly chased through space and time by the Daleks and end up in various locations including the planet Aridus, a viewing platform on the Empire State Building, and a sailing ship. The Daleks so terrify the crew of the boat that they all jump into the sea and, at the end of the episode, it is revealed that the vessel is the famous *Marie Celeste*!

Another episode, *Journey Into Terror*, was set in a haunted house and features Dracula and the Frankenstein Monster. The Frankenstein Monster repeatedly attacks the Daleks and, at one point, lifts one off the ground. It is invulnerable to the Daleks' exterminator guns for reasons that are never explained. At the end of the episode it is revealed that the 'haunted house' is a theme park-type attraction at a World Fair in Ghana, and the monsters are presumably robots. Terry Nation's original idea was that all the events in this episode were happening in someone's subconscious mind. This notion was vetoed by producer Verity Lambert, who felt Nation's concept was too way-out, and she insisted on a more 'rational' explanation for what happened. But I have always felt that Nation's original concept was brilliant.

The last episode of *The Chase* featured creatures called the Mechonoids, which had some similarities with the Daleks – including the fact that they were also designed by Raymond Cusick. The Mechonoids were large polygonal robots armed with a flame gun, and (like the Daleks) were actually trundled along by the operators' feet. Terry Nation hoped they would be as popular as the Daleks but, although a Mechonoid toy was produced in 1965, the creatures never re-appeared in the series. One reason was that the casings were too big to get in the lift at the BBC Lime Grove studios.

There is one further connection between *The Chase* and the Dalek movies. When *The Chase* was being shot in mid-1965, the BBC was short of Dalek casings, so they borrowed three of the movie Daleks from the first film for use in *The Chase*. As mentioned earlier, these were taller than the BBC originals, so two of them had their large fibreglass fenders removed to make them shorter. All three were used as static set dressing and didn't have operators inside. As *The Chase* was broadcast before the premiere of the first Dalek movie, this was their first screen appearance. One of the former movie Daleks – by then owned by Terry Nation – was used to depict the Dalek Supreme in the *Doctor Who* story *Planet of the Daleks* (1973).

Journey to the Center of Time (1967) was a remake of *The Time Travelers* (1964), which starred Scott Brady and Anthony Eisley. It was written, directed and produced by David L. Hewitt, with Ray Dorn as co-producer.

The plot is similar to the original. Stanton (Scott Brady) is in charge of a company which is engaged in time travel experiments. He is helped by Mark Manning (Antony Eisley), 'Doc' Gordon (Abraham Sofaer) and Karen White (Gigi Perreau).

During their experiments, they travel 5000 years into the future and meet aliens led by Vina (Poupee Gamin) who want to colonize another planet. But they find no welcome on Earth, which is in the midst of a global war. She urges them to go home to warn the human race, but is then killed.

The time travellers head back to the present in their machine but then detect another craft which is on a collision course. After attempts to communicate with the other vessel fails, Stanton destroys it.

Unfortunately the time travellers overshoot and end up in the age of the dinosaurs. A giant ruby – which forms a key component of their machine – is destroyed, and they are left stranded. When they explore a nearby cave they find it is full of jewels, including rubies. Stanton is overcome by greed, grabs some rubies, installs one in the time machine and takes off without the scientists. Again he encounters another machine on a collision course and, when he hears a radio broadcast, he realises he is heading towards an earlier version of his own craft. He is then killed by the blast that his earlier self had caused.

Back at the cave, the scientists are leaving when Gordon falls into some molten lava and is killed. Mark and Karen are astonished when the time machine reappears. They get on board the craft but it takes them to a point in time a day before their original departure. They are now in a parallel universe in which they can see their past selves living at a slower rate. They realise this could disrupt the space-time continuum so they return to their machine, but end up lost in time and space. The film ends with the machine, with Mark and Karen aboard, drifting among the stars.

The last time travel movie of the sixties was the well-known original version of *Planet of the Apes* (1968), which starred Charlton Heston and was directed by Franklin Shaffner. The film was based on Pierre Boulle's 1963 novel *La Planete des singes*, which described French journalist Ulysse Merou's voyage to a distant planet where apes are the dominant species and humans are slaves. Boulle got the idea for his book when he visited a zoo and noticed the 'humanlike' expressions of the gorillas.

The first draft of the screenplay was by respected American writer Rod Serling (best known for *The Twilight Zone* TV series), who introduced an important plot twist that turned the film into a time travel movie. At the end of the film, American astronaut George Taylor (Charlton Heston) discovers the broken remains of the Statue of Liberty lying in a desert and realises that the 'alien planet' is really Earth in the future, and that his spacecraft must have travelled through time.

The final draft of the film was by screenwriter Michael Wilson, who had previously worked on the cinema version of another of Boulle's books, *Bridge Over the River Kwai* (1958). Wilson retained Serling's ending, thus turning it into a time travel movie.

The film was a great success, and there was much praise for the very realistic prosthetic makeup. As a result a sequel followed, *Beneath The Planet of the Apes* (1970). Charlton Heston was uninterested in becoming involved in the movie but agreed to film a few brief scenes. A new character – Brent (James Franciscus) – was introduced, and he followed Taylor into the future, landing on the same planet as in the original film.

Further sequels followed. *Escape from the Planet of the Apes* (1971) featured a further plot twist in which three apes repair George Taylor's spacecraft and use it to travel back to 1973. *Conquest of the Planet of the Apes* (1972) was set in a near future in which man has turned apes into slaves, while *Battle of the Planet of the Apes* (1973) dealt with the conflict between humans and apes.

That was the end of the original *Planet of the Apes* films but, in 1974, CBS broadcast a 14-part television series based on the movies. This was ultimately cancelled, but the following year NBC made a 13-episode animated series called *Return to the Planet of the Apes.*

Over the next few decades there were repeated attempts to remake the original film which culminated in *Planet of the Apes* (2001), which starred Mark Wahlberg and was directed by Tim Burton.

***Planet of the Apes* (1968):** APJAC Productions/20th Century Fox

This was generally considered a critical and commercial failure, but in 2011 a new picture premiered. Entitled *Rise of the Planet of the Apes* it was followed by two sequels, *Dawn of the Planet of the Apes* (2014) and *War for the Planet of the Apes* (2017).

This rebooted version of the *Planet of the Apes* franchise draws on elements of all the original films. It also employs the latest developments in CGI to depict the creatures themselves; techniques that were used in Peter Jackson's remake of *King Kong* (2005). Time travel has not featured in these most recent *Apes* films, but further entries in the franchise are likely.

Slaughterhouse Five (1972) was based on a novel of the same name by Kurt Vonnegut, and was inspired by his own experiences as a prisoner of war in WW2 when he experienced at first hand the fire-bombing of Dresden. The film was directed by George Roy Hill, with a screenplay by Stephen Geller. It is very similar to the novel, as it presents a first-person narrative from the point of view of Billy Pilgrim (Michael Sacks) who becomes 'unstuck in time' and experiences the events of his life in a random order, including a spell on the planet of Tralfamadore.

In particular, he recalls his time as a prisoner of war when (like the book's author) he witnessed the Allied bombing of Dresden which resulted in huge civilian casualties. He also remembers other aspects of his time spent with other POWs, who included Edgar Derby (Eugene Roche) and the sociopathic Paul Lazzaro (Ron Leibman). Other memories he recalled include being a husband to Valencia (Sharon Gans) and having a daughter, Barbara (Holly Near), and a son, Robert (Perry King). On the planet Tralfmadore he encountered a young starlet, Montana Wildhack (Valerie Perrine).

Although it was not a huge commercial success, *Slaughterhouse Five* won the Prix du Jury at the 1972 Cannes film festival as well as a Hugo Award and a Saturn Award.

Idaho Transfer (1973) was directed by Peter Fonda (brother of Jane Fonda), who is best-known for the cult motorbike movie *Easy Rider* (1969). The film was produced by William Hayward and Anthony Mazzola, and written by Thomas Matthiesen.

The plot of the movie is relatively simple. Disturbed teenager Karen Braden (Kelley Bohanon) is admitted to an establishment close to the Craters of the Moon lava fields in Idaho. Originally this facility was created to investigate matter transference, but instead its staff discovered how to travel in time. They also learned through experimentation that civilisation was going to be wiped out by an ecological catastrophe.

Unfortunately time travel is found to be damaging to health. Adults over twenty die from renal haemorrhage during the process, so the scientists concentrate on sending only young people fifty-six years into the future where they can build a new civilization.

Eventually the US Government takes over the project. The time machines are switched off, and many subjects are left trapped in the future. With no way of getting back, they explore their new world. The last survivor is captured by a family who put her in the boot of her car, with the implication that she will be used as fuel. A child in the back seat asks what will happen when they run out of time travellers, and she is told that they will have to use each other for fuel.

As is well-known, producer Peter Fonda was very keen that ecological issues should be promoted in films. The movie was made by his own company – Pando – in association with Marrianne Santas, and was copyrighted to Kathleen Film

Production Company in 1973. The end credits conclude with the Latin phrase *Esto Perpetua*, meaning 'It is Forever', which is also the motto of the state of Idaho.

Ivan Vasilievich Changes Profession (1973) is a Russian film which was released in the USA with the title *Ivan Vasilievich: Back to the Future*. The film was based on the play *Ivan Vasiliecich* by Mikhail Bulgakov, and was the most popular film in the USSR in 1973 with over 60 million tickets sold.

The film open in Moscow in 1973. Engineer Alexander 'Shurik' Timofeev (Aleksandr Demyanenko) is building a time machine in his flat. He accidentally sends Ivan Vasilevich Bunsha (Yuri Yakovlev) and George Miloslavsky (Leonid Kuravlev) back to the era of Ivan the Terrible. The two reluctant time travellers are forced to disguise themselves. Bunsha dresses as Ivan IV, and Miloslavsky becomes a fake duke.

Simultaneously, the real Ivan IV is transported by the time machine to Shurik's apartment in 1973 and has to deal with modern-day life. Meanwhile Shurik tries to fix his machine so that everyone can be returned to their original time zones. Many comic situations result from Bunsha and Miloslavsky being stuck in a past time. Eventually Shurik manages to get everyone back to their original points in time, and then it is revealed that the entire episode was a dream by Shurik – or was it? The plot device of 'strange things happening which are eventually revealed to be a dream' was one which was often used by Gerry Anderson in his various puppet and live action shows, e.g. *Ordeal,* an episode of *UFO* (1969-70).

Sleeper (1973) is a futuristic science fiction comedy film directed by Woody Allen and produced by Jack Grossberg. The screenplay was by Marshall Brickman and Allen.

Allen also stars as the main character, Miles Monroe, a health food shop owner who is cryogenically frozen in 1973 and then brought back to life 200 years later. Two scientists (Bartlett Robinson and Mary Gregory) have revived Miles in the hope that he can help the resistance to overthrow the dictatorship which controls the USA by infiltrating a top-secret operation called the 'Aries Project'.

The plot is discovered by the authorities, and the scientists are captured and tortured. However, Miles escapes by impersonating a robot butler and works in the house of socialite Luna Schlosser (Diane Keaton). Unfortunately Luna wants to replace his head, so Miles is forced to reveal his true identity and then kidnap her.

Miles and Luna start a relationship, but then Miles is captured and brainwashed. He is eventually rescued by the resistance, who reverse his conditioning. With Luna's help, he infiltrates the Aries Project. The Leader had been killed by a rebel bomb some months previously, with only his nose surviving. The authorities hope to clone a new Leader from the nose, but Miles thwarts their plans by dropping the nose in front of a road roller. The film ends with Miles and Luna kissing.

The movie was released on 17th December 1973 and did well, making more than $18 million at the box office set against a budget of $2 million. It was also well-received by critics, who appreciated the mix of slapstick humour and one-liners.

One of the best lines in the movie comes early in the film, when Luna tells Miles that 'It's hard to believe you haven't had sex for 200 years'.

'204, if you count my marriage,' replies Miles.

The film has an odd feel, particularly as the incidental music (apparently composed by Allen himself) consists of 1920s-style ragtime music, almost as though Allen had sought the most incongruous music possible as a subtle joke.

Superman (1978) was the first of four films featuring the superhero which starred the late Christopher Reeve, who also starred in one of the greatest time travel movies – *Somewhere in Time* (1980) – which is discussed in detail in a later chapter. Directed by Richard Donner, the movie is not really a time travel picture as such, but it does feature a scene near the end in which Superman travels back in time to save Lois Lane by flying round the Earth at a tremendous speed. How this causes a time jump is never explained. According to Einstein's Special Theory of Relativity, an astronaut who travels close to the speed of light will age more slowly than his twin brother back on Earth (time dilation), but that does not mean that you can travel back in time simply by moving at a very high speed. But of course, the *Superman* films were never meant to be scientifically accurate as they are set in a fantasy world.

The last time travel film of the 1970s was the excellent movie *Time After Time* (1979), and this is reviewed in the earlier chapter on *The Time Machine*.

4
Somewhere in Time

S *OMEWHERE in Time* (1980) occupies a unique place in the history of time travel movies. Made on a relatively small budget of just $4m, it initially underperformed at the box office and was derided by critics when it was first released in October 1980. Much of the criticism centred on the powerful emotional core of the film —and its very sentimental tone – which was enhanced by John Barry's magnificent score, now considered one of his greatest works.

Yet, several months after its release – when it was first shown on cable television in the USA – it developed a fan following. It also proved a very popular hire at video rental shops, which were springing up all over the USA and UK in the early eighties. In 2018 it is now considered a cult classic, with its own website and a very active appreciation society – the International Network of *Somewhere in Time* Enthusiasts (I.N.S.I.T.E.) – with many members worldwide. I.N.S.I.T.E.

has organised a number of conventions to celebrate the film, which have been held every October at the main shooting location, the Grand Hotel on Mackinac Island in Lake Michigan.

The film now has a huge fanbase, not just among women – who are often fascinated by the story of eternal love enduring through time – but also among men, and this is probably because the story is told from the viewpoint of the male protagonist, playwright Richard Collier. I must confess that I am a great fan of the film. It is one of these movies which never dates, and actually improves with further viewings. The subsequent tragedies which befell one of its stars (the late Christopher Reeve) have made the movie even more poignant.

Somewhere in Time started life as a 1975 novel, *Bid Time Return*, by prolific science fiction, horror and fantasy writer Richard Matheson. Born in 1926 in Allendale, New Jersey, Matheson was interested in writing from a very early age and had his first short story published when he was just eight years old. After graduating from Brooklyn Technical High School, he served in the US Army during WW2. After the war he studied journalism at the University of Missouri, graduating with a Bachelor of Arts degree in 1949.

Matheson's career as a writer really took off in 1950 when his short story *Born of Man and Woman* was published in *The Magazine of Fantasy and Science Fiction* and, over the next three decades, he wrote a huge number of short stories, novels and film and TV screenplays.

Some highlights from this period of Matheson's life include *The Shrinking Man* (1956), which was filmed as *The Incredible Shrinking Man* (1957), and the science fiction vampire novel *I Am Legend* (1954) which has been filmed four times, including the most recent (2007) version which starred Will

Smith, and an earlier production – *The Omega Man* (1972) – which featured Charlton Heston.

Matheson also wrote sixteen scripts for *The Twilight Zone* TV series, including *Nightmare at 20,000 feet* (1963) which starred William Shatner as a nervous passenger. He also wrote an episode of *Star Trek, The Enemy Within* (1966), and the short story *Duel* (1971), about a motorist being pursued by a monster truck, which he adapted into a TV movie directed by Steven Spielberg.

In 1975 Matheson wrote a

RICHARD MATHESON
Bestselling author of HELL HOUSE

Bid Time Return

Bid Time Return by Richard Matheson (1975): First published by Viking Press

novel, the aforementioned *Bid Time Return*, in which playwright Richard Collier falls in love with a photograph of a Victorian actress called Elise McKenna and decides to travel back to 1896 – using a form of self-hypnosis – in order to woo her. Collier is actually suffering from an incurable temporal lobe brain tumour, and it is later implied that his whole experience may have been a fantasy created by his diseased brain. The book takes the form of a journal supposedly written by Collier himself in the first person, and ends with the author dying of his brain tumour. The last section of the book is supposedly written by Richard's brother, Robert, after his death.

Matheson based much of the book on his own experience when he discovered an old portrait of an actress called Maude

Adams in Piper's Opera House in Nevada and wondered what might happen if he travelled back in time to the 19th century to meet her. The book's original title comes from a line in Shakespeare's *Richard III* (Act III, Scene 2): *'O call back yesterday, bid time return'.*

To prepare for writing the novel, Matheson resided for several weeks at the Hotel del Coronado in San Diego (where most of the novel is set) and dictated his thoughts into a cassette tape recorder while playing the role of Richard Collier. These original tapes still exist, and copies are available from the fan organisation I.N.S.I.T.E. Much of the biographical information on his heroine, Elise McKenna, was based on Maude Adams, while the character of William Fawcett Robinson – McKenna's very controlling manager – was inspired by Adams' own manager, Charles Frohman, including the fact that he died when the liner RMS *Lusitania* was torpedoed by a U-boat in 1915.

Four years after the publication of *Bid Time Return*, Universal Studios made a film adaptation with a screenplay by Richard Matheson. The producers were Stephen Deutsch and Ray Stark. There were a number of significant changes from the original novel, though. The title was changed from *Bid Time Return* to *Somewhere in Time*, as it was felt that modern American audiences would not understand what *Bid Time Return* meant as the meaning of the word 'bid' had changed since medieval times. The revised title was suggested by Deutsch and, in fact, the words 'somewhere in time' appear in a passage towards the end of Matheson's original novel.

In addition, the location had to be changed, as the Hotel del Coronado was now surrounded by modern structures such as TV aerial masts. Eventually the producers settled on The

Grand Hotel on Mackinac Island on Lake Michigan. Most of the film was shot in and around the hotel. In addition, some scenes were shot on the former Mackinac College (now Mission Point Resort) on Mackinac Island, which had conference rooms and sound stages, and four days of shooting were also carried out in Chicago. The budget was originally set at $8m, but was reduced to just $4m which was not a lot for a period drama.

The subplot about Richard Collier dying from a brain tumour was also deleted as it was felt that most audiences would not like this, and so in the film Richard dies of a broken heart. The dates in the movie were also changed. In Richard Matheson's original novel, Collier time travels from 1971 to 1896 to meet Elise. In the film, he starts off in 1980 and then goes back to 1912. This change was done to allow the inclusion of a character, Arthur, who is present in both time periods.

The screenplay was by the book's original author, Richard Matheson, and is generally considered superior to his original novel. Some editing was carried out to bring the film in at just one hour 39 minutes running time, which adds to its appeal.

The lead role of playwright Richard Collier was played by American actor Christopher Reeve, who at that point was best-known for playing the lead role in *Superman* (1978). As the actor himself admitted, he had a relatively puny physique before playing The Man of Steel and had to put on a large amount of muscle for the role. This required him to spend several hours a day weight-training under the supervision of bodybuilder, fitness expert and actor Dave Prowse, who is best known for playing Darth Vader in the original *Star Wars* (1977). At the time of filming *Somewhere in Time* in 1979, Reeve still maintained the magnificent physique he had acquired for the *Superman* films, and this is very noticeable in some shots.

Elise McKenna was played by English actress Jane Seymour (real name Joyce Penelope Wilhelmina Frankenberg), whose big break had come as the female lead Solitaire in Roger Moore's first James Bond film, *Live and Let Die* (1973), when she was just 21. Her manager – William Fawcett Robinson – was portrayed by Canadian actor Christopher Plummer, who was best-known for playing Von Trapp in *The Sound of Music* (1965). Plummer has had a long career in film, television and the theatre, and is still acting at the age of 88 with his most recent cinema role being John Paul Getty senior in Ridley Scott's film *All the Money in the World* (2017), in which he replaced Kevin Stacey at very short notice.

The director was Jeannot Schwarz, who had mainly worked in American television and had helmed the *Jaws* sequel *Jaws 2* (1978). A major coup, though, was the hiring of English composer John Barry who was at the pinnacle of his success, having written the musical score for a huge number of big-budget pictures, including several James Bond films. Barry was persuaded to write the score for *Somewhere in Time* by Jane Seymour – who was a close friend – and eventually agreed to a deal in which he received a percentage of the royalties of the soundtrack album rather than a flat fee. This proved to be a wise move, as the album eventually became a bestseller and the *Somewhere in Time* suite became an important part of John Barry concerts. At the time he wrote the score for the film, John Barry was still grieving for his parents, who had both died within a few months of one another. His emotional state actually helped him to compose what would now be regarded as his best-ever and most poignant film score.

The film opens with the Universal logo. Then the titles appear as simple white text set against a black background. There is no opening theme music, but after a moment or two there is the sound of a party in full swing, which plays over the remaining titles. A caption reads 'Millfield College, May 1972.' Then the film proper begins. Playwright Richard Collier is celebrating the launch of his first play. An old woman (Susan French) is sitting at the back of the room. She can't be seen clearly as she is in shadow and has a shawl round her head.

The old woman gets up from her seat and (filmed entirely from behind) heads towards Richard, who has his back to her. The crowd of people parts to let her through and she touches the playwright on his right shoulder, making him turn round. The old lady (who we later discover is the elderly incarnation of Elise McKenna) puts a Victorian pocket watch in Richard's right hand and utters her sole line of dialogue in the movie:

'Come back to me!'

Richard is stunned by this incident and doesn't understand what has happened. 'I never saw her in my life,' he blurts out. But, in a deeper part of his mind, he knows she is important to him.

The woman swiftly leaves the party and returns to the Grand Hotel, sitting in the back of an old, black saloon car. Her housekeeper, Laura Roberts (Teresa Wright), lets her in to her apartment at the hotel and asks her how the play was – and whether she enjoyed it. But the elderly Elise says nothing. Instead, she puts on a record (The 18th variation of Rachmaninoff's *Rhapsody on a Theme of Paganini*), studies the cover of the programme of Richard's first play (*Too Much Spring*), and sits in a chair. Later in the film we learn that the elderly

Elise died soon afterwards, her task complete, but this is not depicted on screen (the death of Elise was filmed, but was later cut out during editing).

Susan French, who played the elderly Elise, had worked before with director Jeannot Schwarz on *Jaws 2* and had a remarkable resemblance to Jane Seymour – not just facially, but in height and build as well. In fact, the first time I saw the movie I thought the elderly Elise was actually Jane Seymour wearing old-age make-up!

A caption then appears on screen: 'Chicago, Eight Years Later'. Playwright Richard Collier is looking out the window of his apartment at the city landscape. The camera pans left to reveal all his certificates and diplomas. He is clearly a successful writer, but is restless and unhappy because he is suffering from writer's block. He rips a blank sheet of paper out of his electric typewriter, crumples it up and throws it into a wastebasket. Then he puts on a jacket and leaves his apartment. As he is going downstairs in the lift, he meets his agent (Ted Liss) and tells him that he is taking a break. His agent reminds him about his commitment to the play, but Collier says it is not happening at present. He also reveals that he has broken up with his fiancé.

Collier goes for a drive along the shoreline in Chicago in his car, a silver 1979 Fiat Spider 2000 open-topped sports car. He heads out of the city and eventually comes across the Grand Hotel. (In reality the Grand Hotel is on an island in Lake Michigan, but in the film it is implied that it is on the mainland just along the coast from Chicago.) Richard is so intrigued by the striking appearance of the hotel that he parks his car and checks in, signing the hotel register. The enormous, magnificent 19th century Grand Hotel – which was made mainly of wood and painted a brilliant white – is really one of the stars of the film, and greatly contributed to the authentic period atmosphere of the production. R.D. Musser, the hotel's owner, allowed Universal to film free-of-charge provided the hotel was depicted in a favourable light. As the hotel was at almost full capacity, many scenes (particularly those set inside) had to be filmed at night. The shooting schedule proved quite gruelling as filming was carried out up to sixteen hours a day, six days a week, with Sunday as a day off.

The bellboy Arthur (Bill Erwin), who looks about 75 years old (though Erwin himself was only 64 at the time of filming), carries Richard's bag and takes him up in the lift to his room (313). Arthur opens the curtains to show Richard the view over the lake and reveals that he has been at the hotel since 1910, when he was just five years old. Richard is interested to hear this and gives Arthur a generous tip. Arthur mentions that he lives in a bungalow behind the hotel and – as he leaves – he turns towards Richard, a quizzical expression on his face. He asks Richard if he has previously met him, since he seems familiar, but the young man says they have never met before.

Richard consults his old pocket watch (which he now carries everywhere) and decides to visit the hotel restaurant, but is told by the head waiter that it doesn't open for forty minutes so he decides to kill some time by having a wander round the hotel. He soon discovers that the hotel has a small museum known as the *Hall of History*. As Richard looks at the exhibits, the sound of Rachmaninoff plays on the soundtrack and he is aware of a presence behind him. He turns round to see a framed photograph of a young, beautiful woman with dark hair, which has an oval surround. Reeve's look of surprise in this scene is genuine, as the photograph was kept covered until the last moment.

As Richard moves slowly towards the picture, he is momentarily dazzled by a flare of light but continues towards it. Unfortunately the nameplate beneath the photo is missing, but he still feels drawn towards the picture. It is as though Elise is calling out to him through time.

Richard goes out to the verandah of the hotel to find Arthur, who tells him that the picture is of an actress called Elise McKenna who performed a play at the hotel's theatre in 1912. Richard is astonished to learn that the hotel has its own theatre down by the lake.

Richard returns to the Hall of History to gaze at the photo of Elise again. That night he cannot sleep, tossing and turning, and gets up twice to look at the picture. The next morning, as Arthur is putting his luggage into the boot of his sports car, Richard tells him to put the cases back into his room as he will not be going home just yet. He also asks Arthur where the nearest library is, and the old man tells him that there is one in a nearby town. Collier drives there in his car and soon finds out a lot about Elise McKenna by studying reference books, old magazines and theatre programmes.

He soon learns that she was regarded as one of the greatest talents in American theatre, but had a very domineering manager called William Fawcett Robinson. A change seemed to have occurred in her personality in 1912 after she had performed in a play at the hotel theatre, and she was rarely seen in public after this. Richard comes across the last photo ever taken of her and realises it is the same white-haired old woman he encountered at the post-play party in 1972: the woman who gave him the pocket watch he still carries everywhere to this day.

Later, on a rainy night, Richard knocks at the door of the apartment belonging to Miss Laura Roberts (Teresa Wright), Elise McKenna's former companion and housekeeper. Initially Richard claims he is planning to write a play on the life of Elise McKenna. Roberts tries to close the door on him but Richard pleads with her to listen. He is not actually writing a play: it is something more personal. He shows Roberts the watch and she is astonished as she knew that it belonged to Elise, who had regarded it as precious and carried it everywhere with her. It had mysteriously vanished on the night she died in 1972. Richard mentions that Elise had given it to her at the party. It then dawns on him that she must have died that very same night.

Realising that Richard is not a crank, Roberts invites her in and shows her some of Elise's belongings, including an old costume. Richard then asks what she was really like, and Roberts replies that she was 'kind and thoughtful but within herself'. A personality change seems to have occurred in 1912 after she performed at the hotel theatre. In Matheson's original novel, Richard realises that his proposed time journey back to 1896 may cause Elise some trauma and have resulted in this personality change, but he decides to go ahead regardless; this plot point does not appear in the screenplay. Roberts then shows Richard a photo of Elise's manager, William Fawcett Robinson, and the young playwright asks if he was really as strange as reports suggest.

Then he sees a book by Gerard Finney called *Travels Through Time* and picks it up. Richard is amazed as – by a curious coincidence – Finney was his philosophy teacher when he was at college. Roberts mentions that Elise had read the book many times and had become fascinated by it.

Richard then notices a music box which is an exact replica of the Grand Hotel, and Roberts reveals that Elise had that specially made. When Richard opens it, the tune it plays is Rachmaninoff's *Rhapsody on a Theme of Paganini*, and he reveals that that it is his favourite music of all time.

The next scene is set in Richard's old college, where he intercepts his former teacher Gerard Finney and asks him quite bluntly if time travel is possible. Finney is initially taken aback, but then tells Richard about an occasion when he was staying in a very old hotel in Venice in 1971.

All his surroundings had an aged feel, and Finney thought that if he fed the suggestion into his brain that the year was 1571 not 1971 – using a self-hypnotic technique – then he might travel back in time. Finney did this very thing *over and over again*, making himself exhausted. Then, just for a moment, he felt that he *really had travelled back in time to 1571*. It was a transient and imperfect experience, but he felt convinced that what he had achieved was real and not an illusion. He wasn't sure if he ever wanted to try this again, but if he did he would remove all trappings of the present day from the immediate environment to avoid the time travel process being sabotaged. In other words, he would have to 'dissociate from the present moment'.

The character of Gerard Finney is a nod to the works of author Jack Finney, whose 1970 novel *Time and Again* employed a similar time travel technique (involving self-hypnosis) to that used by Richard in *Somewhere in Time* and the novel it was based on. Matheson's original novel, *Bid Time Return*, included an intellectual appraisal of some of the best-known tomes on the subject of time, such as *An Experiment With Time* by J.D. Dunne and *Man and Time* by J.D. Priestley.

Later, Collier goes to a vintage coin shop and buys some US currency from the year 1912. (In the book he acquires some banknotes, but in the film he only purchases coins.) He also obtains some early 20th century clothes and cuts his hair in an Edwardian style using period photos as a guide. To complete his ensemble, he wears a hat (as almost everyone did in the 1900s).

At the time of the filming of *Somewhere in Time* in the late spring and early summer of 1979, Christopher Reeve still maintained the magnificent muscular physique he had developed for the *Superman* films. To try and disguise this, costume designer Jean-Pierre Dorleac created a beige three-piece suit for Reeve which incorporated vertical stripes, emphasising Reeve's height and apparently lessening his bulk.

Now that he has achieved a period look, Richard makes his first attempt to travel back in time using pre-recorded suggestions on a cassette recorder. No actual hypnotic induction is depicted in the film, as filmmakers have always had a fear that someone might watch the staged induction and then go into a trance themselves. Instead, Collier listens to what a hypnotist might describe as 'direct suggestions'; i.e. they are presented in the *present tense as though the desired change had already happened*. This is actually quite accurate and, if you want to read up more about this subject, I suggest that you read another of my books, *Practical Hypnotherapy* (New Generation Publishers, 2018).

The suggestions that Collier listens to include the following statements:

It is June 27, 1912.
You are lying on the bed. It is 6.00 p.m.
Your mind accepts this.

As Collier listens to these pre-recorded suggestions, he empties the room of any objects which remind him of 1971 and puts them in a closet. Collier has the suggestions recorded on a C-120 cassette, which gives him one hour's playing time per side. (In the novel, he uses a C-90 cassette.)

Despite listening to the suggestions repeatedly over a long period of time, and even saying them out loud as affirmations, Richard remains stuck in 1971 and is unable to make a time jump. In Richard Matheson's original book, Richard makes many abortive attempts before he makes a successful journey through time.

In desperation, Richard visits the Hall of History once more to gaze at Elise's photo. Then he notices an old guest registration book in a glass case and has an idea. Although it is late at night, he runs outside the hotel and knocks on the door of Arthur's bungalow. The old man answers the door wearing his pyjamas.

Richard asks Arthur if the hotel has a storeroom which contains old artefacts such as guest registers, and Arthur confirms that they are kept in the attic. Soon afterwards, Richard enters the attic of the hotel – torch in hand – and locates the old, dusty guest register from 1912. He is so afraid of what this might reveal that he initially keeps his eyes closed, but then opens the book and discovers that he did in fact check into the hotel on 28th June 1912 at 9.18 a.m. and was given room number 416.

Having obtained concrete evidence that his time travel experiment did eventually work, Richard returns to his room and lies on the bed. He puts the cassette player under the bed, but continues to repeat the suggestions. Eventually he falls asleep, a smile on his face. When he awakens, the ambient lighting has changed direction and there is the sound of whinnying horses. To subtly emphasise the change between 1980 and 1912, a different film stock was used. Scenes set in 1980 were filmed using Kodak/Eastman stock, while those in 1912 employed Fujifilm which gave a softer image and different colour saturation.

After checking he still has his period coins, Richard prepares to leave the suite of rooms, but there is a problem as he is not alone. A lady – Maude (Victoria Michaels) – is in the room, and Richard is forced to hide behind a curtain. Her husband Rollo (William P. O'Hagan), wearing a top hat, arrives in the room, and the couple engage in a heated argument. Richard seizes the opportunity to leave the room, but Rollo hears the door shutting and goes out into the corridor. Richard had turned left on leaving the hotel room but, on hearing the door opening, he does a U-turn and walks back towards the room. Rollo asks Richard if he has seen anyone leaving through the door, and Richard said he went 'that way', pointing to the far end of the corridor. This scene differs considerably from Richard Matheson's book, in which Richard arrives in the hotel in 1896 in a relatively small room and finds himself locked in without a key. Eventually he gets out by cutting away part of the door jamb with an open razor which he finds in the bathroom.

Having narrowly escaped detection, Richard makes his way to Room 117. He already knows that Elise is staying in that room, as he saw her details in the register. Richard knocks on the door, but it is answered by Elise's maid – Marie (Maud Strand) – who says she has no idea where the actress is.

Richard then goes down to the main foyer of the hotel in a lift. When he arrives, he discovers the reception area is crowded with people. Among them is a young boy who is about seven years old. It is the young Arthur (Sean Hayden), the 1912 incarnation of the old bellboy who Richard had met in 1980. Arthur is playing with a large rubber ball and is admonished by his father (John Alvin) for doing this in the lobby. Eventually the young Arthur sits on the large ball, looking rather disconsolate. Sean Hayden was chosen for the role of the young Arthur because he looked very like Bill Erwin when he was a child.

Richard visits the theatre near the hotel, but still cannot find Elise. He asks the director of the play, who offers to give a message to her. Then he knocks on the door of a dressing room and meets another actress, who suggests he goes to the shore of the lake where Elise is out walking.

Richard walks out of the theatre, and the audience catches their first glimpse of Elise as a reflection in a multi-paned window behind Richard. She is walking along the shore as the camera zooms in on her reflected image. Richard walks down to the shore as John Barry's powerful theme kicks in. The playwright approaches Elise as she stands by a tree, she turns to see him and then utters the immortal line of dialogue: 'Is it you?'

As Jane Seymour later recounted in the 'Making of' documentary on the DVD release, a whole day of shooting was spent getting this short scene right, particularly Christopher Reeve's movements just prior to the meeting. Despite this, when Seymour uttered her immortal line of dialogue she accidentally fluffed her line and said: 'Is it Jew?' The mistake was corrected later by overdubbing the correct words. This scene is considered one of the emotional highpoints of the film, and the fan organisation I.N.S.I.T.E. later paid for a commemorative plaque to be installed at that exact spot on the shoreline where this first meeting of the two lovers took place.

Richard answers Elise's query with a simple 'Yes', and then apologises for startling her. At this point, her manager Robinson appears and announces that he wishes to take her to dinner. Richard tells Elise that he wants to talk to her, but she ignores his request and walks back towards the hotel with Robinson as Richard follows them. This annoys Robinson, who turns round and asks Richard if he is a guest at the hotel. If he is, he will have him put out. A red vintage car can be seen in the background in this shot. Mackinac Island is normally free of motor vehicles – rather like Sark in the British Channel islands – due to local legislation, and special permission had to be obtained to allow the use of cars on the island for the duration of shooting. The film crew were allowed just one motor vehicle, and extensive use was made of bicycles and horse-drawn transport during shooting.

Richard, Elise and Robinson make their way to the hotel dining room, which is enormous. In fact, the dining room at the Grand Hotel was one of the largest in the USA. As Richard is wondering what to do, a red-haired woman comments on his suit, pointing out that it is ten years out of date.

Eventually Elise finishes dinner, and Richard sees his chance. As she is dancing with another man, Richard cuts in and takes his place. Elise is perturbed at this breach of etiquette and asks him what he is doing. A moment later, Robinson arrives with some hotel staff and declares that Richard is an intruder and must be escorted off the premises. Richard is taken away, but then Elise announces that she is going to speak to him, reassuring Robinson that she 'will return momentarily'.

Elise talks to Richard and discovers he is a playwright. She also refuses to believe that he knows everything about her. 'You are a complete stranger to me,' she says. Richard then asks why she said 'Is it you?' when they first met. She refuses to answer and, when he asks when he will see her again, she simply replies, 'I don't know'.

The next scene is set in Elise's dressing room, and is a shot of a mirror which is reflecting Elise's image as she brushes her hair while sitting down. This suggests non-verbally that Elise is reflecting on what has happened.

'Is he the one, William?' she asks her manager.

'Only you can tell for certain.'

Robinson then discusses her pending performance the following night and gives her some advice. 'Keep ahead of them,' he says, and reminds her of the importance of mystery.

The next scene is set early the following morning as Richard wakes up, having spent a rather uncomfortable night on a cushioned wicker couch on the verandah of the hotel. He makes his way to Room 117 and knocks on the door.

Elise answers. Richard wishes her 'Good morning', and asks if she slept well. Rather sarcastically she replies, 'wonderful', and Richard points out that he didn't sleep well either but will get a room at 9.18 a.m. Richard invites her to have breakfast with him, but she points out that it is only 6.00 a.m. and she never eats breakfast on performance days. She also points out that her maid Marie is still sleeping in the other room, but she eventually agrees to meet him at 1.00 p.m. for a walk.

A couple of hours later, Richard is sitting at an outside table on the huge lawns outside the hotel when Robinson approaches and sits down. He wants to find out more about Richard and what his motivations are. When he learns that he is a playwright, he concludes that he must be interested in having Elise appear in one of his plays. 'Is it money?' he asks.

Having sized up Richard, and wrongly concluded that he does not have the best of intentions, he storms off saying that 'there is a law' and that 'the matter is concluded'.

At 9.15 a.m., Richard arrives at the reception desk to book a room. He is told that the cost will be three dollars a day, and he has been allocated Room number 420. Richard is perturbed because he knows from looking at the register in 1980 that he is meant to reside in room 416. What has gone wrong? Suddenly, another of the reception staff points out that room 420 has already been reserved and he is given 416 instead. Richard signs the register exactly as he previously saw it, and gives the clerk the correct time – 9.18 a.m. Things are now exactly as he had seen them. The young Arthur is sitting on a couch looking rather down in the dumps, so Richard gives him his ball.

Later, Richard comes out of a toilet, his face covered with a dozen tiny bits of paper which are covering shaving nicks as he doesn't know how to use an open razor correctly. He is carrying his shaving tackle in front of him inside his hat. He meets a gentleman going into the toilet, who makes a one-word comment: 'Astonishing'. This Edwardian gentleman was played by Richard Matheson, making a brief cameo as an 'Astonished Man'.

Shortly after this, Elise is on the steps of the hotel, about to leave with Richard. Robinson arrives, but is unable to prevent the couple from departing in a horse-drawn buggy. That afternoon, Richard and Elise spend some time at various locations near the hotel, including a picturesque lighthouse and grassy lawns where artists are working on easels. These are some of the most visually impressive scenes in the movie, and look like impressionist paintings.

Gradually, Elise falls in love with Richard, who once more asks her why she said 'Is it you?' when they first met. This time Elise is more open, and tells Richard that Robinson had predicted that one day she would meet a man who would change her life forever. 'He knows things,' says Elise. This section of dialogue has lead to speculation on the Internet that Robinson must be clairvoyant, but if you read the small article on this subject on the I.N.S.I.T.E. website you will see that the author of the piece has concluded that this is not the case and that Robinson was merely making an obvious deduction. However, in Richard Matheson's book it is suggested that two psychics – an Indian woman and a gypsy's daughter – had previously told Elise that she would meet a man who would change her life. This detail is omitted from the film.

Later, the couple go for a brief sail on the lake in a rowing boat and Richard hums a piece of music, which is none other than the Rachmaninoff composition which recurs repeatedly throughout the film. Elise loves this piece of music and it be-comes the couple's signature tune. In Matheson's original novel the music in question is a piece by Mahler and is even used by Richard to assist his journey through time, but – for the film – composer John Barry felt that Rachmaninoff would work much better.

After the couple have sailed on the lake, they rest on the shore. Elise tells Richard to stick out his tongue so that she can moisten a handkerchief to wipe away the dried blood and paper from his face. She asks Richard what time it is. He tells her it is 4.30 p.m., and she announces that she must rest before her performance. She is fascinated by his pocket watch and asks him where he got it. He replies that it was given to him.

Elise walks down a hotel corridor towards her room and explains that her entire theatre company will be leaving that evening for Denver after the performance. (In Matheson's book Elise has her own private railcar, but this detail is omitted in the film.) Richard asks Elise if he can talk with her a little more, and she agrees to this. He lets her into her room and Richard puts his arms around her, kissing her passionately.

Suddenly there is a knock at the door. It is Robinson, who has been wondering where she has been all afternoon. For the first time in the film, Elise stands up for herself in an assertive way.

'Our relationship is strictly professional... I'm involved with you as an actress, not a doormat,' she says. Richard moves to leave, and Elise tells him that she will meet him at the theatre door after the performance. Robinson leaves the room and goes downstairs, looking rather downcast. He knows that he will never have the same control over her again.

A few hours later, Richard is sitting in the audience near the front watching Elise's performance in a play – *Wisdom of the Heart* – in the hotel theatre. The rather humorous play is about Elise's character being forced into an arranged marriage with a much older and unattractive man.

'There must be something you like about him,' says the maid.

'Yes, his absence,' replies Elise.

Richard laughs heartily but then Elise ignores the script and delivers what fans of the movie have called the 'man of my dreams soliloquy', as she stares at Richard and gives a spontaneous oration inspired by her love for him:

The man of my dreams has almost faded now.
The one I have created in my mind.

The sort of man each woman dreams of in the deep-
est and most secret reaches of her heart.
I can almost see him now before me.
What would I say to him, if he were really here?
Forgive me, I have never known this feeling –
I've lived with it all my life.
Is it any wonder then, that I failed to recognize you?
You – who brought it to me for the first time.
Is there any way I can tell you how my life has
changed?
Any way at all to let you know what sweetness you
have given me?
There is so much to say... I cannot find the words.
Except for these –
I love you.
Such would I say to him, if he were really here.

This speech is one of the emotional highpoints of the film, and is enhanced by John Barry's magnificent music. Robinson and the rest of the theatre production company are aghast at this unscripted piece of improvisation, but the audience loves it and gives Elise a standing ovation.

During the intermission following the first act, Elise goes backstage for a publicity photograph. As she is getting into the right pose for the picture, she looks at Richard with love in her eyes as the camera shutter clicks. A ghost-like oval frame is superimposed on the picture at this point to tell the audience that this is the very same photo of Elise that Richard had seen in 1980 in the Hall of History. She was looking at him when the photo was taken.

In reality, the photo of Elise was taken before shooting be-gan, and Seymour had to recreate the pose exactly for this scene. The photo of Elise is rather like the famous Leonardo

Da Vinci portrait of the Mona Lisa in the Louvre, as the subject's eyes appear to be looking at you regardless of the angle from which you view the picture.

After the intermission, Richard watches the second act but is then given a hand-written note. It is from Robinson, and asks the playwright to meet him immediately in the gazebo behind the hotel. The note says it concerns Miss McKenna and is a 'matter of life and death'.

Richard walks to the gazebo where Robinson is waiting but the manager keeps his back to him to begin with, suggesting (non-verbally) that he has not accepted his presence. Robinson starts his diatribe by asking Richard if he knows how long he has been looking after McKenna's career. Richard replies that he knows he has been her manager since March 1903. Robinson says that is correct, and that he had first seen her on a 'dingy stage in a pathetic play'.

Richard asks Robinson if he wants to marry Elise, but he denies that he merely wants her as his wife. Instead he wants to nurture her, care for her and ensure that she reaches her full potential as an actress. Richard is relieved to hear this, and tells Robinson that he owes him an apology. He too wants Elise to become a star, but with him at her side. She will continue to act and grow, but with him as her husband. Unfortunately Robinson rejects his proposal and claims that he 'came to destroy her'. Two of Robinson's men then overpower Richard and take him away.

After the play is finished, Elise realises that Richard is missing – and when Robinson arrives in her room – she accuses him of being involved in his disappearance. But he denies it, saying that he has done nothing and that Richard has now left the hotel – and her life!

However, Elise declares that she loves Richard – he is going to make her very happy, and she will find him. Before leaving her room to allow her to change, Robinson reminds Elise that the theatre company will be departing for Denver in an hour.

Meanwhile, Richard recovers consciousness in a nearby barn. He is tied up with ropes and a horse is looming over him. Eventually he dislodges an oil lantern from the wall of the barn and uses it to cut through the ropes. He makes his way back to the hotel, where he meets Arthur's father who confirms that the theatre company has left. Feeling despondent, Richard sits on a white wooden bench on the verandah, facing the hotel. After a moment we see Elise on the lawn in the far distance. She eventually spots Richard and runs up the steps towards him. This shot proved a technical challenge, as both Richard and Elise had to be in focus simultaneously and

Somewhere in Time (1980): Rastar/Universal Pictures

the problem was solved by using a split-dioptre lens. Another way this shot could have been done would have been with a split-screen method.

The reunited couple make their way back to Room 117 where Elise pulls out a hairpin, allowing her long tresses to fall on her shoulders. Richard and Elise then make love, although this is depicted in a very tasteful and non—explicit way without any nudity being shown. I think this was a correct decision on the part of the director, because a gratuitous sex scene would not match the tone of the rest of the movie. By comparison, the corresponding scene in the book is quite overt.

Their lovemaking over, the couple have a picnic on the floor of the room and discuss their future. Elise says she wants to know everything about Richard and perform in one of his plays. They are going to get married. Elise looks at the pocket watch which she is holding in her hand. It is 5.00 a.m., but neither of them feel tired.

Elise says she is going to buy Richard a new suit, as the one he has is out of fashion. But Richard is a bit put out, pointing out that his existing garment has a lot of good features, including many handy pockets. He pulls a penny out of one pocket but, as he looks at it, he discovers it is dated '1979'. Immediately his world starts spinning round him. It appears that this concrete reminder of his original time zone has broken the spell. He tries to get rid of the penny and reaches out, but as Elise screams his name she fades into the distance, surrounded by blackness.

A moment later, Richard regains consciousness. He is lying on his bed in room 117 where he last saw Elise. He is clearly back in 1980, as evidenced by the sounds of a radio programme and motor traffic. He is distraught at what has happened and makes his way back to room 313 where he attempts to repeat his time jump, affirming to himself that it is June 29, 1912. However, he is unable to replicate his earlier success, perhaps because his distraught mental state prevents him from going into trance. Feeling devastated, he drops the troublesome penny onto the floor.

An interesting plot point is that back in 1912, Elise has retained the pocket watch which she eventually gives to Richard in 1972. He then takes it back to 1912 and gives it to her. But where did the watch come from in the first place? The answer is really that the watch is in its own time loop, existing between 1972 and 1912.

Having returned to 1980, Richard revisits some of the locations where he had been with Elise in 1912. The tree on the beach where they first met. The shore, where he sits on a bench as a ferry passes. The Hall of History, where he touches Elise's photograph. He stares endlessly out the window at the lake.

He stops eating and drinking and ends up in his room in a catatonic state, his eyes fixed open and his body rigid. This is a truly wonderful piece of physical acting by Reeve, who apparently meditated to achieve the desired result. His body remains so motionless in these scenes, with open eyelids, that you would think that a highly realistic mannequin had been used. But in fact all these shots were done with the actor himself.

Eventually, Arthur and the hotel's manager (David Hull) realise that something is amiss and gain entry to Richard's room using a pass key. The playwright is close to death, but is lifted onto the bed and Dr Hull (Paul Cook) is summoned. Richard is given oxygen and an ambulance is called. 'Such a fine man... I wonder what happened,' says Arthur as the doctor attempts to resuscitate him. A moment later, Richard smiles and then dies and floats out of his body, where he is surrounded by a white light which is emanating from the window. In a white void representing heaven, he is reunited with his beloved Elise as John Barry's magnificent end title theme plays, accompanied by simple black titles against a white background (the exact reverse of the opening titles). Elise and Richard have been reunited once more... somewhere in time.

The ending reflects Matheson's own interest in the afterlife and paranormal phenomenon. Matheson later wrote a book set in the afterlife, *What Dreams May Come* (again with a title taken from Shakespeare), which was eventually made into a film in 1998 starring Robin Williams.

Somewhere in Time premiered in October 1980, but was not a commercial success. There were a number of reasons for this. One was an actors' strike, which prevented the stars from publicising the movie. Another was the hostile reaction from most critics, which damaged the movie's reputation. Critic Vincent Canby described Christopher Reeve as 'looking like a helium-filled canary' and John Brosnan – writing in the British *Starburst* magazine – wrote a very damning review of the film. Brosnan didn't like the film because of its sentimental tone and pointed out that when he saw it the cinema was almost empty, such was its unpopularity.

However – as described at the beginning of this chapter – the film became very popular because of cable television and video rentals, and now it is more admired than ever. Rather like a good wine, the film has actually improved with age and is now appreciated as the masterpiece it is.

What is even more interesting is how similar the movie is to *Titanic* (1997). Both are set in 1912, but have scenes set in

97

the present day. Both involve a love triangle, with one of the men being young and the other being older and more controlling. Both films end with the hero dying and the two lovers being reunited in the afterlife. It has been suggested that James Cameron may have been influenced by *Somewhere in Time* when he scripted *Titanic* and, if you want to read up more about this subject, I suggest you read the two articles on the topic which can be found on the I.N.S.I.T.E. website.

Actor Christopher Reeve remained passionate about the film but – as is widely known – he suffered a devastating spinal injury on 27th May 1995 when he was thrown from his horse. Reeve remained paralysed from the neck down for the rest of his life, and had to breathe using a ventilator. He eventually died from an allergic reaction to an antibiotic on 10th October 2005.

A sequel to the film has been mooted many times. Original director Jeannot Schwartz had his own idea for this. It would start with Richard finding the 1979 penny in his waistcoat in 1912 and travelling back to 1980 while Elise remained in 1912 in possession of the pocket watch. The rest of the film would be Elise's story from 1912 to 1972 and would end with her giving Richard the watch in 1972. It is an interesting idea, but with Christopher Reeve having passed away in 2005 and Jane Seymour now being 67, the parts would have to be recast. It is interesting that a sequel to *Titanic* (1997) was proposed in which Jack has somehow survived and meets Rose again a few years later, but this film was never made.

My own view is that a prequel, sequel, remake or reboot of *Somewhere in Time* should never be made, because the original achieved perfection in every area. Rather like *Casablanca*, *Vertigo* and *Psycho*, *Somewhere in Time* is a classic movie which should never be re-made.

For further information on the fan organisation International Network of *Somewhere in Time* Enthusiasts (I.N.S.I.T.E), the 1980 film and the 1975 book *Bid Time Return*, please visit: **www.somewhereintime.tv**

5

Quality Time
The 1980s

THE first time travel movie of the 1980s was *The Final Countdown* (1980), which was directed by Don Taylor and starred Kirk Douglas, Martin Sheen, Katharine Ross, James Farentino and Charles Durning.

The screenplay was by Thomas Hunter, Peter Powell, David Ambrose and Gerry Davis. Davis was no stranger to science fiction, as he as the script editor of *Doctor Who* from 1966-67, co-creator of the Cybermen, and co-writer of the first three Cybermen stories (though he wasn't always credited as such). He also created the BBC TV series *Doomwatch* (1970-72) with Kit Pedler before moving to the USA.

The plot of *The Final Countdown* could have come from an episode of *The Twilight Zone* TV series. A US aircraft carrier, the real-life USS *Nimitz*, is on exercises near Hawaii when it encounters rough weather. Captain Yelland (Kirk Douglas) orders the escorting destroyers to return to Pearl Harbour, leaving the *Nimitz* to face the storm alone.

But this is no ordinary storm. The crew become engulfed by a multi-coloured mist and the *Nimitz* is silhouetted against a glowing, swirling pattern of lights. The sailors don't know it, but they have entered a naturally-occurring time vortex which takes them back in time to 6th December 1941, the eve of the Japanese attack on Pearl Harbour.

If you think the time storm sequence in the film looks a bit like the titles of a James Bond film, you would be right because they were done by the same person – Maurice Binder. The shot where the *Nimitz's* hull is silhouetted against a coloured background is very similar to many of Binder's Bond title sequences.

After a few minutes, the 'time storm' subsides and the *Nimitz* resumes its patrol... but things aren't right. All VHF and UHF radio transmissions have stopped, and the radio operators on *Nimitz* can only pick up old-fashioned AM radio broadcasts. The crew can hear an old Jack Benny radio show, which they assume to be an archive recording. They cannot contact Pearl Harbour using normal frequencies.

Captain Yelland (Kirk Douglas) wonders if a nuclear war has broken out and orders an RF-8 Crusader reconnaissance aircraft to overfly Pearl Harbour and take some photos. It returns having taken photos of vintage US battleships lying at anchor, as they were just before the attack by the Japanese on 7th December 1941.

Meanwhile, a pair of Grumman F-14 Tomcat fighters has been sent aloft to investigate a surface radar contact which turns out to be a civilian motor yacht. As the two American pilots watch from high overhead, a pair of Japanese Mitsubishi A6M Zero fighters arrive and make repeated strafing runs, forcing its occupants, Senator Samuel Chapman (Charles Durning) and his personal assistant Laurel Scott

(Katharine Ross), to take to the water in lifejackets. The two Zeroes in this scene were replicas based on North American T-6 trainers which were originally built for the film *Tora, Tora, Tora* in 1968 and were subsequently acquired by the Confederate Air Force, based at Harlingen, Texas.

The American Tomcat pilots request permission to intervene, but Yelland will only give them authority to disrupt the Zeroes' attacks without opening fire. The two jets dive down and 'mix it' with the Zeroes, spoiling their attack. Yelland doesn't want to shoot down the planes, but one of his bridge officers points out that the Japanese fighters are getting closer to the *Nimitz* which has fuelled planes on deck. Reluctantly, Yelland gives the pilots the order to 'splash the Zeroes'. One is speedily despatched with a Sidewinder heat-seeking missile, while the second is hit by a burst of 20mm Vulcan cannon fire and crashes into the ocean. The pilot stands on the wing of his downed plane and is rescued by a US Navy Sea King helicopter.

The two rescued American civilians and the Japanese pilot are taken back to the *Nimitz*. Commander Richard T. 'Dick' Owens (James Farentino), the commander of the carrier's air wing, is an amateur historian who is writing a book on the Pearl Harbour attack and recognises Senator Chapman. He was going to be President Franklin D. Roosevelt's running mate (and possible successor), but had disappeared on 6th December 1941 and – by rescuing him – the crew of the *Nimitz* have changed history.

Captain Yelland had initially been sceptical about what has happened, but is now convinced that the *Nimitz* really has gone back in time to the eve of the attack on Pearl Harbour. Warren Lasky (Martin Sheen), a civilian contractor who works for Tideman Industries – who designed and built the

"...THIS IS THE U.S.S. NIMITZ...
WHERE THE HELL ARE WE?.."

Trapped outside the boundaries of time and space —
102 aircraft...6,000 men...all missing.

The Final Countdown (1980): Optical House Inc./United Artists

carrier – points out that they have an opportunity to change history by thwarting the Japanese attack. Yelland realises that his duty is to serve the President of the USA, even if that is now Franklin D. Roosevelt.

Yelland makes plans for all *Nimitz*'s aircraft to get airborne at dawn and attack the Japanese air group. He orders Owens to land Senator Chapman and Laurel Scott by helicopter on a nearby island, where they will be safe. But they can only do this by tricking the Senator into believing he is being taken to Pearl Harbour. The Senator sees through the ruse and tries to take control of the Navy Sea King helicopter using a flare pistol. A fight breaks out, the helicopter is destroyed and Chapman killed, while Scott and Owens are left stranded on the island from where they can see the Japanese air fleet approaching.

Meanwhile, the *Nimitz's* entire air group has got airborne and is heading directly for the approaching Japanese strike force. This is where I have issues with the plot, as a more effective way of blunting the Japanese attack would have been to hit the six carriers *before* they could launch their aircraft, in a devastating night attack. As depicted in the movie, the American plans involve shooting down as many of the Japanese planes as possible. But even if all the F-14s managed to fire off all their missiles and every one scored a hit, only a fraction of the attacking force would be shot down – especially as many of the American planes were Grumman A-6 intruders which had no air-to-air capability whatsoever as they did not carry Sidewinder or Sparrow missiles or cannon.

The American planes are just about to fire their missiles when the time storm reappears near the *Nimitz.* Yelland makes a snap decision and recalls the planes. The time storm envelops the carrier and it returns to 1980. Soon afterwards, the air group reappears overhead and lands back on the carrier. Everything is as it was, although Commander Owens has been left back in 1941. And Laurel Scott's dog, Charlie, is now on board the *Nimitz.*

As Lasky leaves the carrier and walks along the quayside, followed by Charlie, the door of a limousine opens and a familiar voice calls out. Charlie runs up to the car, where he is reunited with his former mistress. Rather perplexed, Lasky walks up to the limousine and discovers it contains 'Richard Tideman' – who is none other than Commander Owens – plus Laurel Scott, who is now 'Mrs Tideman'. 'Come in, Mr Lasky; we have a lot to talk about,' says Tideman.

The Final Countdown was well-received by critics, although some felt it looked like a Navy recruiting film as it featured many scenes of life aboard an aircraft carrier. One criticism of the plot, though, was that the audience was expecting a big air battle with modern jets downing Japanese propeller-driven aircraft but (apart from the brief dogfight involving four aircraft) it never happened, and instead things were put back to the way they were – giving the film a *coitus interruptus* feel! Personally, I feel a more satisfying ending would have depicted the climactic air battle and then have the time storm return and 'wind time back' so that things returned to the way they were. Obviously this would have been more spectacular, but also more expensive to produce.

Some years ago it was announced that a new version of *The Final Countdown* was to be made, again featuring the USS *Nimitz* and set in the waters off Japan, but to date it has not yet appeared.

The next time travel film of 1980 was *Somewhere in Time*, which is discussed in great detail in an earlier chapter. The only other time travel film to appear this year was *The Day Time Ended* (1980) which was directed by John Cardos and produced by Charles Band, Paul Gentry, Steve Neill and Wayne Schmidt. The screenplay was by J. Larry Carroll, Steve Neill, Wayne Schmidt and David Schmoeller. The budget was just $600,000.

The film tells the story of the Williams family, who have moved to a new home in the Sonoran Desert in order to be closer to their grandparents. But there are news reports of a supernova in the sky, and one of the grandchildren has seen a glowing light behind a barn. One night a UFO is spotted in the sky. It lands in the nearby hills. It appears that the supernova has opened up a rift in space and time. Electrical appliances stop working, and the youngest daughter in the family apparently achieves telepathic contact with an alien. The grandmother also has a transient contact with one of the creatures, which then disappears.

As the grandfather is trying to start his car, he sees an odd-looking animal approaching. He goes back inside the house and warns his family. Soon, a number of alien creatures appear outside the property. They attack each other and then try to break into the house in order to kill the family.

After this has gone on for some time, the UFO re-appears and uses its teleportation facility to transport the creatures to a different location. The family flee from the house to the barn, but then become separated from one another. As dawn breaks, they realise they have travelled thousands of years into the future and eventually meet the daughter from whom they had become separated. Somehow she knows that everything is going to be all right in the end.

Eventually they spot a domed city in the distance and take shelter in it, and the grandfather declares that there must be a purpose to all this. As they walk into the distance they realise that they have survived 'the day time ended'.

The film, which was released in November 1980, had a cast of largely unknown actors. The only exception would be Dorothy Malone, playing Ana, who had appeared in a large number of American films and TV series including *Peyton Place* (1964-69). One of Robert Mitchum's sons, Christopher Mitchum, also appeared in the movie as Richard Williams.

Time Bandits (1981) was a British film about an eleven-year-old boy, Kevin, who travels through time with the help of six dwarves who have acquired the ability to jump through time portals. It was produced and directed by Terry Gilliam and written by Gilliam and Michael Palin. The movie was produced by HandMade Films.

The roots of this film go back to the late sixties. Terry Gilliam was originally an artist and provided animated cartoons as links between the sketches for all four seasons of *Monty Python's Flying Circus* (1969-74). He also designed the title sequence. Later, he appeared in some of the sketches and then became the co-director (along with Terry Jones) of the second Python film, *Monty Python and the Holy Grail* (1975). The Pythons' next project, *Monty Python's Life of Brian* (1979), was nearly scrapped after EMI withdrew funding, but was saved when ex-Beatle George Harrison – who was a Python fan and close friend of Eric Idle – offered to fund the project by re-mortgaging his house. This led to the establishment of the production company HandMade Films, which then went on to make many other movies, one of which was *Time Bandits*.

The film opens with eleven-year-old Kevin (Craig Warnock) asleep at home. Suddenly an armoured knight on horseback emerges from his wardrobe and then retreats back through the time portal within. The following night Kevin is in bed when six time-travelling dwarves burst out of the wardrobe carrying a worn map which they have stolen from the Supreme Being. The map enables them to travel in space and time. One of the dwarves is played by Kenny Baker, who was R2D2 in *Star Wars: A New Hope* (1977).

The young boy then accompanies the dwarves in a series of adventures at different locations in space and time, and meets historical figures including Napoleon Bonaparte (Ian Holm) and Robin Hood (John Cleese). Unfortunately their travels are being monitored by Evil (David Warner), who wants to steal the map.

Kevin becomes separated from the group and meets King Agamemnon (Sean Connery) in Ancient Greece. He is then rescued by the dwarves and has further adventures in space and time, including a meeting with the Supreme Being (Tony Jay) and a confrontation with Evil. That creature is destroyed, but a part of him remains as a smoking rock which causes Kevin's house to catch fire. Kevin's parents are killed, but a group of firemen arrive – including one who is clearly a grinning Agamemnon. The film ends with the Earth now in a map being rolled up by the Supreme Being.

The movie was a box office success, making $40 million against a budget of $5 million, and was also acclaimed by critics. A proposed *Time Bandits* TV series was announced in July 2018.

Time Rider: The Adventures of Lyle Swann (1982) is an action movie about a motorbike rider – the eponymous Lyle Swann (Fred Ward) – who accidentally travels back to 1877. It was directed and produced by William Dear and written by Dear and Michael Nesmith, who also provided the music. Michael Nesmith is, of course, best-known for being one of The Monkees, a pop band first created for a TV comedy series in 1966. The band still exists as a trio, although the fourth member – Davy Jones – died in 2012.

The film opens as Lyle Swann, a dirt-bike motorcycle racer, is in the desert competing in the Baja 100 cross-country race. Swann accidentally veers off course in his Yamaha XT500 bike and comes across a time travel experiment which uses a maser (microwave amplification by stimulated emission of radiation) to send rhesus monkeys back in time.

Swann rides through the time field and gets sent back to 5th November 1877. Before the scientists in 1982 can bring him back to the present, he rides off and is now stuck in 1877.

Later, as he is taking a swim in a pond, a bunch of local outlaws led by Porter Reese try to steal his bike, but Swann escapes and travels to the village of San Marcos. The locals are scared by his bike and red suit and think he is the devil.

A local woman, Claire Cygne (Belinda Bauer), befriends him and they become lovers. She shoots one of the pursuing gang, Carl (Tracey Walter), but she is later kidnapped by another of the gang members – Claude Dorsett (Richard Masur) – and the criminals steal Swann's bike. Swann gets some help from two US Marshalls, Potter (L.Q. Jones) and Daniels (Chris Mulkey). He retrieves his bike and frees Claire, but Potter and Daniels are killed.

In a final confrontation atop a plateau, a helicopter appears which has been sent back in time by the scientists in 1982. All of the gang flee, but Reese himself remains and shoots at the helicopter, damaging it. It lands heavily, but is still able to rescue Swann while Reese is killed by the spinning tail rotor. As the helicopter pulls away, Claire snatches a pendant from Swann's neck. It has been in the family for years, and Swann realises that – as he had made love to Claire – he must be his own great-great-grandfather. (This plot point has some similarities with the pocket watch stuck in its own time loop in *Somewhere in Time* and also the plot of the 1980 BBC play *The Flip Side of Dominic Hyde*, in which Dominic travels to 1980 from the future and makes love to a woman, resulting in him becoming his own father.)

The film only made $6 million at the box office and received lukewarm reviews, but it is interesting that it has many plot similarities with the highly acclaimed series of *Back to the Future* films – particularly *Back to the Future: Part III*, which also dealt with time travellers going back to the Wild West in a modern vehicle.

Twilight Zone: The Movie (1983) was a big screen adaptation of the famous science fiction and fantasy TV series which was originally broadcast from 1959 to 1964 and was created by Rod Serling, who also wrote many of the scripts. The film consisted of a brief prologue, *Something Scary*, in which a car passenger turns into a monster. This is then followed by four brief segments, *Time Out, Kick the Can, It's a Good Life* and *Nightmare at 20,000 Feet*, and concludes with an Epilogue.

The last three segments were all remakes of original *Twilight Zone* episodes, but *Time Out* was a brand-new story and incorporated a time travel plot. Directed by John Landis, it starred Vic Morrow as the bigot William Connor. Morrow is best-known for playing Sergeant 'Chip' Saunders in the long-running TV series *Combat* (1962-67), which was set in France in World War II.

This segment starts with a narrative which uses some text borrowed from *Twilight Zone* episodes *What You Need* and *A Nice Place to Visit*, and tells the story of Mr Bill Connor who 'carries on his shoulder a chip the size of the national debt... Mr William Connor, whose own blind hatred is about to catapult him into the darkest corner of The Twilight Zone'.

Connor is angry because he has been passed over for promotion in favour of a Jewish colleague. As he is drinking in a bar with friends, he utters disgusting racist comments about Asians, blacks and Jews. A black man sitting nearby is offended and asks him to stop.

Bill storms outside the bar and finds himself in Nazi-occupied France during WW2. He is approached by two SS officers who interrogate him, but Bill cannot answer them as he does not speak German. The SS men chase him and he is shot and falls off the ledge of a building.

He now finds himself in the Southern USA during the fifties. Some Ku Klux Klansmen try to lynch him even though he claims to be white, but they will not listen to him. Bill tries to escape and falls into a lake. When he comes to the surface, he finds he is in the jungle during the Vietnam War. American soldiers are shooting at him, and one throws a grenade. It explodes but, instead of being killed, he is catapulted back to occupied France. He is captured by SS officers and put on a freight train which is going to a concentration camp along with a large number of Jewish prisoners. He can see his friends standing outside the bar, but they cannot see or hear him and the train leaves for the death camp.

This segment of *The Twilight Zone* proved very controversial, as star Vic Morrow was accidentally decapitated by the rotor of a Bell UH-1 Huey helicopter during the filming. Two child actors also died in the same incident. This meant that the original ending – in which Connor returns to his own time after saving two Vietnamese children – had to be dropped.

The Philadelphia Experiment (1984) was supposedly based on a real incident on 28th October 1943 when the US Navy destroyer USS *Eldridge* vanished from its moorings at Philadelphia Navy Yard and reappeared in New York. This allegedly happened because of a scientific experiment to make the vessel radar invisible (or even optically invisible) using high-frequency current, which inadvertently caused a warp in the space-time continuum in accordance with Einstein's Unified Field theory.

It must be said at this point that there is no real evidence that the incident actually happened. Also, the physical effects of this alleged experiment don't conform to what we know about physics. Nonetheless, it has been the basis of many fascinating books, articles, documentaries and two feature films.

The first mention of this incident came in 1955 when astronomer and UFO buff Morris K. Jessup, author of the book *The Case for the UFO*, received two letters from Carlos Miguel Allende (aka Carl M. Allen) who claimed to have witnessed a secret WW2 experiment at Philadelphia Navy Yard in 1943 in which the USS *Eldridge* was rendered invisible, teleported to New York and then to another dimension, where the crew encountered aliens and were then transported through time, resulting in the deaths of several sailors, some of whom ended up fused with the ship's hull.

This rather unbelievable story subsequently appeared in a 1963 book, *Invisible Horizons: True Mysteries of the Sea*, by Vincent Gaddis. It also formed the basis for a 1978 novel, *Thin Air* by George E. Simpson and Neal R. Burger, in which a Naval officer investigates wartime experiments in matter transmission and technology to create invisibility.

The Philadelphia Experiment became widely known through the publication of a 1979 book by author Charles Berlitz, who had previously written a volume about the Bermuda Triangle. *The Philadelphia Experiment: Project Invisibility* purported to be a factual account, quoted Einstein's Unified Field Theory, and alleged there had been a government cover-up.

This book formed the basis of a film, *The Philadelphia Experiment* (1984), which starred Michael Pare and Nancy Allen and was directed by Stewart Raffill.

The film begins in 1943. Two US Navy sailors, David Herdeg (Michael Pare) and Jim Parker (Bobby De Cicco), are assigned to the destroyer USS *Eldridge* which is involved in a project to make it invisible to radar. Unfortunately the experiment goes wrong, and the two men find themselves in the middle of the desert in the year 1984.

David and Jim eventually meet a lady called Allison (Nancy Allen). The time travel process is badly affecting Jim, who starts having frequent seizures and eventually disappears from his hospital bed in a corona of energy.

David subsequently discovers that Jim is still alive in 1984, but as an old man as he had gone back to 1943 after he vanished from his hospital bed. He also finds out that a Dr Longstreet, who was involved in the original experiments in 1943, is still around and using the same technologies to create a shield against ICBM attack. Unfortunately the original 1943 experiment has created a time vortex which is sucking matter into it. The only solution is to enter the vortex, go back to 1943 and shut down the generator on the USS *Eldridge*. David volunteers to do this and, having completed the task and saved the world, he jumps over the side of the ship and is catapulted back to 1984.

In 1993 a sequel to this film, *The Philadelphia Experiment II*, was made with a completely different cast. This time David Herdog was played by Brad Johnson and the plot involved a scientist sending an American Lockheed F-117 stealth fighter back in time to 1943 Nazi Germany. As a result, the Nazis bomb Washington with nuclear weapons in 1943 and win the Second World War in a new timeline.

With his ability to travel through time and space, David Herdeg finds himself in this parallel world in which the Nazis have conquered the USA. In this respect the film is a bit like the BBC production *SS-GB* (2017) or *The Man in the High Castle* (2015-present). David realises that the solution is to travel through the time vortex and destroy the captured stealth fighter before it can carry out the mission. He achieves his goal and returns back through the time vortex to his original world, where he is reunited with his son.

In 2015 the original *Philadelphia Experiment* film was remade with a mostly new cast. Michael Pare returned – this time playing a character called Hagan – and the main difference between this version and the original was that all the visual effects were done using CGI rather than more traditional optical methods, which had been employed in the earlier film. This meant that the new version was inferior to the original. A shot depicting the USS *Eldridge* stuck high up a tall building looked particularly phoney.

Non ci resta che piangere (*Nothing Left to Do but Cry*) is a 1984 Italian comedy film starring Roberto Benigni and Massimo Troisi, who also directed the movie. The plot concerns a school janitor, Mario (Massimo Troisi), and a teacher, Saverio (Roberto Benigni), who are forced to so spend the night in an inn following a car accident. When they awaken they find themselves in 15th century Florence, where they have a series of adventures.

Trancers (1984), also known as *Future Cop*, was directed by Charles Band and starred Tim Thomerson, Helen Hunt and Art Le Fleur. The plot concerns a 23rd century cop called Jack Deth (Tim Thomerson) who has the ability to travel back to the 1980s to bring his old foe, Martin Whistler (Michael Stefani), to justice. His method of time travel is rather unusual as it involves him injecting himself with a drug.

The film opens in 2247. Jack Deth is on the trail of Martin Whistler, a criminal who uses his psychic powers to turn people into 'trancers' who can then carry out his orders. Deth can locate 'trancers' by scanning them with a special bracelet. 'Trancers' can appear as to be normal humans but, once activated, become violent killers with distorted features.

As a way of escaping justice, Whistler travels back to 1985 using the special drug, and his mind inhabits the body of a contemporary Los Angeles detective called Weisling (Michael Stefani). But Deth is on his trail and destroys Whistler's body in 2247, which means the villain has nowhere to return to. He then follows him back in time, ending up in the body of one of his own ancestors, a journalist called Phil Dethton (Tim Thomerson again).

Aided by Phil's girlfriend Leena (Helen Hunt), Deth goes after Whistler, who has started to 'trance' other victims. The villain has embarked on a scheme to kill the future governing council members of Angel (as Los Angeles will eventually be called) by killing all their ancestors. Deth is unable to prevent most of the murders and can only save Hap Ashby (Bill Manard), who is the ancestor of the last surviving council member, Chairman Ashe (Anne Seymour).

Deth receives some high-tech equipment from the future, which includes a pistol containing two hidden vials of time drugs plus a special wristwatch which can slow down time, stretching one second to ten. He fights with Whistler, and one of the drug vials is smashed. He is now faced with a dilemma, as he only has enough of the pharmaceutical agent to send one person back to the present. He has a choice between killing Weisler (who is possessed by Whistler) or using the last vial to send the villain back to 2247, which would result in him being stranded in the present. He chooses to inject Whistler, but his decision comes at a great cost as he is now stranded in 1985 with no prospect of returning to his original body. There is one consolation, as he remains with Leena while his future boss McNulty is also in 1985 in the body of a young girl.

Cavegirl (1985) is a little-known movie which was written and directed by David Oliver. It tells the story of a clumsy high school pupil, Rex (Daniel Roebuck), who gets lost in a cave while on a class excursion. A time portal opens, and he is sent back to the Stone Age where he meets a young woman called Eba (Cynthia Thomson). He gets involved in a series of adventures as he attempts to get Eba to sleep with him.

My Science Project (1985) was an American comedy science fiction film which was directed by Jonathan R. Betuel. It was designed to cash in on the success of other similar but higher-budgeted movies such as *Real Genius*, *Weird Science* and *Back to the Future*.

The film begins in 1955 when the US military captures a flying saucer and conceals it in a US Air Force hangar. President Dwight D. Eisenhower views the craft and then orders the military to dispose of it.

In 1985 a high school senior pupil – Michael Harlan (John Stickwell), who is interested in powerful cars – is looking for a subject for his science class project. He goes on a date with another pupil, Ellie Sawyer (Danielle von Zerneck), during which they visit an aircraft boneyard (a large collection of scrapped airframes lying in the desert) and discover a nuclear fallout shelter. Inside, Michael finds a glowing globe and steals it as a guard approaches.

The next day, Michael cleans the device in a car maintenance class and accidentally activates it. To his surprise it drains power from a nearby ghetto blaster. Michael wonders what might happen if he connected it to a twelve-volt car battery. He goes ahead and does this, causing the globe to emit a glow of energy that forms into the shape of a Greek vase as the battery melts. The two young men leave the car class, but then realise they have moved forward two hours and have missed their final science exam.

Michael takes the strange device to his science teacher Dr Roberts (Dennis Hopper), who examines it and believes it is a portal to another dimension. He plugs it into a mains socket and promptly vanishes in a glow of energy. All that is left is his peace symbol medallion. Michael tries to unplug the device, but cannot do so. It seems the only solution is to destroy the high-voltage electricity power lines leading to the town.

Drastic situations call for drastic remedies, and so Michael and Vince obtain some dynamite from a hardware store owned by Michael's father (Barry Corbin) as a wave of energy moves along the electricity lines heading for the nearby power plant. They manage to blow up a single high tension pylon, which stops the waves, but it causes a blackout and they are arrested for causing Dr Roberts' disappearance.

Michael phones Ellie and asks her to fetch the globe from the school, as he hopes it will help him prove his innocence. Unfortunately she is too late, as Sherman (Raphael Sbarge) has connected the globe to the mains, causing another blackout and creating a massive time warp. Vince and Michael escape in the confusion. When they reach the school, they find it is enveloped in a time vortex and people from the past and future are milling around. Sherman has become very disturbed.

Mike and Vince grab M-16 rifles from fallen Vietnam War soldiers and go to the science lab while battling a T-Rex and mutants on the way. Eventually they reach Ellie and manage to turn the globe off. Things return to normal, and Dr Roberts returns – having enjoyed a trip to Woodstock in 1969. He tells Michael he is going to give him an 'A' in his science project, but he must destroy the time globe.

Michael returns the globe to the junkyard. On the return journey with Ellie their car breaks down, but Michael is happy to abandon it as he now regards it as 'just a car.'

The Blue Yonder (1985) was relatively simple science fiction film, just 89 minutes long. Directed and written by Mark Rosman and produced by Alan Shapiro, Annette Handley and Susan. B. Handley, it told the story of Jonathan Knicks (Huckleberry Fox), an eleven-year-old boy who travels from 1985 to 1927 in a time machine built by his neighbour Henry Coogan (Art Carney). Coogan has created the device using blueprints drawn up by Jonathan's grandfather, Max (Peter Coyote). On travelling back to 1927, Jonathan discovers that he must prevent his own grandfather from embarking on a solo trans-Atlantic flight which could change the course of history.

Peggy Sue Got Married (1986) is an American comedy film directed by Francis Ford Coppola about a woman on the verge of divorce who finds herself transported back to her last year at high school in 1960. It was written by Jerry Leichtling and Arlene Sarner and produced by Paul R. Gurian. The musical score was by John Barry, making this his second time travel picture (he also composed the music for 1980's *Somewhere on Time*).

The film opens with Peggy Sue Bodell (Kathleen Turner) setting off for her 25-year reunion in 1986. She is wearing the same dress she wore for her 1960 prom, and has recently separated from her husband Charlie (Nicholas Cage) because of his infidelity.

The reunion's MC invites Peggy Sue to come up on stage along with Richard Norvik (Barry Miller), who is now a millionaire inventor. But after a special cake is wheeled on stage,

Peggy Sue faints and finds herself back in 1960 where she has just passed out after donating blood.

At first she is stunned by what has happened, but then decides she can turn the situation to her advantage. She talks to Richard Norvik about time travel, as she believes he is the only person who will understand. She knows it will be a mistake to marry Charlie, as she already knows how things will end, and takes an interest in other male classmates including Michael Fitzsimmons (Kevin J. O'Connor). However, she does learn that Charlie had an interest in singing and gaining a record contract and only gave it up because Peggy Sue fell pregnant. Richard proposes to Peggy Sue, but she declines.

Charlie and Peggy Sue are eventually reconciled. They make love, Peggy Sue falls pregnant, and she is transported back to 1985 where she wakes up in hospital. Charlie is by her side. He tells her his relationship with his girlfriend Janet is over, and the couple decide to make a go of it.

The film was moderately successful, making $41 million at the US box office. It was Coppola's first hit since *Apocalypse Now* (1979), and received considerable acclaim. Kathleen Turner has since criticised Nicholas Cage's behaviour during filming in her 2008 memoir. However, this angered Cage, who sued her for defamation and won. Turner was forced to make a public apology and a donation to charity after her publisher admitted that the claims were false.

Biggles (known as *Biggles: Adventures in Time*) was a 1986 British film in which a time traveller goes back to WW1 to help the famous aviator. As is well known, James 'Biggles' Bigglesworth was a fictional character created by Captain W.E. Johns, who featured in a large number of aviation novels mostly set during the First and Second World Wars and the interwar period. The time travel sub-plot was an addition by the filmmakers, as it was not a part of any of Captain W.E. Johns' books.

The plot was fairly simple. In 1986 a New York catering salesman (Alex Hyde-White) passes through a time hole and finds himself in France in 1917, where he saves the life of Royal Flying Corps pilot 'Biggles' after he is shot down during a photo-reconnaissance mission. Jim is then catapulted back to 1986 and subsequently discovers that he and Biggles are 'time twins'. Any time one of them is in danger, the other spontaneously travels through time to help the other. He is helped in his endeavours by Biggles' former commanding officer, William Raymond (Peter Cushing, in his final screen appearance). Ferguson and Biggles eventually team up to thwart the Germans – who are planning to change history with a 'sound weapon' – using a stolen police helicopter.

The film was not a success at the box office, and it received a lukewarm response from critics. Many other attempts have been made to produce a *Biggles* film since the 1950s, but all had foundered due to the high cost of hiring vintage aircraft and filming the aviation sequences. If Biggles had been American and not English then it is likely that Hollywood would have greenlighted such a production.

Star Trek IV: The Voyage Home (1986) was the fourth motion picture to be based on the classic *Star Trek* TV series which originally ran for just three seasons from 1966 to 1968. It was directed by Leonard Nimoy, who also played Mr Spock, and its plot follows directly on from the events of the previous film, *Star Trek III: The Search for Spock* (1984).

The crew are returning to Earth in a captured Klingon Bird of Prey (renamed the *Bounty*) to face trial for their actions in the previous film. But there is a problem. The Earth is in danger from an alien probe with enormous destructive capabilities, which is trying to contact humpback whales that (it believes) are the true inhabitants of Earth. Unfortunately these whales are now extinct, and the only remedy is for some of the *Enterprise* crew to travel back in time and bring some whales back to the future. Time travel had featured in the original TV series on a number of occasions, notably in the episode *The City on the Edge of Forever* which was scripted by Harlan Ellison and featured Joan Collins.

The *Bounty* arrives in San Francisco in 1986 and the crew hide it in San Francisco's Golden Gate Park using its inbuilt cloaking device. The crew then split up, as they have different tasks. Kirk and Spock have to locate the whales. Scott, Dr McCoy and Sulu have to build a transportation tank to takes the creatures to the 23rd century, while Uhura and Chekov have to find a nuclear reactor to power the *Bounty*.

Kirk and Spock find a pair of whales in the Sausalito aquarium which are under the care of Dr Gillian Taylor (Catherine Hicks), while Uhura and Chekov locate a suitable atomic reactor aboard the aircraft carrier USS *Enterprise*. After overcoming a series of mishaps, the crew manage to transport the whales to the 23rd century where they are released into the sea and make contact with the alien probe, which then returns home. Gillian Taylor has also been taken to the 23rd century and is assigned to a Starfleet science vessel. All charges against the *Enterprise* crew are dropped, although Kirk is demoted from Admiral to Captain for disobeying orders. The film ends with the *Enterprise* crew departing on the new USS *Enterprise* (NCC-1701-A).

The screenplay was by Steve Meerson, Peter Krikes, Nicholas Meyer and Harve Bennett. Meyer had previously written and directed *Time After Time* (1979), which was mainly set in San Francisco in 1979. He also wrote and directed one of the best *Star Trek* films, *The Wrath of Khan* (1982).

The Flight of the Navigator (1986) was an American science fiction film directed by Randall Kleiser and written by Mark H. Baker, Michael Burton and Matt McManus.

The film opens on 4th July 1978 in Fort Lauderdale, Florida. Twelve-year-old David Freeman (Joey Cramer) is on his way to collect his younger brother, Jeff, from a friend's house when he falls into a ravine and is knocked out. When he regains consciousness it is now 1986 and Jeff is sixteen.

An alien spaceship crashes nearby, and scientist Dr Faraday investigates David. He discovers that David knows a lot about alien technology and had been taken to the planet Phaelon, 560 light years away. He had experienced time dilation as predicted by Einstein, and so had not aged.

The next day David boards the spaceship and meets the robotic commander, 'Max'. He learns the alien ship was on a scientific mission. They had found David and put a lot of information into his brain. They now need to retrieve this, as the ship's computer has crashed. Max carries out a mind transfer to retrieve the information from David, who they now call 'The Navigator'.

Eventually, the aliens agree to return David to 1978. He wakes up to find everything as it was – except that he now has a memento of his experiences in his backpack, a bat-like creature called Puckmaren.

Masters of the Universe (1987) was an American science fantasy film directed by Gary Goddard and produced by Menahem Golan and Yoram Globus. Golan and Globus were big players in the eighties, as they were in charge of the now-defunct Cannon group which owned about 1,500 cinemas and made a huge number of action pictures including many starring Chuck Norris or Charles Bronson. The film was written by David Odell, based on Mattel's toy range *Masters of the Universe*.

The plot involves two teenagers who encounter the mighty warrior He-Man who has arrived from the planet Eternia, and they help him to defeat his nemesis, the evil Skeletor. The film opens on the planet Eternia where Skeletor (Frank Langella) and his army capture Castle Grayskull and the Sorceress (Christina Pickles). Skeletor's arch-enemy, He-Man (Dolph Lungren), and his daughter Teela (Chelsea Field) rescue Gwildor from Skeletor's forces. He reveals that Skeletor has acquired a 'Cosmic Key' which can open a portal to anywhere in the Universe by using sound keys.

After a battle, He-Man and his friends are forced to flee to Earth. Two American teenagers, Julie Winston (Courteney Cox) and Kevin Corrigan (Robert Duncan McNeill), find the Key on Earth and accidentally send a signal that allows Evil-Lyn (Meg Foster) to track the Key and recover it. After a series of adventures, Skeletor is defeated while Julie travels in time to prevent her parents going on a flight which will end in a crash.

Masters of the Universe was released in the USA on 7th August 1987 but flopped at the box office, making just $22 million set against a budget of $17 million. However, it is now regarded as a cult film.

Timestalkers (1987) is a film which combines Wild West mythology and time travel. It was directed by Michael Schultz and written by Brian Clemens, based on a novel entitled *The Tintype* by Ray Brown. This was a rare Hollywood outing for Brian Clemens, who is best-known for his work on a number of classic British TV series including *The Avengers*

(1961-69), *The New Avengers* (1976-77), *Thriller* (1973-76) and *The Professionals* (1977-83).

The story begins in 1986. Dr Scott McKenzie (William Devane) is a college professor who is a fan of the Wild West. His life has been blighted by tragedy, as a year earlier his wife and child had been killed in a car crash caused by a drunken driver. McKenzie and his friend Joe Brodsky (John Ratzenberger) buy a pair of old cases at an auction of Wild West memorabilia. As this is happening, the audience sees flashbacks showing what had happened to the cases' contents during the 19th century. A man called Joseph Cole (Klaus Kinski) had been involved with a gunfight with three thugs. He shot all three dead, and one bullet had entered the trunk.

When McKenzie examines the contents of the case, he finds a photo of Cole and the three men he had killed. When he looks closer, he sees that Cole is carrying a modern .357 Magnum revolver and concludes he must be a time traveller. Georgia Crawford (Lauren Hutton) approaches McKenzie, saying she also has a similar theory, and so the two agree to work together.

Georgia then retrieves a strange device from a barn and uses it to travel back to the 19th century. She fails to locate Cole, but he sees her and is able to work out what time she has come from. When she returns to the present, she meets McKenzie and admits she is from the 26th century. Her mission is to stop Cole, who is a renegade time traveller. She believes he intends to kill Matthew Crawford (John Considine), an advisor to President Grover Cleveland.

The pair learn that Cole is planning to travel back to 11th July 1886, when a mysterious 'star-handled stranger' helped protect President Cleveland. Georgia and McKenzie travel back in time to 1886 and witness the attack. This time things end differently. Though the stranger is killed, McKenzie takes his weapons and eventually kills Cole. McKenzie sends information to McKenzie's earlier self in the 20th century, which enables his wife and child to avoid their fatal car crash.

The Navigator: A Medieval Odyssey (1988) was an Australian/New Zealand co-production produced by John Maynard and directed by Vincent Ward, who also wrote the script along with Geoff Chapple and Kelly Lyons.

It tells the story of a group of 14th century villagers in Cumbria in North West England who engage in tunnelling activities and end up in contemporary New Zealand. The film opens in the 14th century as the village is affected by plague. In an attempt to save themselves, the villagers rely on the visions of a young boy called Griffin (Hamish McFarlane) who has clairvoyant abilities. With the assistance of Connor (Bruce Lyons), they dig a tunnel, climb a ladder and find themselves in modern day New Zealand, at which point the film changes from black-and-white to colour.

Vincent Ward apparently got the idea for the film when he attempted to cross a German autobahn and got stuck on the central reservation. The experience made him wonder how a medieval person would react if he found himself in the modern world. Although the film was not a huge commercial success, it won several New Zealand and Australian awards including the Australian Film Institute Award for best film.

Field of Dreams (1989) was written and directed by Phil Alden Robinson and produced by Lawrence and Charles Gordon. It was based on the book *Shoeless Joe* by W.P. Kinsella. It is probably star Kevin Costner's most critically-acclaimed film.

It tells the story of Ray Kinsella (Kevin Costner), an Iowa farmer who hears voices and sees visions which convince him to turn part of his land into a baseball field. He hears a voice which says 'If you build it, he will come'. His daughter Karin (Gaby Hoffman) is sceptical, but one day she sees a vision of a deceased baseball player, Shoeless Joe Jackson (Ray Liotta), standing in the field. Later he returns with seven other players who had been banned from playing as a result of the 'Black Sox Scandal' in 1919.

Ray has various strange experiences. At one point he finds himself in 1972 and meets Archie Graham (Burt Lancaster), who had been a doctor as well as a baseball player but had died in 1973. Eventually a team of ghost players is assembled from the past, and people come from miles around to watch the games. The message of the film is really that no-one should give up on their dreams as they can come true.

Bill and Ted's Excellent Adventure (1989) was a comedy time travel film directed by Steven Herek and written by Chris Matheson and Ed Solomon. It starred Keanu Reeves, Alex Winter and George Carlin. The story concerned two American high school seniors (played by Reeves and Winter) who travel back in time in a machine to gather several historical figures for a high school history

***Bill and Ted's Excellent Adventure* (1989):** Interscope Communications/ Nelson Entertainment/Orion Pictures

presentation. It is regarded as one of the cult movies of the late 80s, and reflected contemporary teenage culture.

The film opens in San Dimas, California in 1988. Two lazy high school seniors, Bill (Alex Winter) and Ted (Keanu Reeves), are more interested in their rock band *The Wyld Stallyns* than their schoolwork. The pair have a couple of amusing habits – they keep describing everything as 'excellent' (hence the film's title), and strum their 'air guitars' frequently.

Ted's father – who is also a local police chief – has threat-ened to send Ted to a military academy if he fails his history exam. The two teenagers have a plan for a project – which is to describe how historical figures would view modern-day San Dimas – but they are struggling.

But salvation is at hand. In 2688 the music of the *Wyld Stallyns* has led to the creation of a Utopia, and the supreme beings in this future world instruct Rufus (George Carlin) to go back in time in a machine disguised as a telephone box (a nod to *Doctor Who*) in order to help Bill and Ted pass their exams.

Rufus arrives in San Dimas in 1989 and introduces himself to Bill and Ted. A moment later, a second identical phone booth materialises nearby, and future versions of Bill and Ted emerge from it. They explain that they are from the future and that their earlier selves must trust Rufus and do what he says.

Rufus takes the pair on a journey back through time to meet various historical figures and then bring them back to modern-day San Dimas. They make the acquaintance of Napo-leon Bonaparte (Terry Camilleri), Billy the Kid (Dan Shor), Socrates (Tony Steedman), Sigmund Freud (Rod Loomis), Ludwig van Beethoven (Clifford David), Joan of Arc (Jane Wiedlin), Genghis Khan (Al Leong) and Abraham Lincoln

(Robert V. Barron). Then they return to 1989 and, when the phone box materialises, they see their younger selves nearby.

Bill and Ted hit on the idea of taking all these historical figures to the local shopping mall to experience life in San Dimas in 1989, while they try to track down Napoleon who had been left in the care of Deacon. They find Napoleon at the Waterloo waterpark but, when they return to the shopping mall, they find that the various historical figures have almost caused a riot and have ended up in jail. They manage to free all the historical figures and they all make their way to the school, giving an impressive presentation which results in the two teenagers getting high marks in the exam.

The film was very popular and made $40.5 million at the box office against a budget of $10 million. A sequel, *Bill and Ted's Bogus Journey*, premiered two years later.

Millennium (1989) was a time travel film directed by Michael Anderson, who is best known for directing classic war movies such as *The Dambusters* (1955), *The Yangste Incident* (1957) and *Operation Crossbow* (1965). It was based on a 1977 short story, *Air Raid* by John Varley, which was later expanded into a novel, *Millennium*.

The film opens in the year 1989. An American passenger airliner is involved in a mid-air collision when another aircraft hits it from above during landing. The flight engineer goes back to check out the passenger cabin, but comes back a moment later screaming, 'They're all dead! All of them! They're burned up!' The aircraft then crashes with a great loss of life.

National Transportation Safety Board investigator Bill Smith (Kris Kristofferson) is hired to determine whether the collision and subsequent crash was due to some mechanical fault or human error on the part of either pilot. They are confused by what they hear on the cockpit voice recorder, as there is no evidence that the plane was ablaze before it hit the ground. Meanwhile, a theoretical physicist – Dr Arnold Maher (Daniel J. Travanti) – is interested in the case. During a lecture, he talks about the possibility of time travellers coming from the future to our world.

In fact, time travellers *are* visiting the present, and abducting passengers from aircraft that are due to crash. They are doing this because the future human race has become sterile. By sending these rescued people into the future, they will be available to repopulate the earth.

One problem is that every trip into the past causes a 'time quake', a disturbance in the space-time continuum. To minimise this, they are abducting people who have no further effect on the future and replacing them with copies of those who would have died. This explains the strange cockpit voice recording in which the flight engineer claimed that all the passengers were burned prior to the crash at the beginning of the film.

Unfortunately Dr Mayer suspects what is going on, because he possesses a futuristic stun gun which was found in the wreckage of an aircraft which crashed in 1963. 25 years later he finds a similar weapon in the wreckage of the plane which crashed at the beginning of the film.

The inhabitants of the future Earth are concerned that Smith and Mayer may change history, so an operative named Louise Baltimore (Cheryl Ladd) travels back to 1989 in the hope that she can discourage Smith from continuing with his enquiries. She seduces him in the hope that this will distract him from his efforts, but unfortunately Louise falls pregnant as a result of this 'one-night stand', creating a temporal paradox. Unfortunately Smith becomes even more suspicious of what has happened. Louise materialises from the future while he is visiting Dr Mayer, and reveals her plans in the hope that they will agree to desist. But Mayer then accidentally kills himself in an accident with the stun gun.

Maher was involved in the development of the technology that led to the development of time travel, so his death results in a serious temporal paradox which causes a severe 'time quake' which threatens to destroy the entire civilisation of the future Earth. The only remedy is to send all the people who have been collected into the far future before everything blows up. Louise and Bill travel into the future through the gate. Just before everything is engulfed in a huge explosion, the android Sherman (Robert Joy) quotes Winston Churchill: 'This is not the end. This is not the beginning of the end. It is the end of the beginning'. These words were actually spoken by Churchill after the successful conclusion of the Battle of Alamein in the autumn of 1942.

Millenium took over a decade to get off the ground and went through various proposed directors, including Douglas Trumbull. At one point Paul Newman and Jane Fonda were suggested for the lead roles. The film was not very successful financially, making only $5.8 million at the box office.

Warlock (1989) is an American supernatural horror film with time travel elements. It was directed by Steve Miner and starred Julian Sands, Lori Singer and Richard E .Grant, with a script by David Tuohy and a music score by Jerry Goldsmith. It told the story of an evil 17th century warlock who flees to the 20th century while being chased by a witch-hunter.

The film opens in Boston, Massachusetts in 1691. The Warlock (Julian Sands) is captured by witch-hunter Giles Redferne (Richard E. Grant). He is put on trial and sentenced for his despicable activities, which have included the death of Redferne's wife. But before the execution can be carried out, the Devil appears and sends the Warlock forward in time to late 20th century Los Angeles. Redferne then follows the evil creature through the time portal.

The Warlock attempts to recreate *The Grand Grimoire*, a Satanic book revealing the true name of God and allowing him to undo all of creation. Redferne and the Warlock then engage in a cat-and-mouse chase with *The Grand Grimoire* and Kassandra (Lori Singer), a waitress who discovers Redferne trying to use a 'witch compass' to attract the Warlock. After explaining the various weaknesses of the Warlock, such as its vulnerability to salt, Kassandra accompanies Redferne as the Warlock has put an ageing curse on her after removing her bracelet.

The Warlock recreates two thirds of *The Grand Grimoire*, and Redferne is astonished to discover that the remaining section is buried in the creature's grave which is outwith church land and protected by a witch's curse. The Warlock reappears and carries a magic ritual to recreate *The Grand Grimoire* in full. After seeing the name of God appear in the book, the Warlock is about to destroy all existence by calling it out loud, when Cassandra (who is a Type 1 diabetic) injects saline into his neck. The Warlock bursts into flames. Redferne expresses his gratitude to Kassandra and returns to his own time. In a final scene Kassandra buries *The Grand Grimoire* in the Bonneville Salt Flats.

The film received poor reviews and was also a financial failure, making only $9 million at the box office set against a budget of $15 million.

6

You Are Terminated!
The Terminator Franchise

THE series of *Terminator* films (1984-present), which began 35 years ago, represents a unique achievement in the history of time travel cinema. Most time travel movies have had relatively small budgets and have not fared terribly well at the box office. A good example would be *Somewhere in Time* (1980), discussed at length elsewhere in this book, which although now regarded as a 'cult classic' was made on a budget of just $4m and initially did poorly at the box office.

Although the first *Terminator* film in 1984 had a relatively small budget, all the subsequent sequels have had huge amounts of cash spent on them, with *Terminator 2: Judgment Day* being particularly expensive to make. At the time of its release, *T2* was considered one of the most costly movies ever produced. On the other hand, the *Terminator* movies have all done very well at the box office. At the time of writing, there have been five movies with a sixth due for release in 2019.

There has also been a spin-off TV series – *Terminator: The Sarah Connor Chronicles* – which ran for two seasons, and there is the possibility that there will be further films and maybe even more TV series.

Thus the *Terminator* series has been responsible for popularising the concept of time travel, particularly the core idea that it might be possible to go back in time and alter events to change the present and future.

The first *Terminator* film was the brainchild of James Cameron, who was then unknown but is now arguably the world's greatest moviemaker, having directed the two biggest-grossing movies of all time, *Titanic* (1997) and *Avatar* (2009) – which itself is set to spawn a number of sequels. Born in 1954 in Kapuskasing, Ontario, Canada, he originally studied physics at Fullerton College in 1973 then switched to English before dropping out of college in the autumn of 1974 to earn a living as a truck driver. However, Cameron was fascinated by film-making and, after seeing *Star Wars* in 1977, vowed to become a film director. He soon learned a great deal about every aspect of the craft and became a special effects designer, model-maker, artist and production designer on several films including John Carpenter's *Escape from New York* (1981).

Later that same year, Cameron was in Rome working as a special effects designer on a low-budget movie called *Piranha II: The Spawning* when he fell ill with food poisoning. During his brief illness he had a bad dream involving a skeletal metal robot emerging from flames clutching two knives. This gave him the inspiration for one of the final scenes in what eventually became *The Terminator*, and was the starting point for his screenplay. Since the robot existed in the future and an entire film set in this period would be very expensive, the answer was to bring the robot to the present – hence the time travel element which forms a key part of the plot.

There was nothing new about the idea of killer robots. A 1965 monochrome episode of the British TV series *The Avengers*, called *The Cybernauts*, involved humanoid metal androids (the 'Cybernauts' of the title) which home in on their victims and kill them with powerful karate chops. The robots – which were created by deranged wheelchair-bound scientist Dr Armstrong (Michael Gough) – zeroed in on a small radio transmitter concealed inside a pen, gifted by Armstrong, which the victim carried in their jacket. Invulnerable to bullets, the Cybernauts smashed their way through doors to get to their targets. Utterly convincing on screen, the principal robot was portrayed by a stuntman wearing a simple blank silver mask with fake rivets, a heavy woollen coat, black leather gloves, black hat and trousers, and dark glasses to conceal the eyeholes in the mask.

The Cybernauts proved so popular that they returned in 1967 in the first colour series of *The Avengers* in an episode entitled *Return of the Cybernauts*. This time, the metal monsters homed in on the heartbeat of their victims using an illicitly-obtained ECG recording, and in one exciting sequence a Cybernaut bashes through a wooden fence, stops a moving car and then hauls its victim out through a hole it has smashed in the roof.

The third and final appearance of the Cybernauts to date came in a 1976 episode of *The New Avengers*, *The Last of the Cybernauts?*, in which the robots are controlled by a joystick and TV link. Eventually the villain, Kane (Robert Lang) – who has overcome paralysis by turning himself into a 'half Cybernaut, half human' – is defeated after being sprayed with quick-setting plastic, an idea possibly borrowed from Episode 3 of the *Doctor Who* Cyberman story *The Wheel in Space* (1968) in which a Cybermat (a small metallic rodent-like creature) is immobilised in a similar fashion.

As I have indicated above, the Cybernauts only appeared three times on British television, but in 2014 footage was posted on *YouTube* taken from a 'Mexican Cybernauts movie' [[sic]]. This came from the 1968 Mexican film *Luchadoras vs el Robot Asesino,* directed by Rene Cardona, which apparently was one of a series of Mexican films involving female wrestlers! Many of the scenes in this movie appear to have been lifted wholesale from *Return of the Cybernauts*, and the appearance of the robot is identical. One wonders why it did not trigger a lawsuit from the makers of *The Avengers?*

The idea of a person travelling back in time to kill someone and thus alter history is also not new. In the 1972 *Doctor Who* story *The Day of the Daleks* (written by Louis Marks), a number of guerrillas from a future Earth ruled by the Daleks travel back to the present moment to assassinate British diplomat Sir Reginald Styles who they (wrongly) believe set off a bomb to destroy a peace conference, thus triggering a nuclear war which gave the Daleks an opportunity to invade the Earth for a second time.

Harlan Ellison's teleplay for a 1964 episode of American sci-fi series *The Outer Limits*, entitled *Soldier*, also features a trooper travelling back in time from a post-nuclear war apocalypse to the present moment, and the similarity between this screenplay and *The Terminator* led to a legal action after Cameron's film was released as I shall describe in more detail later in the chapter.

Science fiction films often have high budgets, but *The Terminator* was originally to cost just $4m (though this was later increased to $6.5m) – not a large sum when you consider the vast amount of special effects, miniature work and stunts in the picture. By comparison, the British action thriller *Who Dares Wins* (1982) cost $6m to make and had relatively few special effects compared with the American picture.

For the role of the Terminator, Cameron cast former bodybuilding champion turned actor Arnold Schwarzenegger, whose career was on the up. Although Cameron had original-ly intended the Terminator to be an averagely-proportioned man who possessed incredible physical strength, he changed his mind after meeting the Austrian-born actor. With his background in bodybuilding, Schwarzenegger brought an in-tense physicality to the role and even his Austrian accent worked to his advantage. As Cameron later said 'his voice had a synthesised quality... as if they hadn't quite got it to work correctly'.

Accounts vary on whether Lance Henriksen was seriously considered for the role. What is beyond dispute is that he did dress up as the Terminator for a meeting with studio execu-tives, with his make-up consisting of gold foil over his teeth and fake cuts. Some concept art for the Terminator with Lance Henriksen's likeness was also prepared by James Cam-eron, but eventually the director opted to have a super-muscular Terminator – a decision which probably contributed greatly to the movie's popularity.

A large number of prominent Hollywood actresses audi-tioned for the role of Sarah Connor and – if reports on the internet are to believed – these included Sharon Stone, Geena Davis, Debra Winger, Kelly McGillis, Kathleen Turner and even Glenn Close. In the end, though, the role was given to the relatively unknown Linda Hamilton.

27-year-old Michael Biehn was cast as Sgt Kyle Reece, the soldier from the future who comes to rescue Sarah and becomes her lover. Biehn became one of Cameron's 'repertory company', playing similar military roles in *Aliens* (1986) and *The Abyss* (1987).

The film was produced by Cameron's then-wife Gale Ann Hurd, who bought the screenplay from her husband for the token sum of one dollar. Gale Ann Hurd, who worked for Orion Pictures, was the producer, with John Daly of Hemdale Pictures as executive producer.

Cameron's screenplay called for extensive creature effects, and these were provided by Stan Winston who had provided the amazing transformations in John Carpenter's 1982 remake of *The Thing* and went on to work on Cameron's next film, *Aliens* (1986). Other effects such as the future war sequences were created by a large team from Fantasy II Film Effects.

The film was originally scheduled for shooting in 1983, but was delayed nine months to allow Arnold Schwarzennegger to meet his commitments on *Conan the Barbarian*. During this recess Cameron wrote the screenplay for his next film, *Aliens* (1986), and also wrote a first draft of *Rambo: First Blood Part II* (1985).

The film opens with a caption which reads 'Los Angeles 2029 AD'. Strange alien-looking hovering aircraft float over a desolate smoke-filled landscape as they shoot at everything that moves with laser cannon. Later in the film, we learn that these craft (plus their tracked, land-based equivalents) are known as Hunter-Killers (HKs), and apparently their appearance and weaponry was inspired by the Martian war machines in *War of the Worlds* (1953). Soldiers in futuristic battledress armed with hand-held laser weapons run for cover as a lengthy caption appears on screen:

'The Machines Rose from the Ashes of a Nuclear Fire. Their war to exterminate mankind has raged for decades. But their final battle would not be fought in the future. It would be fought here. In the present. Tonight.'

Then the titles appear, accompanied by Brad Fiedel's synthesised score with its pounding five-note 'Terminator Theme', supposedly representing a mechanical heartbeat.

After the titles, a caption informs us that it is 'Los Angeles 1984'. Amidst smoke, and what looks like a miniature electrical storm, the Terminator arrives, played by the incredibly muscular Arnold Schwarzennegger. He is naked and immediately confronts three nearby punks (who are clowning around next to a 'pay as you view' telescope), demanding their clothes.

'Give me clothes,' he says.

Two of them refuse to comply and are swiftly killed by the Terminator. The third, played by Bill Paxton, is so terrified he strips off all his clothing and runs away.

Meanwhile, in a nearby alley, another naked man with a more average muscular build materializes from the future. To achieve this effect, a stuntman dropped about four feet from a lying position on a wooden plank mounted between two stepladders, fortunately not injuring himself in the process. The second time traveller is Sgt Kyle Reese (Michael Biehn), a soldier from the year 2029.

Reese immediately confronts a tramp in the alley and robs him of his trousers. He steals a revolver from a policeman and holds him at gunpoint while he asks him the date, which is Thursday 12th May. Before he can find out the year, he is chased by other cops and breaks into a department store where he steals a raincoat and other clothing items. As he makes his way out of the shop, he also manages to purloin a pump-action shotgun from a police car. Reece saws off most of the wooden stock and fits a makeshift sling made from rope to allow the weapon to be easily concealed. Now suitably armed, he finds a phone box and rips out a page from the telephone directory containing the names, addresses and phone numbers of the three people in LA called Sarah Connor.

The next morning (in one of the few daytime shots in the movie, as it was mainly filmed at night), 19-year-old Sarah Connor rides to work on a Honda motor scooter. She arrives (slightly late) at the diner and stamps her card.

Meanwhile, the Terminator steals a station wagon by smashing the driver's window with his fist and then hot-wiring the ignition and starter motor using the usual Holly-wood method of ripping out a few wires and twisting them together.

As the Terminator drives off, Sarah is having a bad day at work. The diner is busy, she is overworked and then she spills food on a customer. As she leans forward to clean the cus-tomer's trousers a young child puts a scoop of ice cream in the pocket of her uniform. One of her fellow waitresses sees her predicament and makes the profound philosophical observa-tion: '100 years from now, who is going to care?'

On the way to his next victim, the Terminator stops at a gun store where he asks for several weapons including a '0.45 Longside laser sighting pistol, a 12 gauge auto loader shotgun, a phased plasma rifle in the forty watt range and an Uzi 9mm sub-machine gun'. The 'phased plasma rifle' is obviously a weapon from the future and so is not in stock, but the propri-etor is able to supply the other items plus copious amounts of ammunition.

The shop owner says he will have to wait a couple of weeks before he can uplift the handgun (due to the paper-work and legalities involved), though he can have the rifles straight away, but the Terminator shoots him with the shotgun and leaves with all the guns. Soon afterwards he turns up at a phonebox, pulls out the occupant and steals a page of the phonebook containing the names and addresses of the three Sarah Connors who live in Los Angeles (though the Terminator clearly hasn't considered the possibility that Sarah has an ex-directory number!).

Later, the Terminator arrives at the address of the first Sarah Connor listed in the phone book. As his station wagon comes to a halt, its left front wheel crushes a toy truck underfoot, hinting at the devastation that is to come later in the movie. The truck is an exact replica of the cab unit of the articulated tanker which appears towards the end of the film. As Sarah answers the door, the Terminator grunts just two words of dialogue:

'Sarah Connor?'

'Yes.'

Having confirmed her identity, the Terminator kills her with a single round from his laser sighted .45 pistol, then fires a few more rounds into her body for good measure.

A few hours later, Sarah is still working at the diner when she hears a news item on the television. A lady called Sarah Connor, 35 – a mother of two – has been killed at her home.

'You're dead,' says one of her fellow waitresses.

But Sarah remains unperturbed.

In the meantime, Reese has stolen a car of his own. As he rests in the driver's seat, parked near a building site, a tracked excavator rolls past and he has a flashback about fighting tank-like HK vehicles in the future. As one of them trundles past, he flings a grenade under one of its caterpillar tracks and blows it up. This was part of the highly realistic miniature filming. Two-dimensional cut-outs were used to represent devastated buildings, and smoke helped to create a sense of

The Terminator (1984): Hemdale/
Pacific Western Productions/
Cinema '84/Orion Pictures

perspective. Actors were added to the foreground of these scenes using both back and front projection.

Now Reese and a soldier colleague jump into an old car, which has been converted into a makeshift anti-aircraft vehicle by cutting off the roof and fitting a laser cannon in the rear (which was apparently a modified Browning M2 0.50" cal machine gun). As the car speeds, off it exchanges fire with a pursuing Hunter Killer aircraft. Suddenly the car is hit and crashes as Reese is jolted back to reality.

Later, Sarah Connor and her flatmate Ginger (Bess Motta) are in their flat preparing for their dates. The phone rings and Sarah picks it up. A man starts talking dirty to her, telling her what he would like to do to her. Sarah realises it is Matt (Rick Rossovich), Ginger's boyfriend, and passes the receiver to her.

In a nearby police station, Detective Hal Vukovick (Lance Henriksen) and Lieutenant Ed Traxler (Paul Winfield) have discovered that a second person called Sarah Connor has been killed and they may be facing a 'pattern killer' who is out to murder everyone with that name.

Meanwhile, Sarah is checking her ansaphone for messages and discovers that her date for that evening (Dan) has cancelled, so she decides to go out on her own using her Honda scooter. The ansaphone message was voiced by James Cameron himself. As she is leaving her flat, Reese follows her in his car.

Just after she has left, the phone rings; it is the police, desperately trying to contact Sarah. But the call is picked up by her ansaphone, as Ginger is busy having sex with her boyfriend while listening to her cassette Walkman with a pair of headphones.

As Ginger and Matt continue with their copulation – unaware of the danger they are in – Sarah is enjoying a meal and a drink in a bar. A TV news item mentions that two people, both called Sarah Connor, have been killed and police are hunting the killer. Suddenly, realising her life may be in danger, Sarah grabs a phonebook from a nearby payphone and deduces that someone is intent on killing all the Sarah Connors in the phonebook and that she will be next.

Feeling anxious, she leaves the bar. As she walks along the street she realises she is being followed by a man (Kyle Reese), so she manages to lose him and ducks into a nightclub, the *Tech Noir*. This nightclub was created especially for the film and was so realistic that many LA citizens wanted to come inside and use its facilities, not realising it was merely a film set. Sarah makes a bee-line for the payphone inside the nightclub. Although it is working, all the lines are busy.

As Sarah continues with her attempts to contact the police, the Terminator has arrived at Sarah's flat. Ginger has finished her lovemaking with Matt and, Walkman headphones still in place, she is dancing as she makes her way to the kitchen to prepare a post-coital snack. As she takes items out of the fridge and food cupboard, the Terminator enters Ginger's bedroom where he starts to fight with Matt. Though an obviously fit and well-muscled man, Matt is no match for the powerful cyborg. He is quickly killed after both him and the Terminator burst through the bedroom door. Ginger screams in terror, but is executed as she tries to flee.

As the Terminator is about to leave the scene, he hears an incoming message on the ansaphone. It is Sarah, saying she is at the *Tech Noir* nightclub. She gives the address. The Terminator knows he has to go there to complete his mission. Before he departs, he rummages through Sarah's drawers and finds her address book and University ID card. He now knows exactly what she looks like. Back at the *Tech Noir* nightclub, Sarah has finally managed to get through to the police and speaks on the phone to Lieutenant Traxler who tells her to stay where she is as help is on its way.

By now Reese has arrived at the nightclub and is stalking Sarah, though at this point she does not know he is trying to protect her. Then the Terminator arrives and quickly identifies Sarah. He aims his .45 Longside pistol at her, projecting a small dot of red laser light on her forehead. Just as he is about to pull the trigger, Reese breaks cover and pulls out his pump action shotgun from beneath his coat. He fires several rounds at the Terminator, knocking him to the ground with the sheer kinetic energy of the projectiles and temporarily stunning him. But the Terminator is not killed and, within seconds, he gets up again and opens fire with his Uzi 9mm sub-machine gun at the fleeing crowds. Sarah is not hit, but is trapped under the body of one of the Terminator's victims. As she lies on the ground, pinned down by the dead body, the Terminator cocks his Uzi and takes careful aim. Just as he is about to pull the trigger Reese fires again, this time knocking the Terminator through a large plate glass window.

Before the Terminator recovers, Reese grabs Sarah by the hand, uttering the immortal line of dialogue: 'Come with me if you want to live'. They run out of the nightclub and down an alley, pursued by the Terminator. At this point we see a 'Terminator's Eye View' of the proceedings, which resembles the HUD (Head Up Display) of a fighter aircraft.

Reese and Sarah get into his car. As they drive off at speed, the Terminator climbs onto the windscreen and tries to smash his way in. Reese reverses at high speed and hits a police car – the impact throwing off the Terminator – and the pair escape. However, the Terminator steals a police car and sets off in hot pursuit. A furious car chase ensues. The Terminator uses the police car radio to find out what is going on, and one of its many capabilities is revealed: it can exactly mimic any human voice it has heard.

As Reese drives like a maniac through the streets of LA, he tries to explain to Sarah what is going on. He is Sergeant Kyle Reese, who has been sent back in time from the year 2029 to try and prevent her assassination by a Terminator – effectively metal robots looking a bit like skeletons. These 'endo-skeletons' are covered with real living flesh to enable them to pass for humans. Though earlier 600-series Terminator models had rubber flesh and could be easily identified, the new T-800 Model 101s have real human skin and muscles and even have bad breath and sweat, meaning they are hard to spot.

Terminators don't feel pain. They have no remorse. They can't be bargained with. Once they have been programmed to carry out a mission, they will execute it.

Sarah asks Reese if he can stop the Terminator and he says he is not sure, bearing in mind the limitations of the contemporary weaponry he is forced to use. Reese drives into a car park and steals another car to try and fox the Terminator. As he breaks the steering lock and hotwires the car, he explains a bit more about what is happening.

The Terminators have been produced by Cyberdyne Systems. In the near future, the machines produced by Cyberdyne – in particular, the Skynet defence satellite system – have become self-aware and decide to eliminate mankind by starting a nuclear war. However, some humans survive and set up a resistance army to fight the machines. Others are used as slave labour, and Reese shows Sarah a tattoo rather like a bar code on his forearm.

One of the key resistance leaders is John Connor, Sarah's as-yet-unborn son, and Skynet wants to damage the future resistance movement by killing Sarah in 1984 – thus preventing the birth of John Connor.

Suddenly the Terminator arrives in a police car, and another car chase on a freeway follows. But this time several police cars arrive and, after an exchange of gunfire, the Terminator eventually crashes his vehicle. Reese and Sarah are surrounded by several police vehicles and are forced to surrender. There is no sign of the Terminator though, as he has apparently fled the scene. Reese and Sarah are taken to the police station where Reese is interrogated by Dr Silberman (Earl Boen), a criminal psychologist.

As this is going on, the Terminator breaks into a building where he carries out some much-needed 'surgery' on his flesh outer body following his car crash. He cuts open the flesh of his right forearm so he can repair some damaged control rods.

The surgery over, he folds back the skin and applies a band-age.

The Terminator also has to do some work on the area around his left eye, which has been damaged. Many of these shots were achieved using a life-sized animatronic puppet of Schwarzenegger's head, which took weeks to build. Totally convincing, the only thing that indicates that it is not the ac-tor's real head is that its movements are slightly jerkier than a real human one. A larger-than-life size model of the Termina-tor's left eye was also created, incorporating a real camera ap-erture. With the left eye now working properly, the Termina-tor covers the damage with a large pair of Gargoyles sunglass-es.

Back at the police station, Dr Silberman continues to ques-tion Kyle Reese but is sceptical about his story. He asks if Reese had really come from the future, why he didn't bring a ray gun with him which would have avoided his reliance on contemporary weapons? Reese explains that the Time Dis-placement Equipment only works with living organisms, so inanimate objects (such as weapons) can't be transported through time.

A little later, Sarah watches a monochrome video record-ing of Silberman's interview with Reece, who comes across as a deranged lunatic. Drexler suggests that the Terminator's invulnerability to bullets and shotgun shells could be ex-plained by the fact that he probably wore body armour, and shows Sarah a Kevlar vest that policemen wear on operations. She is beginning to doubt Reece's story, but is not sure. Sarah asks how the Terminator could punch his hand through a car windscreen, and Vokavich speculates that he may have been taking PCP, a drug which would prevent him feeling any pain. PCP (also known as Phencyclidine or 'angel dust') is an anaesthetic agent which was popular as a recreational drug in the eighties. Vokavich tells Sarah that she must need some sleep, and suggests she has a rest on the couch as there are 30 cops in the building and she is quite safe.

As Sarah is dropping off, the Terminator arrives at the front desk of the police station claiming to be a friend of hers, but the on-duty cop says he can't see her.

'I'll be back,' says the Terminator.

This has become one of the most famous lines in movie history, but was nearly 'I will be back', as Schwarzenegger thought it was more appropriate dialogue for a machine. He was overruled by James Cameron, who wanted the line delivered as scripted. 'I don't tell you how to act, you don't tell me how to write,' he is reported to have said.

A moment later the Terminator drives his car through the front of the police station and jumps out armed with his Uzi machine pistol and an Armalite AR-18 automatic rifle. Quickly, the Terminator rips out the main electricity supply cable with his bare hands, plunging the building into darkness. The police arm themselves with M-16A1 rifles from the armoury, but their guns prove useless against the metal killing machine. In the confusion Reece breaks free, finds Sarah, and they escape in a stolen car and head for the country.

Unfortunately their car soon runs out of petrol, and they have to push it off the road. As they take shelter, shivering, in a nearby culvert Sarah applies a makeshift field dressing to Reece's right forearm as she asks him about her son John.

Reece reveals that he volunteered for the mission as he wanted to meet the legend, Sarah Connor. Sarah is perplexed, because the Sarah Connor Reece talks about is obviously tough and organised whereas she 'can't even balance her cheque book'. Reece is unchanged in his views though, and recites a personal message from her son John telling her she must survive so he can exist in the future.

Sarah asks Reece to tell him more about the future war, and he explains how the Hunter Killers (HKs) use infrared vision to find resistance fighters in the dark. He remembers an incident when a Terminator infiltrated their camp and caused carnage. The Terminator in this sequence was played by Franco Columbu, one of Arnold Schwarzenegger's workout buddies. The alarm was raised by two Alsatian dogs, who were able to detect the difference between humans and Terminators and barked a warning. In the resulting firefight the only photo he had of Sarah (a small Polaroid print) got burned. Sarah falls asleep and dreams about this future war, and – when she awakens – she remembers that the resistance uses dogs to sniff out Terminators.

In the intervening time, the unshaven and rather dishevelled-looking landlord of a cheap guest house knocks on the door of a bedroom as he puffs on a cigar. 'Hey buddy! You got a dead cat in there or something?'

Inside the bedroom, the Terminator considers possible linguistic responses in a 'menu' display inside his head and selects the best option:

'Fuck you, asshole.'

Unperturbed, the proprietor sets off down the corridor, pushing his cleaning trolley before him as the Terminator continues to study Sarah's address book.

Meanwhile, Sarah and Reece have arrived at the Tiki Motel and ask for a room with a kitchen. Sarah says she is dying for a shower. Reece has to go out for supplies, so he gives Sarah a handgun for her protection. A deleted scene reveals that this weapon was given to him by Lieutenant Traxler during the police station massacre.

Later, having had her shower, Sarah is sitting on the bed wrapped in a towel on the phone to her mother who implores her to give her her contact number. Though she knows she shouldn't really do this, she gives her the Tiki Motel's phone number. Unbeknown to Sarah, her mother is dead, killed in her cabin, and she is speaking to the Terminator who can impersonate anyone's voice with pitch-perfect accuracy. After Sarah has hung up, the Terminator rings the number he has been given and finds out the address of the motel. He immediately leaves for the motel on a motorcycle.

Back at the Tiki Motel, Reece arrives with two paper bags of groceries. Sarah wonders if he has bought food for dinner, but his provisions include mothballs, corn syrup and ammonia, the ingredients required to make home-made explosives.

Reece gets to work with Sarah's assistance and prepares six pipe bombs. As they construct the munitions, Sarah asks Reece if he has a special person in the future. To her surprise he reveals he fell in love with Sarah after seeing her Polaroid photo. The couple then kiss and make love. Soon after they have finished having sex, the Terminator arrives at the motel and they are forced to flee the building.

Reece steals a pick-up truck, and a high-speed car chase follows in which they are followed by the Terminator who is firing bursts from an automatic weapon. While travelling fast, Reece swaps places with Sarah so that he can attack the pursuing Terminator with his stock of pipe bombs. Reece lights the bomb fuses with a cigarette lighter and flings them out the passenger window one at a time, resulting in near misses which do not damage the Terminator. As he is about to throw a fourth bomb he is hit by a burst of gunfire, causing him to drop the ordnance next to his truck. The device explodes, injuring him further. By now the Terminator has run out of ammunition for his Uzi and is relying on his pistol.

As his bike comes alongside the pick-up truck, Sarah pulls on the wheel, causing the vehicle to swerve and knock down the Terminator's bike. Unfortunately Sarah's sudden manoeuvre also makes the pick up overturn, and the couple (by now both injured) have to climb out the vehicle.

A large articulated fuel tanker of the JG Oil Company (the J and G stood for James Cameron and Gale Ann Hurd) drives past at speed and runs over the Terminator, who grabs onto the underside of the vehicle, showering sparks everywhere. The truck driver brings his vehicle to a halt and jumps out to find out what has happened. He is immediately killed by the Terminator, who jumps into the cab and tells the other occupant to get out. Quickly, the Terminator starts the vehicle, turns it round and chases after Sarah, mounting the kerb as he does so.

Reece races after the vehicle and shoves a lit pipe bomb into an open metal tube at the rear of the tanker, then dives into a large metal bin to take cover. Within seconds the tanker explodes in a massive conflagration. This was one of the most impressive pieces of miniature filming in the entire production, and is totally convincing. A one-sixth model of the fuel tanker was built and destroyed using 42 separate charges. The first take was a failure because a wire pulling the model accidentally ripped the front axle from its mounting, and a new miniature vehicle had to be built in just a few days.

The Terminator staggers through the inferno as its outer flesh body is consumed by the flames. Then, apparently killed, it collapses on its funeral pyre. The distributors wanted to end the film at this point, but Cameron put his foot down and insisted that the final scenes he had scripted be shot and included in the final cut. He was right, because the last few minutes include some classic moments of cinema.

Sarah wanders amongst the wreckage and discovers the wounded Reece. Then, as the couple embrace, the Terminator comes back to life like a malevolent phoenix rising from the ashes. For the first time we see the Terminator endoskeleton in its full technological glory: a glistening metal robot with glowing red eyes and skull-like head. Some scenes featuring the endoskeleton were achieved using a full-sized animatronic puppet, which only existed from the waist up and was worked from below by an operator. For shots showing the robotic Terminator in its entirety, a complete stop-motion puppet was used, and in these scenes the movement is a little more jerky.

Despite their injuries, Sarah and Reece make their way into a nearby factory which employs robot machine tools (rather like the Fiat Strada factory which appeared in TV commercials in the early eighties). Reece switches on the machinery in order to impede the Terminator's tracking devices and bolts the door behind them. This does not deter the robot, who starts breaking down the door. Eventually he makes a hole large enough to put a hand through, lets himself in, and then chases the couple through the factory.

Reese tries to fight the skeletal Terminator with a metal bar, but is unable to damage it. He then lights his last pipe bomb and sticks it into the waist of the Terminator. A few seconds later it explodes, effectively amputating the robot's body below the waist. Reece is killed, and Sarah receives a large shard of metal in her left thigh. But the Terminator is still alive and crawls towards Sarah, determined to kill her with his metal hands. With the last of her energy, Sarah crawls under a large hydraulic press. As she escapes out the far side, the Terminator follows her and Sarah presses a large rubber button which brings the press down on the machine creature.

'You're terminated, fucker!' she says as the press squeezes the last bit of life out of the robot and its glowing red eyes fade to black. For this scene, a simple mock-up of the Terminator was made using foam-core and metal foil. The smoke is actually from a cigarette. Sarah collapses, exhausted, as the sound of police car sirens is heard in the background.

In the next, penultimate scene Sarah is lifted into an ambulance as Reece's corpse is taken away in a body bag (which was actually a suit bag obtained from the trunk of James Cameron's car). Scenes deleted from the final cut of the picture revealed that the factory was owned by Cyberdyne Systems, and that the Terminator's CPU chip had been found in the wreckage and was sent to Cyberdyne's research and development division, thus leading to the eventual creation of the Terminator in a future time. Thus this chip was itself in a time loop, rather like the pocket watch in *Somewhere in Time* (1980).

The final scene of the movie is set in Mexico, several months later, where a heavily pregnant Sarah has stopped at a gas station in her CJ-7 Jeep. She has an Alsatian dog on the passenger seat (obviously to detect Terminators), a revolver in her lap, and is dictating a series of audiocassettes to advise her unborn son.

A Mexican boy approaches her and takes a Polaroid picture of her for five dollars. The resulting print is the very same photo which John Connor gives to Kyle Reece in 2029. Sarah drives off along the highway as dark clouds gather on the horizon and end title credits roll.

The Terminator premiered on 26th October 1984 and proved to be one of the most successful films of the year. It has also proved very popular on VHS, DVD and Blu-Ray formats.

Author Harlan Ellison loved the film but felt it was too similar to *Soldier*, a 1964 episode of *The Outer Limits* he had written. As a result he took out a legal action which meant that all future releases of *The Terminator* credited his works as a source of inspiration.

In 1991 a sequel, *Terminator 2: Judgment Day*, with a budget of $102m followed. In this new story, set 10 years after the original, Skynet tries to interfere with the past for a second time by sending another Terminator back in time. But this is a T-1000 'liquid metal' shape-shifting Terminator which is even harder to stop than the original. Arnold Schwarzenegger returned in this sequel, playing a reprogrammed T-800 Terminator sent back in time by the resistance to protect John Connor while the T-1000 was played by Robert Patrick. This harked back to Cameron's original 1984 concept for the T-800, which was that it should be played by a relatively skinny actor. As mentioned earlier in the chapter, the relatively slim actor Lance Henrikssen had originally been considered for the part of The Terminator but in the end Cameron decided to go for a bulky cyborg played by Schwarzennegger.

James Cameron had originally planned to include a T-1000 Terminator in the 1984 original, but discounted the idea as special effects technology wasn't up to the job in the eighties. Some early primitive Computer Generated Imagery (CGI) had been used in *Tron* (1982), and Cameron had also gained some experience of the technique in *The Abyss* (1989). By 1991 CGI technology had advanced to the point where it could be used to create the shape-changing 'liquid metal' T-1000 terminator.

Terminator 2 also featured a number of ideas which were filmed for the 1984 original but were subsequently deleted, such as a technician discovering a microchip in the wreckage of the Terminator at the factory and Sarah's suggestion that they blow up the HQ of Cyberdyne Systems.

The movie opens in the present day (1991), with John Connor living in Los Angeles with foster parents. His mother Sarah has prepared him well for his role of future resistance leader, but is now banned from seeing John as she has been sent to a psychiatric hospital after attempting to blow up a computer factory. Linda Hamilton returned as Sarah Connor, but looked considerably different from her earlier incarnation as she had put on a lot of muscle thanks to a low-fat diet and a weight-training routine.

In 2029, Skynet sends an advanced T-1000 'liquid metal' Terminator back to 1991 to kill John. The T-1000 materializes under a freeway, kills a policeman and assumes his identity. Meanwhile, another Terminator – an earlier T-800 model – is sent back in time from 2029 to protect John.

The two Terminators meet at a shopping mall, where the T-800 is trying to kill John. Although initially wary of the T-800, John eventually realises he has been sent back in time by his future self to protect him. The T-800 saves John, and they make their escape on a motorbike. But John insists that the T-800 helps him to free his mother from the psychiatric hospital where she has been held.

At the hospital, Sarah realises that the only way she will ever be released and reunited with her son John is if she pretends that she has now recovered from her 'mental illness', which has led her to claim that a Terminator cyborg from the future has tried to kill her and that 'Judgement Day' is imminent. In fact, what Sarah is saying is the truth, but her psychiatrists believe she is suffering from delusions and realise she is telling them what she needs to say in order to convince them she has recovered. Unfortunately her psychiatrists see through her deception, and she is told she will have to stay in hospital for the time being. But Sarah won't give up that easily, and plans to escape from the facility.

Just as she is escaping from the facility, John and the T-800 arrive. Sarah is initially frightened of the T-800, but then it starts to battle with the T-1000 which has also arrived. Eventually, Sarah, John and the T-800 escape in a police car and head for a hiding place in the desert, where Sarah has a cache of weapons. At that point Sarah and John are safe, as the T-1000 has lost them, but Sarah is still obsessed with hitting back at Skynet. After she has had a nightmare about Judgement Day, she comes up with a new plan – she will kill Miles Bennet Dyson (Joe Morton), the Skynet designer whose work leads to the creation of Skynet and hence the Terminators.

Arming herself with a variety of weapons, including an assault rifle, she heads for Dyson's house. She succeeds in wounding the computer designer but is unable to bring herself to kill the man in front of his family. At this point John and the T-800 arrive. The cyborg shocks John by cutting open his forearm to reveal the mechanical endoskeleton.

This graphic demonstration shocks Dyson, who now realises that his work will have horrific consequences for the human race. He vows to help Sarah and John achieve their objectives, and points out that much of his work was based on reverse engineering of the right arm and CPU of the very first Terminator which was recovered from a machine press in 1984. It will therefore be necessary to destroy these items.

Dyson, John, Sarah and the T-800 make their way to the Cyberdyne factory, where they retrieve the arm and the CPU and set explosive charges. Unfortunately the police arrive and Dyson is shot dead, but the factory is still blown up. Unfortunately this raid has caused the T-1000 to re-acquire its targets, and the trio are pursued to a steel mill where the two Terminators battle one another. The T-800 is apparently killed, but manages to revive itself using an emergency power supply. Eventually it blasts the T-1000 into a vat of molten steel using repeated shots from an M-79 grenade launcher.

John throws the arm of the original Terminator into the molten steel along with its CPU. The T-800 then asks John to lower it into the molten metal as well, since its own destruction will be necessary to prevent the future nuclear war from occurring.

Further sequels followed: *Terminator 3: Rise of The Machines* in 2003, *Terminator: Salvation* in 2009 and *Terminator: Genisys* in 2015, plus a TV series – *Terminator: The Sarah Connor Chronicles* (2008-2009) – with English actress Lena Headey replacing Linda Hamilton. However, most critics would agree that none of these matched the 1984 original for sheer thrills and originality. It is without a doubt one of the greatest films ever made.

Terminator 2 received widespread critical acclaim, with many reviewers considering it superior to the 1984 original. It was also very successful financially, making $553.7m against a production cost of $102 million. It was the highest-grossing film of 1991, beating its main competition, *Robin Hood: Prince of Thieves*. The film was the first to earn more than $300m dollars overseas, and is rated number 84 in all-time box office earnings worldwide.

Bearing in mind the fantastic success of this film, it was surprising that a whole twelve years elapsed before the next sequel *Terminator 3: Rise of the Machines* (2003). This featured the return of Arnold Schwarzenegger as the T-800, but otherwise had an all-new cast. Nick Stahl replaced Edward Furlong as the young John Connor. Linda Hamilton also did not appear in this sequel, with her character Sarah Connor supposedly dead. James Cameron was also not involved in the film, though he received an on-screen credit for creating certain characters.

On this occasion, the directorial reins were handed to Jonathan Mostow, who is best known for directing the controversial war thriller *U-571* (2000).

The plot followed the continuing story of John Connor, who was living 'off the grid' in Los Angeles following the death of his mother Sarah Connor. Because of the actions of John and Sarah in the previous film, the nuclear war which was to have been started by Skynet in 1997 has not happened, but John is still fearful that it may kick off at some point in the future and so is hiding from Skynet.

As Skynet is unable to locate John, it sends another Terminator – the T-X – back to 2004 with orders to find and destroy him. The future Resistance responds by sending a T-850 Terminator (Model 101) back to the same time period to protect John. This time the T-X is programmed to kill not just John but also his future wife Kate Brewster (Claire Danes). This film was Danes' big break, and she has since become very well-known for playing the disturbed CIA analyst Carrie Matheson in *Homeland* (2009-present).

After killing several people, the T-X (Kristanna Loken) tracks down Kate and John at a veterinary hospital where

John has been stealing medication. Fortunately the T-850 arrives and helps them to escape.

The next day, they travel to a cemetery where there is a mausoleum which supposedly contains Sarah's body. In fact, it contains a cache of weapons which Sarah had stored many years before in case they were needed. The T-850 manages to retrieve the guns, despite interference from the police. The T-X also tries to stop them, but they manage to escape.

The T-850 later reveals that Sarah and John's previous actions had only delayed Judgement Day, not stopped it altogether, and that the nuclear war is due to start at 6.18 p.m. John orders the Terminator to take him and Kate to see Kate's father, a Lieutenant General who is rebuilding Skynet.

Initially the Terminator refuses, but agrees to do so once Kate orders him to. It then admits that it had killed John in 2032 but had then been captured, reprogrammed and sent back by Kate, who is now the only person he will obey.

In the meantime, the Chairman of the Joint Chiefs of Staff is trying to persuade General Brewster to activate Skynet in order to counter a virus which is affecting servers all over the world. He doesn't realise that the virus is actually Skynet doing its work.

Skynet becomes active, and various machines start assaulting Brewster and his staff. He is then attacked by the T-X. Just before dying, he hands over a crucial code book to John, Kate and the Terminator.

John and Kate plan to fly to a military base known as Crystal Peak, which is deep inside the Sierra Nevada. The T-X fights with the T-850 and wins this round. She then reprograms the Terminator to attack the youngsters. The T-X attempts to pursue John and Kate, but is immobilised by the magnetic field of a particle accelerator. The Terminator attacks the pair, but then John manages to persuade it to reject the T-Xs control. It responds by shutting down, allowing them to escape.

The two youngsters reach Crystal Peak and attempt to gain entry by entering access codes. Suddenly the T-X arrives by helicopter, closely followed by the Terminator who is also flying a rotorcraft. He attempts to destroy the T-X by flying his aircraft into its helicopter, but the T-X survives the crash and attempts to follow Kate and John into the bunker. The Terminator helps John and Kate to get into the facility and then uses its hydrogen fuel cells to destroy both itself and the T-X.

John and Kate discover that the facility is actually a nuclear fallout shelter and control centre for Government officials. They realise that Judgement Day cannot be prevented, as Skynet releases nuclear missiles all round the world, initiating a nuclear holocaust. Billions of people die, but the two of them have survived to create the Resistance.

The film was well-received by critics. Despite the non-involvement of James Cameron and Linda Hamilton, it was regarded as a worthy successor to the two earlier films and even James Cameron praised it. The film was also reasonably successful at the box office, making $433.4 million set against a budget of $187.3 million.

The next event the in the continuing development of the *Terminator* franchise was a TV series which ran to 31 episodes over two seasons in 2008 and 2009. Titled *Terminator: The Sarah Connor Chronicles*, it starred English actress Lena Headey as Sarah Connor with Thomas Dekker as her son John.

With the events of *Terminator 2: Judgement Day* supposedly taking place in 1995, the series begins in 1999 when

Skynet sends another Terminator, a T-888 called Cromartie (Owain Yeoman), back in time to kill John Connor. Sarah and John are joined by another Terminator, a female called Cameron (Summer Glau), who has been sent back in time by the resistance to protect them.

Cromartie fails in his mission and suffers some damage while Sarah, Cameron and John make a time jump to 2007 to escape their pursuer (thus ensuring that the rest of the season is set in 2007). Other characters make an appearance, including resistance fighter Derek Reese (Brian Austin Green), the brother of Kyle Reese (Michael Biehn) who played an important role in the original Terminator film. Other major characters included FBI Agent James Ellison (Richard T. Jones), who is doggedly pursuing Sarah and John. Although initially sceptical, he starts to believe in the existence of the Terminators. The TV series is therefore set in an alternative universe, as it disregards the events of *Terminator 3: Rise of the Machines*. The altered physical appearance of Sarah Connor is also never explained.

Another important character in the series was Catherine Weaver, who was played by Shirley Manson – lead singer with pop band Garbage – who had performed the title track for the James Bond film *The World is Not Enough* (1999). Weaver is the CEO of a high-tech corporation called Zeira Corps, but is eventually revealed to be a shape-shifting T-1001 liquid metal Terminator. Later it is revealed that Weaver is planning to fight Skynet, and may even be considering joining the Resistance.

The first series of nine episodes was well-received by fans and got good ratings. A second series of twenty-two episodes was therefore commissioned. However, ratings soon fell dramatically, and the series was cancelled in 2009.

One problem with the series was that it was lacking in action compared with the original films, and this was purely down to budgetary considerations. Also, so many additional characters and plot elements had to be introduced to fill thirty-one episodes that it soon became incomprehensible. One of the beauties of the original film was that it had a fairly simple plot that was easy to understand.

Not long after *Terminator: The Sarah Chronicles* ended on American television in the spring of 2009, a fourth *Terminator* movie premiered. Titled *Terminator Salvation*, it was the only *Terminator* film which did not feature time travel and star Arnold Schwarzenegger.

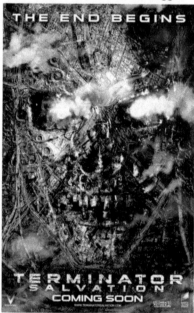

***Terminator Salvation* (2009):** The Halcyon Company/Wonderland Sound and Vision/Warner Bros. Pictures/ Columbia Pictures

Set in 2018, fourteen years after the events of *Terminator 3: Rise of the Machines*, it took place entirely in the post-apocalyptic world first depicted briefly in the original 1984 film and starred Christian Bale as an adult John Connor, with Anton Yelchin playing his younger self.

The film opens in 2003. Dr Serena Kogan (Helena Bonham Carter) who works for Cyberdyne Systems, convinces death row inmate Marcus Wright (Sam Worthington) to allow his body to be used for medical research after his execution. The following year, Skynet becomes self-aware and initiates a nuclear holocaust to eradicate humanity.

Fourteen years later, Resistance fighter John Connor leads an attack on a Skynet facility. He discovers that Skynet is attempting to build Terminator robots, which are covered with human flesh. The resistance blows up the base, but Marcus survives and walks towards Los Angeles.

John makes his way to the Resistance headquarters aboard a nuclear submarine, where General Ashdown (Michael Ironside) tells him that the Resistance has discovered a code which can be used to shut down Skynet's machines. They plan to attack the Skynet headquarters in San Francisco. John also learns that he is on a 'kill list' prepared by Skynet. Also on the list is fellow Resistance fighter Kyle Reese, who he knows will eventually travel back to 1984 and become his father.

In Los Angeles, Marcus meets Kyle and a mute child called Star (Jadagrace Berry). Kyle and Star are subsequently taken prisoner by Skynet following a battle. Meanwhile, Marcus has located a downed pilot, Blair Williams (Moon Bloodgood), whose A-10 aircraft has been shot down during an attack on a Skynet transport.

They travel to John's base, but Marcus is wounded by a land mine. As he is receiving medical attention, the Resistance fighters realise that he is actually a cyborg with a mechanical endoskeleton. John concludes that Marcus must have been sent by Skynet to kill him, but Blair helps the cyborg to escape. Eventually Marcus makes a deal with John – if he will let him live then he will infiltrate Skynet's headquarters in San Francisco to help John liberate Kyle and other prisoners.

John wants the attack on the headquarters delayed so he can come up with a good plan, but General Ashdown refuses to agree to this. However, the Resistance decide to obey John and go along with his scheme. The Resistance fighters encounter the new T-800 (Model 101), which we first saw in the original Terminator film. Marcus destroys the T-800 and John blows up the base, but he realises he has only won one battle and not the whole war. The conflict will continue.

The film got mixed reviews, but made $371.4 million set against a budget of $200 million. It also suffered from many of the annoying stylistic trends of modern cinema such as washed-out colour, jerky camerawork and unrealistic CGI. The plot was also over-complicated and hard to follow, and long-term fans of the series were bemused.

In 2015 a fifth Terminator film premiered. *Terminator Genisys* saw the return of Arnold Schwarzenegger in the title role and was originally intended as a reboot of the series. Directed by Alan Taylor, it used time travel as a way of erasing the events of previous *Terminator* sequels from the timeline of the movie.

The plot is initially similar to the original *Terminator* film. In 2029 the Resistance sends soldier Kyle Reese (Jai Courtney) back to 1984 to protect Sarah Connor. Unfortunately when Kyle arrives in the past he discovers that the timeline has been altered and that Sarah has been raised by a reprogrammed Terminator.

Unfortunately the film has a confusing plot which I have never understood, and comes across as a 'greatest hits' package as it recreated popular scenes from previous *Terminator* films, particularly the first two. It was moderately successful at the box office, making $440.6 million set against a budget of $158 million.

Although, as previously stated, *Terminator Genisys* was intended to be a reboot of the entire series leading to further films and maybe even another spin-off TV series, this never happened and in 2017 it was announced that a sixth *Terminator* film was to be made with a release date of 2019. The exciting news was that the original *Terminator* writer and director, James Cameron, was to be involved in this project which would also see the return of Linda Hamilton, reprising her role of Sarah Connor. Arnold Schwarzenegger also announced that he would be returning as the Terminator.

Most fans of the *Terminator* series of films would probably agree that the first one was excellent, the second was probably even better, the third was good but not excellent, while the fourth and fifth films were disappointing and hard to understand, despite their high budgets.

The news that James Cameron is to return to the series – this time as producer, not as a writer or director – will please many fans, as he has a reputation for being a perfectionist with very high standards. The movie is expected to premiere in November 2019 and, if it achieves the success which everyone expects, then it is likely to lead to further sequels and perhaps even another spin-off TV series. The *Terminator* series of films therefore has a special place in film history, as they are the most financially successful and enduring series of time travel movies ever made. Schwarzenegger's words in the original film, 'I'll be back', were more prophetic than anyone realised.

7

Back to the Future

IN 1985 Universal Studios released a highly successful time travel movie, *Back to the Future*, about a teenage American schoolboy named Marty McFly who accidentally journeys from 1985 to 1955 where he is forced to act to ensure his parents get together and he is born. Although originally planned as a standalone movie, the film proved so popular that two sequels were released in 1989 and 1990. The *Back to the Future* films therefore represent one of only two 'time travel franchises' in the history of the cinema, with the other being the *Terminator* movies which started in 1984 and are still being made, with the sixth due out in 2019.

Co-producer and writer Bob Gale got the idea for the film when he wondered what would have happened if he had gone back in time to meet his own father when he was at high school. How would they have got on? Gale calculated that he would have to go back in time thirty years for this to be possible, so he set the movie in two time zones: 1985 (which was then the present) and 1955.

But how would time travel be achieved in the film? Gale's original idea was that a machine would be required, and his first idea was to make the craft an ordinary domestic refrigerator. Gale soon rejected this notion, partly because he was afraid that this concept might result in children shutting themselves inside refrigerators and coming to harm.

His next idea was to use a motor vehicle with had to reach a certain velocity to jump through time. Eventually the Northern Ireland-built DeLorean DMC-12 sports car was chosen for its futuristic appearance. Gale had already decided that there would be a scene in which the time craft arrived in 1955 and was partially buried under hay in a barn. The gag was that it would be found by locals who mistook it for an alien spacecraft, requiring a vehicle with a futuristic appearance. The DeLorean was ideal for this scene as it had an unpainted stainless steel body and gull-wing doors.

The script was co-written by Bob Gale and Robert Zemeckis, the producers were Bob Gale and Neil Canton and the film was directed by Robert Zemeckis. The executive producer was Steven Spielberg.

The original choice of actor to play the lead, Marty McFly, was Michael J. Fox. Unfortunately Fox was unavailable as he had a long-term commitment to the TV series *Family Ties*, so filming started in 1984 with Eric Stoltz in the lead. After just two weeks of shooting, it became clear that Stoltz was not the right actor for the part, so he was replaced by Michael J. Fox.

Born in 1961 in Edmonton, Alberta, Canada, Fox was already an established actor. Although he was 23 at the time of filming, he had a youthful appearance and was only 5 foot 5 inches tall, so he could play a teenager convincingly.

Fox shot *Family Ties* during normal working hours and then went over to Universal to film *Back to the Future* at night. Typically, Fox would not finish work until 2.30 a.m., and then had only four or five hours of sleep before working on *Family Ties*. Any of his outdoor daytime scenes for *Back to the Future* had to be filmed at the weekend, and his unsocial working hours also explained why much of the film takes place at night. This gruelling schedule took its toll on the young actor, who had to endure considerable sleep deprivation, but it is a credit to his professionalism that he delivered a fine performance despite being exhausted for much of the time.

The film was set entirely in the fictional town of Hill Valley, California, in 1955 and 1985. As two time zones had to be depicted, the producers chose to build the entire town as an outdoor set on the back lot at Universal Studios in Los Angeles. The 1955 version of Hill Valley is spotless and gleaming with highly polished period cars and trucks, advertising billboards, diners and drug stores. The fifties scenes were shot first, and then the outdoor set was dirtied up and made to look rather dog-eared for the 1985 scenes.

Some other locations were used in the production. Interiors of Doc Brown's home were shot at the Robert R. Blacker House, while exteriors were filmed at Gamble House. Shopping mall scenes were filmed at the Puente Mills Mall in the City of Industry at California. All exterior shots and some interior scenes of the Hill Valley School were lensed at the Whittier High School in Whittier, California. The 'Battle of the Bands' rehearsal was filmed at the McCambridge Park Recreation Centre in Burbank, with the dance sequences being shot at the Hollywood United Methodist Church.

Back to the Future (1985): Amblin Entertainment/
Universal Pictures

The film opens in 1985 as teenager Marty McFly and his
girlfriend Jennifer Parker (Claudia Wells) are cautioned by
their school principal Mr Strickland (James Tolkan) for their
poor timekeeping. Marty auditions for the school's forthcoming Battle of the Bands, but is rejected for being too loud.
Meanwhile, Marty's parents are having a tough time. His
father George (Crispin Glover) is being bullied by his supervi-
sor Biff Tannen (Thomas F. Wilson), while his mother Lorraine (Lea Thomson) is overweight and depressed.

Marty is friends with a local inventor, Doctor ('Doc')
Emmett Brown (Christopher Lloyd), who asks him to meet
him in a local parking lot in the small hours. Doc shows him a
time machine he has created, based around a modified De-
Lorean DMC-12 sports car. The craft employs nuclear power
to generate the vast amounts of electricity required for a time
jump, and is fuelled by plutonium which Brown has stolen

from some Libyan terrorists. The key component of the machine is a so-called 'flux capacitor': three flashing glass cylinders arranged like a Mercedes logo and fixed between the two front seats. In order to make a time leap, the DeLorean has to reach a speed of 88 mph.

The DeLorean DMC-12 sports car, which features prominently in all three *Back to the Future* films, was one of the most interesting designs in the history of automotive engineering, particularly as it was originally only produced between 1981 and 1983. Built in a factory near Belfast in Northern Ireland, the car was the brainchild of businessman John DeLorean and employed an unpainted stainless steel body designed by Giorgetto Giugiaro and a steel chassis created by Colin Chapman, which was based on a Lotus design. Although originally conceived as a mid-engined vehicle, production versions had a rear-mounted PRV 2.85 litre V6 engine producing 130bhp and giving the car a top speed of 110mph. (By the way, these were quite good power output and performance figures for a 1981 car, but in 2019 the latest 1.0 litre petrol engines offer similar performance and power with a far lower fuel consumption.)

McFly does not believe Brown's claims, so the inventor carries out a simple demonstration. He sits his dog Einstein in the driver's seat, puts a digital clock around his neck, and then operates the DeLorean remotely using a radio-control unit. The car accelerates up to 88mph in the parking lot and then disappears, accompanied by a lot of glowing visual effects. McFly is distraught because he thinks Einstein has been killed, but a moment later the DeLorean reappears with Einstein unharmed in the driver's seat. Brown shows McFly the clock around Einstein's neck and reveals that all he did was send the car a minute into the future, proving that his time travel machine works.

Brown then sets the digital display on the car's control panel to 5th November, 1955 – the day he first invented time travel. But before he can make his journey back, a group of Libyan terrorists arrive in a Volkswagen Microbus. They are angry that Brown has stolen their plutonium and want revenge, so one of them stands in the rolled-back canvas sunroof opening and shoots at the two Americans with a submachine gun. Brown is hit by several rounds and killed, while Marty flees in the DeLorean. The terrorists now produce a Soviet-made RPG-7 rocket propelled grenade launcher and take aim at the car. Marty knows his only chance of escaping is to outrun his opponents and so he accelerates hard, reaches 88 mph, and travels thirty years into the past.

It is now 1955. The DeLorean crashes into a barn full of hay and, as Marty climbs out the car wearing an anti-radiation suit complete with helmet and visor, some townsfolk see him and think he is an alien.

Marty realises that he is trapped in 1955 without enough plutonium to return to 1985. The next morning he wanders about Hill Valley and is amazed at how pristine it looks – particularly the school building, which was quite grubby in 1985. He enters a local diner and asks for a 'Pepsi Free' (i.e. Diet Pepsi), but the owner is unfamiliar with this term and thinks he wants a free drink. He also sees Marty's body warmer, mistakes it for a life-preserver (life jacket), and assumes he is a sailor.

McFly also encounters the teenage version of his father George, who is unassertive and being bullied by Biff Tannen. Marty saves George from being knocked down by a car. Unfortunately he is injured himself and is nursed back to health by his future mother, Lorraine, who is attracted to him.

Later, when he has recovered, Marty goes to 'Doc' Brown's house. The inventor greets him wearing a contraption on his head, supposedly a mind-reading device, but it soon becomes apparent that it quite obviously does not work.

Christopher Lloyd's eccentric performance is one of the great strengths of the movie, with the actor apparently basing his performance on two people – Albert Einstein and conductor Leopold Stokowski. With his wild hair and mannerisms, Lloyd's portrayal is also reminiscent of many 'nutty professors' in film and TV, such as Edward Burnham's Professor Kettlewell in the classic 1974-75 Doctor Who story *Robot*.

Marty's first task is to convince the Doc that he really has come from the future. The Doc asks who the President is in 1985, and Marty reveals that it is Ronald Reagan.

'The actor?' says a disbelieving Brown. 'And who is Vice President? Jerry Lewis?'

This is one of the funniest lines in the film, and the real President Reagan apparently found it very amusing.

Marty eventually convinces 'Doc' that he has come from the future using his time travel technology. The eccentric inventor then realises that he has to get Marty back to 1985. But how? 1.21 gigawatts of electricity would be required for another time jump, but they have no plutonium left. The only way to get some in 1955 would be to raid a nuclear testing station in Nevada. At an early stage in scripting of the film there was to have been a scene involving the Nevada nuclear facility, but it was scrapped to save money.

Then Marty comes up with an idea. He produces a flyer from 1985 which reveals that the Hill Valley courthouse was struck by a lightning bolt in 1955. The flyer gives the exact date and time of the incident, which happens to be the following Saturday. If they could harness the energy of the lightning strike and feed it into the DeLorean's flux capacitor as it is travelling at speed then Marty could return to 1985.

The Doc tells Marty that he must not leave his house and should not interact with the local population, as there is a risk that he could inadvertently change history. Unfortunately Marty has already done this by preventing George from being knocked down. In his original timeline, George and Lorraine had met as a result of this minor road traffic accident, so Marty will have to find another way to ensure they become a couple. If he cannot do this, he will cease to exist. Marty also realises that he will have to tip off Doc Brown about his death at the hands of the terrorists in 1985 so that he can take precautions. He hands a handwritten letter to the 'Doc' which warns of his pending assassination in 1985 but Brown rips it up, saying that it is wrong to tamper with history.

The Doc starts work on suitable apparatus to capture the power of the forthcoming lightning strike, while Marty conceives a plan to ensure that his parents get together. He will accept Lorraine's invitation to go to the dance and – when he is in the car with her – he will make inappropriate advances. George will then rescue her and that will be the beginning of their romance. Things don't quite go to plan though, as it is a drunk Biff who tries to force himself on Lorraine. This causes an enraged George to overcome his inhibitions and hit Biff, who is knocked out.

Lorraine is delighted that George has shown his assertive side and the couple go into the dance hall where they kiss and fall in love. Meanwhile Marty is playing the guitar with considerable skill and gives a rendition of *Johnny Be Good*, a classic Chuck Berry number. For these scenes, Michael J. Fox received some tuition on the guitar although he was not actually playing.

One of the most memorable features of the film was the rousing musical score by prolific composer Alan Silvestri, who had also provided the music for a number of eighties Hollywood blockbusters including *Romancing The Stone* (1984), *Delta Force* (1986) and *Predator* (1987). The signature tune for the movie was *The Power of Love*, performed by Huey Lewis and the News, which became a smash hit. In the 1980s both Jennifer Rush and Frankie Goes to Hollywood had Top 10 hits with songs called *The Power of Love*, but these were two completely different compositions.

Later, Marty prepares to return to 1985. Doc's plan is to string a cable between the top of the clock tower and a thick electric wire he has strung across the main street of the town. Marty is to accelerate the DeLorean up to 88 mph at which point a contraption on the roof of the car (similar to that found on trams and electric trains) will make contact with the cable and allow the high voltage current to travel into the DeLorean's flux capacitor. In true Hollywood tradition, things don't quite go to plan; the cable gets tangled up, and then two connectors break. Doc is forced to hold two components together to complete the circuit, but at the last moment everything works and Marty returns to 1985. He finds himself back in the parking lot in 1985 and sees Doc being shot by the terrorists. But the Doc survives, as he is wearing a bulletproof vest. I must admit I always groan at this scene, as the 'hero has survived an assassination attempt because he is wearing a bulletproof vest' is such a cliché in films and television. I have lost count of the number of times I have seen this gag used. Two years later it was employed in *Lethal Weapon*. In reality, bulletproof vests aren't as effective as a lot of films imply.

They might stop a small-calibre handgun bullet, but they would not completely stop machine gun rounds.

Doc admits that after Marty had departed for 1985 he had found all the pieces of his letter and taped them back together to reveal the warning message. The Doc then takes Marty home and departs for the future in his DeLorean. The next morning, Marty awakens and finds that George is a successful author and married to Lorraine who is fit, slim and healthy. Biff is working as a car detailer (valeter) and is polishing George's car. (I wonder what real car valeters thought of this scene, as it implies that their job is the worst possible occupation!)

Marty is reunited with his girlfriend Jennifer, but then the Doc reappears in the DeLorean – which is now a flying car. He says he has to take the two of them to the future, as there is a problem with their children. On some home entertainment format releases there is a 'To Be Continued' caption at this point, but this was not a feature of the original cinema release.

Back to the Future was released on 2nd July 1985 and was a smash hit success, becoming the biggest grossing film of 1985. It made $389.1 million worldwide against a budget of $19 million. The movie received generally favourable reviews from the critics. It also scored at the 58th Academy Awards, winning Oscars for Best Sound Effects Editing, Best Original Screenplay and Best Sound Mixing.

As a result of the movie, the phrase 'Back to the Future' entered popular culture and was used by President Ronald Reagan in his 1986 State of the Union Address.

The critical and commercial success of the film lead to two sequels: *Back to the Future: Part II* which was released in

1989, and *Back to the Future: Part III* which premiered in 1990.

The ending of the original film might imply that it was always intended to be the first of a series of three films, but this was not the case and a full five years elapsed before the second movie was made. To save time and money, Part II and Part III were made back-to-back.

Many of the original cast returned for Part II, but Claudia Wells' part of Marty's girlfriend Jennifer was recast with Elizabeth Shue taking over the role. In addition, an agreement could not be reached with Crispin Glover for his return to the role of George McFly, so the part was played by Jeffrey Weissman who wore prosthetic make-up in order to resemble Glover while some footage of Crispin Glover shot for the first film was re-used. These decisions upset Glover, who took legal action against the producers, and one result was that the Screen Actors Guild introduced new clauses in its collective bargaining agreement which stated that film companies could not use such methods to reproduce the likenesses of actors.

Back to the Future: Part II begins with the reprised ending of *Part I*, though this had to be re-shot with Elizabeth Shue replacing Claudia Wells in the role of Marty's girlfriend, Jennifer Parker. The date is 26th October 1985, and Doc Brown has returned in his DeLorean (which is now a flying car) to warn Marty and Jennifer that they must come with him to the future as there is a problem with their children. The three of them depart in the car, but are seen leaving by Biff Tannen.

The DeLorean arrives in Hill Valley on 21st October 2015, where Doc puts Jennifer into a trance electronically and leaves her to sleep in an alley as he does not want her to have too much knowledge of the future. Marty then poses as his own son Marty Junior and declines to participate in a robbery with

Biff's grandson, Griff. By doing this, Marty prevents his own children spending time in prison.

Marty swaps places with Marty Junior (Michael J. Fox again) and rejects Griff's offer, but Griff forces Marty to fight him. This results in Griff and his gang being arrested, saving Marty's future children. One of the challenges facing the film's production team was how to depict the future. Many scenes featured flying cars which, we now know, were not a feature of life in 2015. One of these vehicles – which appears as a taxi – was a modified Citroen DS. By a curious coincidence, the Citroen DS was first produced in 1955 – the year in which the first *Back to the Future* movie was set – and was praised at the time for its futuristic design which included powered hydro-pneumatic suspension. The DS was built until 1974, and later models had additional high-tech features such as swivelling headlights which were linked to the steering. It was eventually replaced by the CX model, which never had the same impact on popular culture.

3D movies are also a feature of the imagined 2015, and one nice visual gag is a holographic advert for *Jaws 19* which is 'directed by Max Spielberg'. Max was the real name of one of Steven Spielberg's children. Marty also comments that 'the shark still looks fake', a reference to the rather unconvincing mechanical shark 'Bruce' which was used in the original *Jaws* film in 1975.

Another gadget which features in 2015 is the 'food hydrator', which appears to serve the same role as a microwave in today's world. Marty also uses a 'hoverboard', a flying version of his original skateboard which plays an important part in the plot of the third *Back to the Future* film.

Before Marty meets up with Doc, he purchases an almanac containing results of sports fixtures from 1950 to 2000. Marty realises that he can use this to make money, as he can go back in time and place bets while knowing the result. Doc warns him about the dangers of interfering with history and plans to destroy the almanac but, before he can do this, the police arrive. They have found Jennifer incapacitated and, scanning her identity, take her 'home' – that is, the home of her future self. The police pursue the time travellers and, in the confusion, Biff gets hold of the almanac. He has overheard the conversation between Doc and Marty and realises that he can use the sports publication to make a fortune.

Later, Jennifer wakes up in her 2015 home and hides from the McFly family. She listens to her future self talking about her life and does not like what she hears. She sees Marty being chastised by his co-worker, Douglas J. Needles, which results in Marty being sacked. Upset, she tries to leave the house, but encounters her 2015 self and faints.

As the Doc and Marty attend to her, Biff steals the DeLorean and returns to 1955 where he gives the almanac to his younger self, pointing out that he can use the book to make a lot of money through betting on sports fixtures. After doing this, Biff returns to 2015 and leaves the DeLorean. Later, the Doc, Marty and Jennifer go back to 1985 in the time machine, unaware of what Biff has done.

The dystopian 1985 they return to is now totally different as a result of Biff's actions. A new timeline has been created. Biff is now very wealthy and lives in a huge skyscraper. Marty's father George is dead, as he was killed before 1985, and Biff has forced Lorraine to marry him. From studying a contemporary newspaper, Marty learns that Doc Brown has been committed to a lunatic asylum. An M-113 armoured personnel carrier patrols the streets of Hill Valley, which is strewn with abandoned cars. One of the wrecked cars is another Citroen DS.

Eventually Doc and Marty work out what has happened. They confront Biff, who admits that he was given the almanac on 12th November 1955. The only way that the Doc and Marty can put things right is by going back to 1955 to retrieve the crucial almanac, and then destroy it. The two adventurers return to 1955 in the DeLorean, leaving Jennifer on her own front porch.

Marty stalks the 1955 version of Biff in what is perhaps the most interesting part of the film, as there are two Martys in some scenes – the original 1955 version playing the guitar that we saw in the first film, and the second incarnation who has travelled from 1985 to put things right. The dance and guitar scenes look exactly as they did in the first film, but were actually meticulous recreations of what was previously filmed five years before.

Marty sees the 1955 Biff receive the almanac from his older self and then follows him in the hope that he can acquire it. He returns to the dance and sees his other self doing his 'Johnny Be Good' routine on the guitar. After a few failed attempts to get hold of the almanac, he finally retrieves the publication and burns it. This immediately changes the timeline and the Doc appears, hovering overhead in the DeLorean. Suddenly, the time machine is struck by lightning and the car vanishes. A Western Union courier then arrives on the scene and gives Marty a letter from the Doc in which he explains that he was transported back to 1885 and is fine. Marty then travels back to the town and meets the 1955 version of Doc, who has just helped the original Marty return to 1985. Doc is so surprised at Marty's sudden (re-)appearance that he faints.

The film ends with a mini-trailer for the third and final *Back to the Future* film, *Part III*, which is set in the Wild West in 1885.

Back to The Future: Part II was released in the USA on 22nd November 1989 (which was the day before the Thanksgiving weekend). It was very successful, making $331 million worldwide against a budget of $40 million, and was the third most successful film of 1989 – beaten only by *Indiana Jones and the Last Crusade* and *Batman*. The film received generally favourable reviews from critics, although most agreed it was not as good as the first film since the novelty of the concept was lost.

Just six months after *Part II* premiered, the third and final instalment of the *Back to the Future* trilogy was released. This third segment of the story was shot back-to-back with *Part II*. While *Part II* was lensed on the Universal back lot in Los Angeles, most of *Part III* was shot at a specially-built Western town set at Red Hills Ranch, near Sonora, California. Some shooting was also carried out in Jamestown, California and in Monument Valley, which has featured in many Westerns. Train sequences were shot at the Railtown 1897 Historic Park.

Part III featured a love story, in this case a romance between Doc Brown and Clara Clayton (Mary Steenburgen). As you will recall from reading the chapter on *The Time Machine*, this actress also starred in another 'romantic' time travel film, *Time After Time*, in which H.G. Wells pursues Jack the Ripper to 1979 San Francisco.

The film opens at the point where *Part II* ended. On 12th November 1955, Marty McFly has just seen Doc Brown apparently killed by a lightning bolt. After reading the letter from the Doc which he received from a courier, Marty learns that Doc is trapped in 1885. In his message, the Doc makes it clear that he is in good health and unwilling to return to 1985. He is keen, though, that Marty should return to his original time as soon as possible. Using the information contained in the letter, the 1955 version of Doc and Marty repair the De-Lorean so that the teenager can go back to his own time period.

However, before returning to 1985 Marty discovers a tombstone in Hill Valley with the Doc's name on it, dated six days after the letter. He learns that the Doc was killed by Biff Tannen's great-grandfather, Buford. He takes a photograph of the tombstone and, rather than heading back to 1985, instead travels to 1885 in order to warn the Doc.

Marty arrives in the desert on 2nd September 1885 and finds himself in the middle of a US Army Cavalry pursuit of some Native Americans. These scenes were shot in Monu-ment Valley. The DeLorean is damaged in the ensuing chase and its fuel line is ripped open, causing it to lose petrol. Marty hides the vehicle in a small cave and walks to Hill Valley town, where he meets his Irish-born great-grandparents: Sea-mus and Maggie McFly. Marty decides to adopt the alias of 'Clint Eastwood', who of course did not exist in 1885. He also encounters Buford and his gang, who try to hang him. Buford attempts to put a noose round McFly, but the teenager is res-cued by the Doc. Later, the Doc and Marty retrieve the De-Lorean and put it in a barn which is serving as the inventor's workshop.

After hearing about Marty's discovery of his forthcoming death, the Doc agrees to return to 1985. But there is a prob-lem, as the DeLorean's fuel tank is dry and petrol is not avail-able in 1885.Without fuel, the DeLorean will be unable to reach the critical speed of 88mph required for a time jump.

The Doc experiments with alcohol as a possible fuel, but it doesn't work.

Then the Doc has an idea. After speaking to the driver of a steam locomotive, he realises that it might be possible to accelerate the DeLorean up to 88mph by pushing it with the steam engine. The Doc's plan involves a rail spur which leads to a bridge over a ravine, which is planned but not yet built. Marty points out that the DeLorean will simply crash over the edge of the ravine, but the Doc is sure they will be safe because the bridge exists in 1985 and the time jump will occur just before the engine reaches the ravine. So the plan should work, if there are no snags.

As they are mulling over the plan, they spot a horse-drawn wagon which is out of control as the horses have panicked and are pulling it at full speed towards the ravine. Doc manages to stop the wagon and save the passenger, Clara Clayton, and the two fall in love. There is a problem, though, as the Doc has interfered with time by altering history. The

The DMC DeLorean (Image Credit: dtavres at Pixabay)

ravine was originally supposed to be named after Clara, who was meant to fall over the edge.

The couple dance at a town festival. The band in these scenes was the popular eighties group ZZ Top. Later, Buford attempts to kill the Doc but Marty stops this happening. Buford is furious and challenges Marty to a duel in two days' time. A furious Marty accepts, but then the Doc notices that his own name has vanished from the photograph of the tombstone – although the date is unchanged. Doc wonders if it is now Marty who is going to be killed.

The Doc and Marty continue with their plan to return to 1985, and the Doc insists that once the DeLorean has returned to its original time zone it must be destroyed as their meddling in time has caused so many problems. The Doc goes to Clara to try and explain that he has to return to 1985, but he is unable to persuade her that he is telling the truth when he says he is a time traveller from the future. She thinks what he is saying is a nonsensical excuse and tells him their relationship is over.

The Doc is devastated by this revelation and goes to the saloon bar to get drunk. But the Doc is incredibly sensitive to alcohol and even a single drink – in this case one shot of whisky – renders him unconscious. The Doc is now lying flat out on the floor, apparently comatose, and Marty realises he must get him awake and sober if they are to escape to 1985 as the clock is ticking.

The bartender makes up a special 'wake-up juice' using various ingredients and gives some to the Doc, who regains consciousness. There is another problem though, as Buford and his gang have arrived and challenge Marty to a duel. Buford shoots Marty and apparently kills him, but the teenager is really still alive as he is wearing a metal plate under his clothing. (This is really a re-use of the plot point about Doc Brown's 'bulletproof vest', which was used in the first film and which – as previously explained – is a familiar Hollywood cliché.)

After fooling Buford, Marty rips off his metal plate and knocks Buford into a wagon full of horse manure. This another running gag in the *Back to the Future* films, as all feature a scene in which Biff/Buford gets buried in dung. Soon after this, Buford is arrested by the town marshal and charged over a robbery.

In the meantime, Clara is on a train leaving town when she overhears another passenger having a conversation about how he had met a man in the bar who was devastated at the break-up of his relationship. She enquires about what this person looked like and realises it can only be Doc. In a flash the truth dawns on her – the Doc really does love her and was trying to tell her the truth. She applies the train's emergency brake, leaves the carriage, and returns to the Doc's workshop where she finds a model of the DeLorean and the railway track. Putting two and two together, she rides out to the railway and chases after the locomotive which has been stolen by the Doc and Marty and is heading out along the spur, pushing the DeLorean.

Clara arrives on the scene and climbs onto the engine's tender, which is full of chopped logs. She begs the Doc to take her with him, but to do this she will have to climb over the logs and then make her way to the front of the engine where she can board the DeLorean. Unfortunately she nearly falls off, but Marty hands the Doc his hoverboard and the inventor uses it to rescue Clara. In the nick of time, the DeLorean reaches 88mph and jumps to 1985, but the railway locomotive plunges over the ravine and is destroyed. The Doc and Clara are saved by the hoverboard, but they have been left behind in 1885.

The DeLorean arrives on the railway track on 27th October 1985 with Marty on board. But it is now powerless as it has an empty fuel tank, and – just after Marty has jumped out – it is destroyed completely by a passing freight train. Marty soon finds that everything in 1985 has now returned to the way it was originally. Jennifer is sleeping on the front porch. And he avoids his future car accident by refusing to get involved in a road race with Douglas J. Needles.

Back to the Future: Part III was released on 25 May 1990 and was a great success, making $244.5 million at the box office set against a production cost of $40 million. It also received very positive reviews, with most critics agreeing that it was better than the second film and wrapped things up neatly.

The series of three *Back to the Future* films had a great influence on popular culture. They lead to various spin-offs including an animated TV series in 1991-92, comic books, novelisations, a proposed musical in 2015 and a theme park ride at the Universal Studios backlot.

So far no remake of the original film or its sequels has been suggested but – with Hollywood's current penchant for remakes, reboots, sequels and prequels – anything that made money the first time round may be considered for a reimagining. So who knows?

One positive legacy of the film, though, was that it restored the reputation of the DeLorean DMC-12 car which might otherwise have been regarded as a failure since its original production run was only from 1981 to 1983.

Three DeLoreans were used in the original film. The A car was highly detailed and used for close ups. The B car was employed for stunt work, and the C car was a version which could be split in half for process shots. Of these three vehicles, only the A car survived the shooting of the trilogy. It spent many years sitting out in the open on the back lot at Universal Studios where its condition gradually deteriorated. Between 2012 and 2013 it underwent a thorough restoration by a team of technicians lead by Joe Walser, and is now kept in a glass case in pristine condition.

Production of new DMC-12 cars has also resumed in Humble, Texas, using old stock and reproduction parts. On 27th January 2016 DMC (Texas) announced that it planned to build 325 replica DMC-12 cars, which would sell for about $100,000 each.

8
Time Marches On
The 1990s

THE 1990s saw a boom in time travel movies. It was also an era which saw a great change in the way visual effects were created. At the start of the nineties, most movies used miniature and optical effects techniques which had not changed much since the 1930s. By the end of the decade, Computer Generated Imagery (CGI) methods had become the norm, with the breakthrough movie being *Terminator 2: Judgment Day (1991)* and its depiction of the T-1000 'liquid metal' Terminator.

Frankenstein Unbound (1990) was a science fiction horror movie based on the novel of the same name by prolific British SF writer Brian Aldiss. The so-called 'King of the B movies', Roger Corman, directed the film and was also co-producer along with Jay Cassidy, Kobi Jeager, Laura J. Medina and Thom Mount. The script was written by Corman and F.X. Feeney.

The film opens in 2031. Dr Joe Buchanan (John Hurt) has developed a prototype energy beam weapon. Unfortunately it is causing rifts in space and time, and Dr Buchanan and his car are transported to Switzerland in 1817 where some of the events of Mary Shelley's *Frankenstein* novel are happening for real. He meets Victor Frankenstein (Raul Julia), who reveals that his young brother has been killed. The boy's nanny is the chief suspect, but a monster has been spotted in the woods and Joe sees Mary Shelley (Bridget Fonda) taking notes at her trial.

The nanny is found guilty of murder, but Joe knows the monster must have done it. Victor Frankenstein refuses to listen to his pleas, while Mary does not want to become involved. Later, Joe drives over to Victor's workshop and finds the doctor talking to the monster (Nick Brimble).

The monster wanted Frankenstein to create a mate for him. When he refused, he killed the doctor's fiancée Elizabeth (Catherine Rabett). Now the doctor wants Joe to use his knowledge of electricity to revive Elizabeth. Buchanan agrees and tells the monster to run an electric cable to the weather vane on the roof, but he re-routes some of the wiring to the energy weapon fitted in his car.

When the lightning strikes, Elizabeth is resurrected. But the energy weapon becomes fully charged and Buchanan destroys the castle. Unfortunately, another space time rift is created and the four characters arrive on a snowy mountain top. Frankenstein kills the woman, and he in turn is murdered by the monster. Buchanan follows the creature in the hope he can destroy it.

The creature is eventually trapped in a cave filled with computers, and Buchanan triggers an alarm which causes the monster to be burned to death by lasers. As Buchanan trudges through the snow to a nearby city there is a voice-over from the monster which states that he cannot now be killed as he is 'unbound'.

The film was a financial flop, making just $335,000 set against a budget of $11.5 million. It was of great interest to film historians though, as it combines the key elements of Mary Shelley's classic novel with ideas found in other time travel films such as *Back to the Future* (1985) and *The Phila-delphia Experiment* (1984).

Mr Destiny (1990) is a fantasy-comedy film which starred James Belushi. It was directed, produced and written by James Orr, with Jim Cruickshank as co-producer and co-writer. The story begins as Larry Burrows (James Belushi) celebrates his 35th birthday. Larry believes that all his problems stem from a single event exactly twenty years earlier when he struck out during a high school baseball championship game. He now wishes he had reacted differently.

His wish is granted when a guardian angel figure called Mike (Michael Caine) appears. Mike has the ability to mani-fest himself in various guises, including a taxi driver and a bar-tender. Mike (appearing as a barman) gives Larry a home-made drink called 'spilt milk' which makes his wishes come true. He has actually transferred Larry to an alternative reali-ty in which he has won an all-important high school baseball game. He is now very wealthy and married to Cindy Jo Bumpers (Rene Russo). But he realises that his new life has many disadvantages, and he misses his wife Ellen (Linda Ham-ilton).

Everything is different in this new reality. Ellen is married to another man. Jewell (Courteney Cox), who is a forklift operator in the other world, is now Larry's mistress and secre-tary. Ellen, a shop steward, is threatening to bring all the staff in Larry's company out on strike. Larry offers to meet all her demands providing that she has dinner with him. Reluctantly she agrees, and learns that they were married in a parallel existence.

But his department head, Niles (Hart Bochner), is angry at what has happened and takes his revenge by telling both Cindy Jo and Jewel about Larry's dinner date with Ellen. He then decides to murder Larry. Niles kills company owner Leo Hansen (Bill McCutcheon) by mistake and tries to pin the crime on Larry, who is chased by the police and runs into 'The Universal Joint' bar. He can't find Mike, so he makes some of the 'spilt milk' himself. After drinking it, Larry arrives back in his own world. He goes over to the company headquarters and punches Niles, exposing his scheme before he can sign the deal. The company president, Jackie Earle Bumpers (Jay O. Sanders), offers Niles' job to Larry and he accepts. The film ends with a scene set twenty years earlier. As a young Larry is about to leave the stadium, he is approached by Mike who reassures him that everything will be all right.

Bill and Ted's Bogus Journey (1991) was a sequel to the earlier *Bill and Ted's Excellent Adventure* (1989). It starred Keanu Reeves, Alex Winter and George Carlin, who reprised their roles from the first film. Although it received mixed reviews, the movie now has a cult following largely because it contained a spoof of Ingmar Bergman's classic film *The Seventh Seal* (1957) – particularly the depiction of 'Death' as a hooded figure (a.k.a. 'The Grim Reaper').

The plot of the film continues directly from the previous movie. The music of Bill and Ted's band *The Wyld Stallyns* has created an ideal world and youngsters emulate the duo's speech, mannerisms and dress. Bill and Ted's enemy, Chuck De Nomolos (Joss Ackland), steals a time travelling phone booth and sends two evil robot duplicates of Bill and Ted back to 1991 to prevent the duo from winning the San Dimas Battle of the Bands.

The *Wyld Stallyns* are preparing for the Battle of the Bands, but Ted's father is threatening him with military school if the two fail the contest. At this point, the two evil robot duplicates arrive, take the place of the two teenagers and kill them by throwing them over a cliff at the famous Vasquez Rocks, which has featured in many movies and TV series, includ-

Bill and Ted's Bogus Journey (1991): Nelson Entertainment/ Interscope Communications/ Orion Pictures

ing several episodes of *Star Trek* – notably *Arena*, which has the distinction of being the first *Star Trek* episode to be shown in colour on British television in November 1969.

Bill and Ted have died, but their spiritual selves meet Death (William Sadler) who engages in a game for their souls. Bill and Ted escape and try to warn their families about what has happened, but cannot do so in their current spiritual form. They arrive in Hell, and are tormented by the Devil. The only way to escape is to go along with Death's plan. The entity takes them to his domain and offers them several games to play. Bill and Ted choose modern games like 'Battleships' and 'Twister' and easily beat Death. He is forced to admit defeat and becomes their servant. Bill and Ted realise their only chance of survival is to build 'good' robots to fight the evil ones. Death takes them to Heaven, where they meet an extra-terrestial being called Station who agrees to help Bill and Ted.

Death returns them to the real world, where they participate in the Battle of the Bands. As the evil robots take to the stage, Station's 'good' robots defeat the evil ones. The duo are reunited with their fiancées Elizabeth (Annette Azcuy) and Joanna (Sarah Trigger), who they refer to as their 'Princesses'. But they find they are still bad musicians, so they go back in time and have sixteen months of guitar training. They then return to the present and perform a stunning rock ballad accompanied by Death, Station and the good robots. The concert is broadcast across the world, creating harmony across the globe, and the film ends with the *Wyld Stallions* planning to take their act to Mars. The film was well-received, and a third movie has been under development since 2010. On 8th May 2018 it was revealed that the title would be *Bill & Ted: Face the Music*, though no release date has yet been announced.

Godzilla versus King Ghidorah (1991) was a Japanese science fiction film featuring the well-known monster Godzilla, which included a time travel plot. It was made by Toho Studios, who were well-known for creating excellent miniature sequences.

The story begins in 1992. A science fiction writer, Kenichiro Terasawa (Kosuke Toyohara), is writing a book about Godzilla and learns that a group of Japanese soldiers were stationed in Lagos Island during the Gilbert and Marshal Islands campaign in WW2. The Japanese servicemen were saved from death at the hands of American forces in February 1944 when a mysterious dinosaur appeared. He believed that the creature mutated into Godzilla in 1954 as a result of an American H-bomb test on the island.

The story becomes even stranger. A UFO lands on Mount Fuji, and its inhabitants are revealed to be humans from the year 2204. Godzilla has completely destroyed Japan, so these future humans – known as the 'Futurians' – plan to travel back to 1944 and remove the creature from Lagos Island, thus preventing this future catastrophe.

The Americans attack Lagos Island in 1944, but the Futurians teleport the dinosaur to a location in the Bering Strait, thus preventing it from being exposed to radiation in 1954. But they also leave three small creatures called Dorats on the island, which then become affected by the H- bomb radiation in 1954 and become a single three-headed creature called King Ghidorah which attacks Japan.

At this point the story becomes much more complicated. The Futurians plan to travel back in time to change Japan's future by creating King Ghidorah and using it to destroy Japan. They also intend to kill Godzilla, which is a threat to their plans. But the dinosaur has grown in size after absorbing radiation from a Russian nuclear submarine that sank in the Bering Strait in the 1970s.

Godzilla travels to Japan and battles with King Ghidorah. The dinosaur kills the creature by blasting off its middle head. It then destroys the UFO. The Futurians retaliate by travelling to the future and bringing back Mecha-King Ghidorah, a cybernetic version of the three-headed monster. Godzilla eventually triumphs over Ghidorah, but both creatures are dumped at the bottom of the ocean. Ghidorah is dead, but Godzilla survives to fight another day.

Army of Darkness (1992) is an American horror comedy film directed and co-written by Sam Raimi. It was a sequel to the two previous films *Evil Dead* (1981) and *Evil Dead II*

(1987), and featured the recurring character of Ash Williams (Bruce Campbell).

After travelling back to the Middle Ages, Ash is captured by Lord Arthur's men. He is thrown into a dungeon with Duke Henry (Richard Grove), and his gun and chainsaw are confiscated. Ash kills a Deadite and recovers his weapons. He learns that the only way he can return to his original time is by using the magic Necronomicon Ex-Mortis book. He clashes with his own clone and is forced to kill it.

Eventually he finds the all-important book. In order to remove it safely he has to mumble the words 'Klaatu Barada Nikto'. (Fans of science fiction films will recognize this as a line from 1951 film *The Day the Earth Stood Still*. It is a command given to Klaatu, the robot in that film.) Unfortunately Ash cannot remember the exact words and mumbles the line. He grabs the book and escapes just as his evil copy and the dead come to life to form the Army of Darkness.

Ash organises the local population into a force to fight the Army of Darkness. He succeeds, and a Wise Man gives him a potion which will enable him to return to the present. To make the time jump, he has to take the potion and repeat the magic phrase.

Ash returns to an S-Mart Department Store in the present, but is then confronted by a Deadite who has followed him through time. The monster kills a customer before being shot by Ash, who then lives happily ever after with a woman he has met in the store.

Freejack (1992) was directed by Geoff Murphy and produced by Ronald Shusett and Stuart Oken. The screenplay was by Steven Pressfield and Ronald Shusett, based on Robert Sheckley's 1959 book *Immortality Inc.* This book was first dramatized as a single one-hour episode of the BBC2 anthology series *Out of the Unknown* in 1969. The cast included Mick Jagger, who is best-known as the lead singer of the The Rolling Stones but has also acted in a few films. His then-wife Jerry Hall has a brief cameo in the film as a TV reporter.

The plot of the film is ingenious. In 2009, wealthy people can achieve immortality by using 'Bonejackers', specialised mercenaries who steal people from the past just prior to the moment of death by using time travel technology. Their bodies are then used to enable rich people to escape death by using a mind transfer process. The resulting beings are known as 'Freejacks'.

Alex Furlong (Emilio Estevez) is a Formula One driver in 1991 who is snatched by mercenaries led by Victor Vacendak (Mick Jagger) just as he is about to die in a fiery crash on the racetrack. He is taken to New York in 2009, but manages to escape. His former fiancée, Julie (Rene Russo), is still alive and working for the McCandless Corporation, which also employs Vacendak.

Alex manages to rekindle his relationship with Julie, but finds himself on the run from various people including Vacendak and his private army, Ian McCandless (Anthony Hopkins) and his guards plus Mark Michelette (Jonathan Banks).

Alex and Julie flee and end up on the 100th floor of the corporate building, where McCandless's mind is in storage. The old man wants to make use of Furlong's much younger body to achieve immortality. He is also motivated by the fact that he is in love with Julie and believes he can win her over if he inhabits Furlong's body. Vacendak arrives as the mind transfer process is happening and Julie shoots at the machine, disrupting the procedure. It is now unclear if McCandless or

Furlong is inhabiting Alex's body. Michelette tries to kill Alex but is shot by Vacendak's men.

Later, Julie and Alex get into one of McCandless's cars and he drives off. They are stopped by Vacendak, who realises that something is wrong as McCandless could not drive. The mind transfer had not been completed. However, Vacendak lets them go and they drive off.

What makes *Freejack* such an enjoyable film is that it has an interesting plot with a love story at its core, but also has frequent well-staged action sequences worthy of a Bond movie. There are gunfights and car chases galore, and many incredible stunts. Particularly impressive are the many futuristic vehicles used in the movie, such as the various armoured cars used by Vacendak's gang of mercenaries which were all created by modifying existing machines such as Cadillac-Gage Commando V100 scout cars. A much-altered British Alvis FV603 Saracen personnel carrier also appears in the film.

One criticism I have of the film, though, is that the future world seems far too technically advanced for 2009. In Sheckley's original novel, the present day was 1959 and the future world was 2110. In the film, the time difference is just eighteen years. This was presumably done for dramatic reasons so that Julie would still be alive and relatively young in the future world. Also, despite extensive dialogue coaching, Mick Jagger's American accent is unconvincing and one wonders why the producers couldn't have solved the problem by making his character English – particularly as villains in Hollywood movies are often played by English actors (e.g. Alan Rickman's Hans Gruber in 1988's *Die Hard*).

Timescape (1992), also known as *Grand Tour: Disaster in Time,* was directed by David Twohy and produced by John

A. Connor. The screenplay was by David Twohy, based on the novel by Henry Kuttner and C.L. Moore.

The film opens as Ben Wilson (Jeff Daniels) – who has recently lost his wife – is renovating an old guest house in his hometown, helped by his daughter Hillary (Ariana Richards). A group of tourists arrive in a bus and stay at the guest house. Soon after this, they are joined by another person named Quish (David Wells) whose clothes are covered with fine ash.

The next day, Quish has a minor accident and Ben becomes suspicious when he discovers that his passport is stamped with various locations decades apart. An X-ray reveals he has a device embedded in his skull. Wilson also notes that the date stamps correspond to various natural disasters such as the 1906 San Francisco earthquake. The ash is presumably related to the 1980 Mount Helena earthquake.

Meanwhile, Ben's father-in-law Judge Caldwell (George Murdock) arranges for Hillary to be taken away, as he considers him to be an unfit father. Ben is forced to stay at a hotel. One of the vacationers, Reeve (Emilia Crow), confirms that they are 'time tourists' who visit the sites of past disasters. She gives him a drug which knocks him out.

Later, Ben is revived by Oscar (Jim Haynie). The town is struck by a meteorite (explaining why the 'time tourists' are interested in it). The hotel is destroyed, but Hillary survives and her school is used as a disaster relief centre. Unfortunately there is a subsequent gas explosion which kills her.

Ben comes round and finds he is a prisoner of the tourists. An official from the future called the Undersecretary (Robert Colbert) has arrived to carry out an investigation. Reeve (Emilia Crowe) gives Quish's passport to Ben. He examines it and finds it contains a time travel device.

199

Ben returns to the previous evening and, with the help of his previous self, manages to prevent the disaster and saves countless lives, including Hillary's. In the final scene, Ben and Hillary are working in the guest house. Ben is reading old love letters from his wife. Suddenly, Ben vanishes and Hillary hears the sound of her mother playing the piano.

Split Infinity (1992) is a little-known film directed by Stan Ferguson. The screenplay was written by Forrest S. Baker III, Sharon Baker and Leo D.Paur, and tells the story of a teenage girl who learns the importance of family unity after falling out of a hayloft and travelling back to the 1930s.

At the start of the film, Amelia Jean Knowlton (Melora Slover), known as A.J. and just fourteen years old, is fixated on making money. She generates her cash by selling confectionery and providing tutoring services. But she is also selfish and judges people by appearances, particularly how they dress.

Her grandfather, Frank (H.E.D. Redford), gives her a locket that had belonged to his younger sister – also called Amelia Jean – who had died aged nineteen. That night, A.J. goes out to the barn and falls through some rotten floorboards. When she recovers consciousness she discovers she has travelled back to 1929 and is now Frank's younger sister (who, as mentioned, is also called Amelia Jean). After spending a day at school, she goes back to the farm and learns that Frank is going to invest some money in the stock market. A.J. knows that the stock market crash will happen in just a few weeks' time, and believes she has been sent back in time to stop Frank from losing his savings.

A.J. has difficulty adjusting to 1929 and wears inappropriate clothes. She also uses her knowledge of the future to build a mini-theme park in the barn called 'Future World' which has various carnival-style rides. Frank plans to sell the farm and invest the money in the stock market. A.J. is unable to stop him, and he loses all the cash. However, he makes some money from 'Future World' which enables him and his wife to save the farm. That night, A.J. returns to the barn and goes on a ride called 'Jaws of Death'. She is knocked out, and wakes up in hospital in 1992. She soon learns that her grandfather took the advice he gave her in 1929 and invested his money in blue chip stocks, including IBM. He uses the money to build a children's hospital, intending that A.J. will eventually run it. They have both learned lessons in life.

Teenage Mutant Ninja Turtles III (1993) was – as the name suggests – a sequel to *Teenage Mutant Ninja Turtles II*, and was written and directed by Stuart Gillard and produced by David Chan, Kim Dawson and Thomas K. Gray. All the Ninja Turtle movies used turtle-like creatures as the heroes, and were inexplicably popular. This particular segment was set in both 1593 and 1993, and incorporated a time-travel element. It was panned by critics, though it was moderately successful, making $42.2 million set against a budget of $21 million.

Les Visiteurs (1993), which translates as 'The Visitors', is a French fantasy comedy film directed by Jean-Marie Poire and produced by Alain Terzian. It was written by Poire and Christian Clavier. The plot concerns a 12th century knight and his servant who travel to 1992. It is therefore a bit like an inverted version of the famous time travel film *A Connecticut Yankee at the Court of King Arthur*, which has been filmed three times.

The film begins in 1123. Count Godefroy Amaury de Malfete (Jean Reno) saves the life of King Louis VI by killing an English swordsman. He is rewarded for this bravery by the

King, who offers him the hand of the beautiful Frenegonde de Poille (Valerie Lemercier). But things go wrong – Godefroy is poisoned by a witch, becomes delirious, and kills his future father-in-law – the Duke of Poille – with a crossbow bolt. Frenegonde then refuses to marry him, so Godefroy attempts to put things right by asking a wizard named Eusebius (Pierre Vial) to send him back in time to a moment before he shot the Duke. But Godefroy and his servant Jacquouille (Christian Claver) are instead transported to 1992.

Godefroy is like a fish out of water, and there are many comic moments when he misunderstands modern technology. For example, he washes his hands in a W.C. After a series of adventures, Godefroy elects to return to 1123. He is helped by Monsieur Ferdinand, a descendant of Eusebius, who gives him some more of the magic potion. Jacquouille decides to stay in 1992 by swapping places with his descendant, Jacquard. Godefroy returns to 1123, just in time to stop himself killing Frenegonde's father, and the deflected crossbow bolt kills the witch instead. Godefroy rides off on horseback with Frenegonde.

Groundhog Day (1993) is one of the most popular 'time loop' movies, and tells the story of a TV weatherman who relives the same day over and over again. Although it was only moderately successful when first released, it had a great impact on popular culture as it led to the words 'Groundhog Day' being used to describe a recurring situation. (I myself often describe my role as my wife's carer as being 'like Groundhog Day', since every day is exactly the same.)

The film starred Bill Murray as weatherman Phil Connors. Murray had previously become well-known for his appearances on the American satirical TV series *Saturday Night Live* (1975-present) and the film *Ghostbusters* (1984).

Groundhog Day was directed by Harold Ramis, who also served as co-producer (with Trevor Albert) and wrote the script with Danny Rubin, who had come up with the original story.

The film begins with Phil Connors (Bill Murray), a television weather presenter, reassuring viewers that a blizzard will miss western Pennsylvania. He travels to the town of Punxsutawney in that state with his news producer Rita Hanson (Andie McDowell) and his cameraman Larry (Chris Elliott) to cover the annual (February 2nd) 'Groundhog Day' event. The centrepiece of the event is a groundhog (a small furry rodent, also known as a woodchuck) which is called Punxsutawney Phil.

The next day Phil wakes up in a guest house in Punxsutawney to the sound of Cher's 'I Got You Babe' playing on the clock radio. He covers the town's festivities in a lethargic way. Although he wants to return to Pittsburgh, he is forced to stay overnight because of a sudden snowfall.

The next morning he awakens once more to the sound of the same song playing on the clock radio. Eventually he realises that he is stuck in a time loop, in which the same day is repeated over and over again. Initially he responds to this development by indulging in reckless behaviour such as binge-drinking, eating huge quantities of unhealthy food and reckless driving. He even commits suicide several times, but always wakes up to find himself back at the start of the same day.

After a few repeating days have elapsed, he turns this odd situation to his advantage and learns various new skills such as piano playing, ice sculpting and speaking French. He tells Rita what has happened. Initially she does not believe him, but he proves his case by accurately predicting what is about to happen a moment before it does. He also uses the repeating nature of the time loop to woo Rita successfully, as he is able to learn from his mistakes.

Phil becomes a changed man and now reports on the Groundhog Day events with great enthusiasm, something which impresses Rita. The two eventually fall in love and end up in bed together... but when he wakes up, he finds Rita is still in bed with him. It is February 3rd, and the snow is gone. He has escaped the time loop and vows to live with Rita.

Time Chasers (1994) – also known as *Tangents* – starred Matthew Bruch, George Woodard and Bonnie Pritchard, and was directed by David Giancola. It tells the story of an inventor who travels through time to stop an evil corporation from changing history for profit. It was made on a low budget of just $150,000.

Physics teacher Nick Miller (Matthew Bruch), who also holds a Private Pilot's Licence, has created a workable method of time travel which involves a Commodore 64 (a home computer popular in the 1980s) and his light aircraft. This attracts the interest of both an executive of Gen Corp and a reporter from a local paper, Lisa Hansen (Bonnie Pritchard), who is an old flame. After a quick trip to 2041 to demonstrate that his method works, the CEO of Gen Corps – J.K. Robertson (George Woodard) – offers Nick a licencing deal.

Nick subsequently makes another trip to 2041 and discovers than Gen Corps has now created a dystopian future. He tells J.K. Robertson but he dismisses his claims, claiming that there will be time to fix this before it happens. Things go from bad to worse as Robertson eventually concludes that Nick's opinions and actions constitute treason.

Nick and Lisa escape from the clutches of Gen Corps and attempt to repair the damage to their timeline. Robertson is incensed at their actions and, with the assistance of Matt (Peter Harrington), he shoots down Nick's plane. Lisa is killed, but Nick escapes by jumping out and finds himself in 1777. This alters his timeline and means that the time machine is never created. At the end of the film Nick deletes all the 5.25" floppy discs containing details of his time travel theory, meaning that the time journeys never happen. He then meets Lisa once more in the supermarket, and it is implied that they have a future together.

A.P.E.X. (1994) is a cult SF movie which was directed by Philip J. Roth. It was written by Roth and Ron Schmidt and produced by Jeffery Beach, Gary Jude, Tallat Captan and Gary Lo Conti.

The plot is fairly simple. In 2073 scientist Nicholas Sinclair (Richard Keats) is working on a time travel project. Back in 1973, a deadly virus attacks the project, activating countermeasures. Deadly robots are sent back in time to kill the people carrying the virus. They fail in their mission, and the Earth of 2073 is ravaged by both the virus and the robots. Sinclair goes back to the ruined project lab in an attempt to prevent the original cause of the accident.

Although the film was not a great commercial success, it was nominated for Best Film in the International Fantasy Film Award at the 1994 Fantasporto International Film Festival in Porto, Portugal.

Star Trek: Generations (1994), directed by David Carson, was the seventh film in the series of *Star Trek* movies which were based on the original TV series (1966-68). It was the first movie to introduce the cast of the highly successful TV series *Star Trek: The Next Generation* (1987-94), plus three members of the original *Star Trek* cast. Time travel featured as a plot device on a number of occasions in both the original series and its various spin-offs and films. In *Generations* it was used as a plot device to enable both Captain James T. Kirk and Captain Jean-Luc Picard to share scenes together.

The film opens in 2293. Retired Captain James T. Kirk (William Shatner), Pavel Chekhov (Walter Koenig) and Montgomery 'Scotty' Scott (James Doonan) are on board the USS *Enterprise-B*, which is under the command of the inexperienced Captain John Harriman (Alan Ruck). *Enterprise* is forced to rescue two El-Aurian ships from a strange energy ribbon, but is severely damaged and Kirk is presumed dead.

78 years later in 2371, the crew of the USS *Enterprise-D* are celebrating the promotion of Worf (Michael Dornan) to Lieutenant-Commander. But mischief is afoot. An El-Aurian, Dr Tolian Soran (Malcolm McDowell) fires a probe at the star Amargosa, causing it to implode. Soran escapes in a stolen Klingon Bird of Prey. Guinan (Whoopi Goldberg) tells Captain Picard (Patrick Stewart) that Soran intends to enter the energy ribbon in order to travel to the 'Nexus', a strange realm where anything you wish can come true. But Soran's plan will involve altering the path of the ribbon, resulting in the destruction of the populated planet Veridian IV. The *Enterprise* ends up battling with the Klingon Bird of Prey, and first officer Commander Riker (Jonathan Frakes) is forced to crash-land it on Veridian III.

Soran launches his missile, and Picard finds himself in the Nexus where he meets Kirk – who is happily chopping wood by a log cabin. He persuades Kirk that the experience is not real, and they travel back in time to Veridian III to confront Soran just before he launches the rocket. Picard and Kirk battle Soran. Eventually they triumph, as the missile explodes and kills Soran. But this victory has a price, as Kirk dies heroically. The *Enterprise* has also been destroyed, but Picard realises that later ships will bear its name.

Timecop (1994) was directed by Peter Hyams from a screenplay by Mark Verheiden, and was produced by Moshe Diamant, Sam Raimi and Robert Tapert.

The film opens in 1994. Time travel has just been developed, and is already being used for criminal purposes. A Time Enforcement Commission (TEC) has been established, overseen by Senator Aaron McComb (Ron Silver). Police officer Max Walker (Jean-Claude Van Damme) is at home with his wife Melissa (Mia Sara) when they are attacked by a gang. The house explodes and Melissa is killed.

Ten years later, in 2004, Walker has joined the TEC. He is assigned a partner named Sarah Fielding (Gloria Reuben), and they investigate Senator McComb. On one journey to 1994 they witness the 2004 version of McComb arriving and killing Jack Walker (Kevin McNulty). McComb tells his 1994 self that they must not touch each other. But Fielding works for McComb and, after a battle, Walker escapes to 2004.

When Walker arrives in 2004 he finds that McComb is now sole

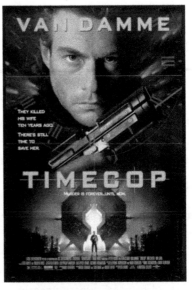

Timecop (1994): Largo Entertainment/JVC Entertainment/ Signature/Renaissance/Dark Horse/Largo International N.V./Universal Pictures

owner of a computer company and is running for President. The cop returns to 1994 and realises that he can save Melissa.

That night both his 1994 and 2004 selves are in the house when the gang attack. They are led by McComb, who is also present in both his 1994 and 2004 incarnations. McComb threatens to explode a bomb, but Walker defeats the evil senator by pushing his older and younger incarnations together. They turn into a gooey mess which then disappears. Walker escapes from the house before the bomb explodes after rescuing an unconscious Melissa.

When Walker returns to 2004 he finds his timeline has changed. McComb no longer exists, Melissa is alive and well, and the couple have a young son.

Twelve Monkeys (1995) was a neo-noir science fiction movie directed by Terry Gilliam which was based on Chris Marker's 1962 short film *La Jetee*, which consisted mainly of a montage of still monochrome photographs and is discussed in an earlier chapter of this book.

The script was by David and Janet Peoples, and expanded the plot considerably. In 1996 a virus has killed most of humanity, and the survivors live underground. It is believed that the virus has been released by a group of anarchists called the Army of the Twelve Monkeys.

In 2035 time travel is a reality, and prisoner James Cole (Bruce Willis) is sent back in time to retrieve an original sample of the virus which will enable scientists to develop a cure. But Cole is troubled by a recurring dream in which he sees a man shot at an airport, and he arrives in Baltimore in 1990 instead of 1996. Unfortunately no-one believes his story, and he is incarcerated in a secure psychiatric unit under the care of Dr Kathryn Railly (Madeleine Stowe).

Cole meets a fellow patient, Jeffrey Goines (Brad Pitt), who has a fanatical outlook. Later, Cole is locked in his cell and then vanishes. He returns to 2035, where the scientists send him on another time trip – this time to World War I, where he is shot in the leg before arriving back in 1996.

Cole kidnaps Railly and persuades her to help him in his quest. He is convinced Goines is behind the outbreak, but when they confront him in Philadelphia he denies everything, claiming that Cole was actually responsible.

Before he can be arrested, Cole returns to 2035 and is then sent back to 1996 where he meets Railly again and wonders if he is insane. But Railly now believes he is a time traveller, as she has seen a photo of him taken during World War I. The pair flee to Florida, but on the way to the airport they learn that The Army of The Twelve Monkeys was not behind the epidemic as they were merely an animal rights' group.

At the airport Cole meets Jose (Jon Seda), who has travelled from the future to give him a gun. They now know that Dr Peters (David Morse), who worked at the virology lab, must have been responsible for the outbreak. Cole forces his way through security as he pursues Peters. He draws his gun, but is then shot by police. As he lies dying in Railly's arms he spots a young boy who is witnessing this traumatic event. It is none other than the young James Cole who is witnessing his own death, and it is this memory which will be replayed in his dreams for decades to come. Peters survives and boards his plane.

The film was very successful, making $168.8 million at the box office against a budget of $29.5 million. Brad Pitt was nominated for an Academy Award for Best Supporting Actor, and also won a Golden Globe for his performance. The movie became a cult classic and eventually spawned a TV series which ran to 47 episodes over four series from 2015 to 2018.

Star Trek: First Contact (1996) was the eighth *Star Trek* film, and the first to be based solely on the *Star Trek: The Next Generation* TV series as the previous movie had involved a combination of the old and new cast. Once again the story had a time travel element and involved recurring foes, the cybernetic Borg who travel back in time to change history. The film was directed by Jonathan Frakes, who also played the Enterprise's first officer, Commander William T. Riker, in *Star Trek: The Next Generation* and various movie spin-offs.

The film begins in the 24th century. Captain Jean-Luc Picard (Patrick Stewart) awakens from a nightmare in which he has recalled being turned into a Borg a few years earlier (an event which happened in the TV series). He is informed about a new Borg threat, but is ordered by an Admiral to instead patrol the Neutral Zone in the new USS *Enterprise* to protect Earth from Romulan aggression.

However, Picard disobeys orders and travels to Earth where a group of Starfleet vessels are struggling to hold off a single Borg Cube ship. With his knowledge of Borg technology, Picard instructs the Starfleet flotilla to concentrate their fire on a single weak point. The Borg ship is destroyed, but manages to launch a sphere-shaped craft which travels back in time through a temporal vortex. Picard then discovers that Earth is now populated entirely by Borg. Somehow the aliens have changed history. The only solution is for the *Enterprise* crew to go back in time and put things right.

The crew travel back to 4th April 2063 and beam down to Earth. It is one day before inventor Zefram Cochrane's first warp flight in his ship, the *Phoenix*, which results in contact with aliens. The Borg intend to prevent this happening.

Unfortunately, the Borg get on board the *Enterprise* and Picard is forced to activate the self-destruct mechanism to prevent the ship from being captured. The crew abandon ship using the escape pods while Picard rescues the android Data (Brent Spiner).

Cochrane (James Cromwell), Riker and engineer Geordi La Forge (LeVar Burton) prepare to activate the warp drive on the *Phoenix*. But there is a problem, as the Borg Queen (Alice Krige) has grafted skin onto Data giving him the sensation of touch. Picard offers to surrender himself to the Borg in exchange for Data's freedom, but the android refuses to leave. He then fires photon torpedoes at the *Phoenix* but they miss, and the Queen realises that Data is still working for Starfleet. Data then bursts open a coolant tank, and the corrosive liquid eats away the organic components of the Borg.

Cochrane completes his first warp flight, and the next day a Vulcan ship lands on Earth. 'First Contact' has been achieved, and the *Enterprise* returns to the 24th century.

The film was released on 22nd November 1996 and was highly successful, making $146 million set against a budget of $45 million. Respected critic Roger Ebert considered it the best of the *Star Trek* series.

Retroactive (1997) is a low-budget film just 91 minutes long which explores the familiar concept of temporal paradoxes. It was directed by Louis Morneau and produced by Jeffrey D. Ivers, David Bixler, Brad Krevoy, Michael Nadeau and Steven Stabler. The screenplay was by Robert Strauss, Michael Hamilton-Wright and Philip Badger.

The plot was simple. Karen (Kylie Travis) is forced to hitch-hike after her car breaks down. She accepts a lift from Frank (James Belushi), who is travelling with his wife Rayanne (Shannon Whirry). Unfortunately he learns that his abused wife has been unfaithful, so he murders her.

Karen escapes after a gun battle, and takes refuge in a laboratory where a scientist named Brian (Frank Whaley) has created a time machine. She uses the apparatus to go back in time to just before Rayanne's murder, but is unable to prevent the woman's death. She repeats the process, and things get even worse as Rayanne's lover, a policeman and a family on holiday also end up dead.

Karen realises that the only solution is to go back in time far enough that she does not become involved with Frank in the first place. This does not result in an entirely happy ending, though, as Frank still kills his accomplice and Rayanne's lover and is then murdered by Rayanne.

The film is now regarded as a cult classic. It explores the problems caused by changing the past in a very grim way. Other movies which covered similar ground (like *About Time* and *Groundhog Day*) had a more humorous approach.

Run Lola Run (1998) is a German thriller which was directed by Tom Tykwer and starred Franka Potente and Moritz Bleibtreu. The plot concerns a woman who has to obtain 100,000 Deutschmarks in twenty minutes to save her boyfriend's life.

The film opens with Lola (Franka Potente) receiving a phone call from her boyfriend Manni (Moritz Bleibtreu), who is in a pickle. He is a 'bagman' for a criminal gang, and accidentally left a holdall containing 100,000 Deutschmarks on a station platform. Unless he can find or raise the money in twenty minutes, he will be killed. He plans to rob a supermarket, but Lola implores him to wait as her father (Herbert Knaup) is a bank manager.

Lola hurries to the bank but her father refuses to help, telling her he is not her biological father and that he has a mistress who is pregnant. She then races to the supermarket and reluctantly helps Manni to steal 100,000 Deutschmarks. But the police arrive and shoot Lola in the chest.

The film then resumes from the point where Lola leaves the house. This time she trips over a man with a dog and arrives at the bank a little later. Meanwhile, her father has now learned that he is not actually the father of his mistress's child. Lola arrives at the bank a little later than previously, overhears the conversation, and grabs a security guard's gun. She robs the bank and gives the cash to Manni, but he is run over by an ambulance.

The action then restarts again from the moment Lola leaves the house. This time she leaps over the man and his dog and ends up at a casino, where she luckily wins the required 100,000 Deutschmarks. As this is happening, Manni retrieves the original money bag from a homeless man and gives it to the criminal gang. Lola arrives and Manni asks her what is in her bag.

The film received much critical acclaim and won a few awards, including the Grand Prix of the Belgian Syndicate of Cinema Critics.

Lost in Space (1998) was an American SF film which was based on the popular Irwin Allen TV series which ran from 1965-68. The original TV series was effectively a version of Swiss Family Robinson set in space, and dealt with a family who end up marooned on an alien planet after their space mission goes wrong. The first season was in black and white and had quite a dark tone, but then became quite cheesy with very sentimental storylines.

In the film version, the principal lead, Professor John Robinson, was played by William Hurt with Mimi Rogers as his wife, Professor Maureen Robinson. The villain, Dr Zachary Smith, was played by Gary Oldman. The plot of the film was similar to the TV series, as it involved Dr Smith sabotaging the Robinson family's Jupiter II spaceship with the aid of a robot. As a result, the spaceship ends up on a distant planet. One addition to the storyline was that Will Robinson (Jack Johnson) builds a time machine, which enables him to make temporal journeys.

The film made $136.6 million at the box office, but as the budget was $80 million this was not deemed enough to warrant the development of a franchise as had originally been planned. However, in 2018 an American TV series of *Lost in Space* debuted on Netflix with British actor Toby Stephens as Professor John Robinson.

Rebirth of Mothra III (1998) was released in Japan as *Mothra 3: Invasion of King Ghidorah,* and is part of a movie genre unique to Japan made by Toho Studios in which various monsters ravage Tokyo. The best-known of these would be the *Godzilla* series.

This particular movie was unusual as the 'hero' monster, the Mothra, developed the ability to travel in time by moving at a speed close to the velocity of light. Actually this is not correct scientifically, and the same error appears in *Superman* (1978). Albert Einstein predicted that if an astronaut travelled close to the speed of light then he would age more slowly than his twin brother back on Earth. He did not actually state that time travel could be achieved by travelling at near-light speeds. Yet many writers who lack scientific knowledge persist in believing this to be the case.

In the film, Mothra travels back in time 65 million years to confront the three-headed dragon Ghidorah during the age of the dinosaurs. The film was a success in Japan, but is largely unknown outside that country.

Austin Powers: The Spy Who Shagged Me (1999) was one of the most successful movies of that year and is arguably better than the first *Austin Powers* movie, *Austin Powers: International Man of Mystery* (1997). Directed by Jay Roach and starring Mike Myers (who also co-wrote the script with Michael McCullers), it describes the continuing adventures of 1960s-era spy Austin Powers.

The Austin Powers films are often described as 'Bond spoofs', which of course they are, and it should be noted that there have been parodies and rip-offs of the Bond movies since the early sixties. Strangely, the original *Austin Powers* film appeared thirty-five years after *Dr No* (1962), even though the original wave of parodies and copies of Bond had occurred some decades earlier. For example, *Licensed to Kill* (1965) – featuring a very Connery-like Tom Adams as Charles Vine – premiered just three years after *Dr No*, and *The Man from U.N.C.L.E.* – which was 'Bond for television' – started in 1964.

The Spy Who Shagged Me starts in 1999 and continues from the events of the previous film. Austin Powers – a British spy from the sixties who has been cryogenically transplanted to the present day – is in bed with his new wife, Vanessa Kensington (Elizabeth Hurley). Unfortunately she turns out to be a 'fembot' (female robot) controlled by Powers' nemesis Dr Evil (Mike Myers again). She unsuccessfully tries to kill Powers and then self-destructs.

Meanwhile, Dr Evil has returned and has developed a time machine which he uses to go back to 1969 and steal

Powers' mojo, the source of his sex appeal. He is assisted by a small copy of himself called 'Mini-Me' (Verne Troyer) and a very obese henchman, Fat Bastard (Myers again) who extracts Powers' mojo from his frozen body at the Ministry of Defence. Powers is left impotent as a result.

Powers goes back to 1969 in a time travelling New Beetle where he meets Felicity Shagwell (Heather Graham). But the famously promiscuous Powers cannot have sex with her because he has lost his mojo.

Powers studies surveillance photos, which show that it was the villainous Fat Bastard who stole his mojo. Felicity seduces Fat Bastard and places a homing device in his rectum. But the obese henchman expels the bug when he uses the toilet at Paddington Station. British spies analyse a stool sample and discover it contains traces of a vegetable which only grows on one Caribbean island.

Dr Evil has a secret HQ in a volcano, and also has a moon base fitted with a laser which can threaten Earth. Austin and Felicity travel to the moon and battle Dr Evil. Austin saves the world, but Felicity dies. However, he uses Dr Evil's time machine to go back ten minutes in time to save Felicity.

Felicity points out that with all the things Austin has achieved he must surely still have his mojo. The pair escape back to 1999 through the time portal. Dr Evil survives to fight another day.

The film was very popular and had an influence on popular culture as it led to the widespread use of the word 'mojo' and the phrase 'getting your mojo back'. The term 'Mini-Me' also came into common use as a result of its employment in the film. The title of the film also proved controversial, as the word 'shagged' was considered too coarse for use in UK newspapers at the time and the word was asterisked out in many adverts. A third *Austin Powers* film, *Goldmember*, followed in 2002 but was not as well-received despite the inclusion of Michael Caine as Powers' father. A fourth *Austin Powers* film has been mooted for years, but has not yet entered production.

Galaxy Quest (1999) was once described as 'the best Star Trek movie of 1999', even though it didn't have the words 'Star Trek' in the title. It is a brilliant spoof of the original *Star Trek* TV series, and is regarded as an affectionate parody.

The film begins with the members of the cancelled space-adventure TV series *Galaxy Quest* attending a fan convention. This part of the plot mirrors reality, as the original *Star Trek* TV series was cancelled in 1968 and the first movie *Star Trek: The Motion Picture* did not premiere until the end of 1979.

The lead – Jason Nesmith (Tim Allen) – who played Commander Taggart, is in conflict with his other cast members, who include Gwen De Marco (Sigourney Weaver), Alexander Dane (Alan Rickman), Fred Kwan (Tony Shalhoub) and Tommy Webber (Daryl Mitchell), who all resent his egotistical attitude. Alexander Dane plays a character in the series called 'Dr Lazarus', who is clearly based on *Star Trek*'s Mr Spock.

During the convention, Nesmith is approached by a group of people called the Thermians who want his help. Nesmith believes they are just fans, but they are actually real aliens who have adopted human holographic disguises. The next day, while suffering from a hangover, Nesmith is taken to the NSEA *Protector* – the ship from the *Galaxy Quest* TV series – and helps the Thermians to defeat General Sarris (Robin Sachs). Nesmith is then transported back to Earth.

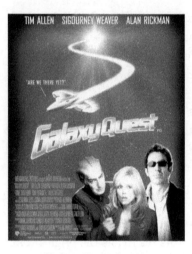

Galaxy Quest (1999):
DreamWorks Pictures/Gran Via
Productions

The following day, Nesmith explains what happened to the rest of the cast but they don't believe a word of it. The Thermians then reappearm and everyone is transported to the *Protector*. It transpires that the Thermians had picked up TV signals in deep space and had assumed the events of *Galaxy Quest* were real. They had then built a spaceship to the same specification as the fictional *Protector*. The actors engage in battle with Sarris, but the ship's crucial beryllium sphere is damaged.

The humans take a shuttle to a nearby planet to acquire a new beryllium sphere. But when they return they find that Sarris has taken over the *Protector*. After a series of battles, Nesmith is forced to activate the 'Omega-13', a device which reverses time, and he manages to knock out Sarris when he first appears. In the meantime the *Protector* has started to break up, and the crew escape in a command module which falls to Earth and crashes into the auditorium of a conference centre where a *Galaxy Quest* convention is being held. The crew emerge and the fans go wild, assuming it is a pre-planned stunt. Sarris comes out of the ship and Nesmith vapourizes him with a ray gun.

The film ends with a trailer for the new TV series of *Galaxy Quest*, called *Galaxy Quest: The Journey Continues*.

The last time travel movie of the 1990s was the little-known *Teen Knight* (1999), which was directed by Phil Comeau and produced by Cris Andre. The screenplay was by Antony Anderson and Christopher Mollo. This production barely qualifies as a cinema film, as it had a very limited theatrical release on 1st October 1998 and was issued on VHS video on 19th January 1999. It 2013 it was released on DVD by Moonbeam Films with a different title, *Medieval Park*.

The story involves a seventeen-year-old schoolboy, Peter (Kris Lemche), who wins a 'Medieval Adventure' competition sponsored by a soft drinks company. The prize is a night in an old castle with the whole experience being captured by a film crew. Unfortunately a spell cast 600 years before transports the castle and all its occupants back to 1383. The dastardly Lord Raykin (Marc Robinson) tries to capture the castle, and the time travellers are forced to stop him. Eventually they succeed and return to the 20th century with the help of the former court magician Percival (Paul Soles).

9

Time for a Change
The 2000s

THE first time travel movie of 2000 was *Frequency*, which was released on 28 April. Directed by Gregory Hoblit – who was also one of the co-producers – along with Hawk Koch, Bill Carraro and Toby Emmerich (who also wrote the screenplay), the film used an interesting plot device – a radio which can communicate with people in other times.

The movie begins in October 1969. Firefighter Frank Sullivan (Dennis Quaid) dies in a warehouse fire, leaving behind his wife Julia (Elizabeth Mitchell) and sixteen-year-old son John (Jim Caviezel).

Thirty years later, John – now a New York Police Department detective – is presented with his father's old Heathkit ham radio but cannot get it to work. However, it starts operating on the night before the anniversary of Frank's death, and John discovers that he can communicate with his father back in 1969 so he warns him of his impending death in an accident. This time Frank escapes from the warehouse without injury.

Unfortunately (in a plot twist familiar to fans of time travel movies) Frank's survival in 1969 alters the timeline. His mother Julia now lives at a different address and his ex-girlfriend Samantha (Melissa Errico) doesn't recognize him, while John also learns that his father died of lung cancer in 1989. Also, a serial killer called 'Nightingale' kills ten nurses instead of the three he murdered in the original timeline. Frank communicates with his father, who saves the first victim, but is then framed for the second murder.

John talks to Frank again by radio and realises that his father's wallet has the killer's fingerprints on it. He tells him to wrap it in plastic and leave it somewhere where he can find it in 1999. This action results in John discovering that 'Nightingale' is Jack Shepard (Shawn Doyle).

Back in 1969, Frank accidentally knocks over the Heathkit radio – damaging it in the process – and he is arrested for the murders. But he escapes from custody after activating the fire sprinkler system and travels to Shepard's apartment, where he finds jewellery belonging to the murderer's victims. He struggles with the killer, who apparently dies.

Frank repairs the radio, but then a deranged Shepard appears and attacks him and John in both 1969 and 1999. Frank shoots off Shepard's right hand (in 1969), causing it to vanish in 1999. He now cannot harm John. The 1999 furnishings change as the timeline has been altered, and Frank is now alive as he had given up smoking. The film ends with the whole family watching a baseball match. Samantha is now John's wife, and the couple have a son.

Frequency was moderately successful making $68.1 million at the box office against a budget of $31million and received generally favourable reviews.

Happy Accidents (2000) is a little-known low-budget film which was written and directed by Brad Anderson and produced by Caroline Kaplan. The plot is fairly simple. Ruby Weaver (Marisa Tomei) – who has a history of failed relationships – meets Sam Deed (Vincent D'Onofrio) in a park. The two start a relationship, but Ruby has some concerns about her new lover. He keeps talking about a 'Chrystie Delancey' and 'causal effect'. Eventually he admits that he is from 2470 and is what he describes as a 'back traveller' (a time traveller).

Ruby is initially sceptical, but his growing agitation convinces her that he needs to see a therapist. She takes him to see Meg Ford (Holland Taylor), and Sam then admits that all his actions were an attempt to change her life. In a final plot twist, it is revealed that both Deed and Ford are time travellers, and a fatal accident involving Ruby is prevented.

The film was first shown at the Sundance Film Festival on 25 January 2000 and was favourably received. It then had a limited release in the USA, grossing just $688,253.

Ditto (2000) is a little-known South Korean science fiction film directed by Kim Jung-kwon. It has some plot similarities with the high-budget movie *Frequency* (2000), as it involves two people who are in different times but can communicate by radio.

The film opens with Yoon So-eun (Kim Ha-neul), a student at Silla University meeting Dong-hee (Park Yong-woo) outside her amateur radio club room.

That night So-eun is woken by a call on her radio from another HAM enthusiast, Ji In (Yoo Ji-Taye). They agree to meet in front of the school clock tower. So-eun waits in front of an unfinished clock tower while Ji In stands in front of a completed one. Each is disappointed that the other person has not turned up, but the explanation for this anomaly comes a little later as they discover that they are in different time zones, standing next to the same clock tower. So-eun is in 1979, while Ji In is in 2000.

So-eun tracks down Ji In in 2000 and finds that she is a professor of English at another University. She is still single, though happy. He tries to contact her again by radio but finds it no longer works. Ji In settles down with his girlfriend Hyeon-ji (Ha Ji-won), while So-eun realises that her future does not lie with Dong-Hee. The film won several awards in South Korea, but is almost unknown in the West.

Timequest (2000) is an American science fiction film directed and written by Robert Dyke and produced by Gary Bloom, Charles F. Cirgenski, Ron Cook, James A. Courtney, Mary Petryshyn and Tom Van Scycoc. It has a plot familiar to fans of time travel films – a person goes back in time to prevent a murder, in this case the killing of President John F. Kennedy in 1963.

The film opens on the morning of 22nd November 1963. An old man (Ralph Waite) wearing a spacesuit materializes in a hotel suite occupied by Jackie Kennedy (Caprice Benedetti). The time traveller shows Jackie future TV footage of the assassination of her husband, President John F. Kennedy (Victor Slezak). He then talks to the President and his Attorney General brother, Bobby (who in our timeline was assassinated in 1968). The time traveller won't reveal his name but claims to have been born that day.

The three Kennedys drink a toast with the time traveller, but at exactly 12.30 p.m. (the time that JFK would have been shot) he vanishes, leaving only a broken glass. Bobby recovers a fingerprint from the glass and then takes action. The two gunmen on the grassy knoll are killed (drawing on the well-known conspiracy theories about the killing), and Lee Harvey Oswald is arrested.

Bobby Kennedy subsequently uses the fingerprint evidence to identify the time traveller as Raymond Mead (Joseph Murphy), who had was arrested at age sixteen for burglary. Bobby Kennedy (who is not killed in 1968 in this new time-line) has him pardoned.

In 2001 JFK dies of old age, his wife having died some years earlier. The film ends with a sequence set in 1964 with Raymond as a toddler. He sees Jackie emerging from Parkland Hospital, where she has just had a baby called James Robert Kennedy.

The Kid (also known as *Disney's The Kid*) is a 2000 fantasy comedy film directed by Jon Turteltaub and scripted by Audrey Wells. It was produced by Hunt Lowry, Arnold Rifkin, Christina Steinberg, David Willis and Jon Turteltaub. It was one of star Bruce Willis's lesser known pictures, although it was a financial success.

Russ Duritz (Bruce Willis) is the central character of the film, an image consultant in Los Angeles who has a difficult relationship with his father. One day, Russ comes home to find a strange boy outside his house. He chases the boy to the Skyway Diner, but the young man vanishes. Russ thinks he may have had a hallucination and sees a psychiatrist, but the next day he finds the same boy on his couch, eating popcorn and watching TV. Russ concludes that the kid, Rusty, is a younger version of himself.

Russ's co-worker Amy (Emily Mortimer) finds out about Rusty the following day and concludes that Russ and Rusty are father and son. Rusty implores Russ to tell Amy the truth, but Russ refuses as he thinks she won't believe him. Eventually Amy notices that the pair have similar mannerisms and guesses the truth.

The next day, Russ is driving through a tunnel when he remembers an incident when he fought some bullies who were abusing a three-legged dog called Tripod. When he emerges from the tunnel, he is back in 1968 and helps Rusty to win the fight. Unfortunately there are consequences. Rusty's father scolds him for getting into trouble, and the trauma gives the boy a lifelong facial tic. Russ tells Rusty that his mother will die before his next birthday, and that his father's cruel behaviour was a result of him being afraid of how he was going to bring him up on his own.

Russ and Rusty go to the Skyway Diner to celebrate their birthday. A dog called Chester comes up to Rusty and he discovers that the owner is an older version of Russ, who has a family with a woman who is none other than Amy. So Rusty's appearance in his life was intended to change his ways. Russ returns to his original time (2000) and settles down with Amy.

Il Mare (2000) is a South Korean film made on a budget of $2.5 million, which was directed by Lee-Hyun-seung, about two protagonists of opposite gender who both live in the same house – *Il Mare* (The Sea) – but in different time periods, namely 1997 and 1999. They soon discover that they can communicate through a mailbox which sends letters forwards or backwards in time. The couple fall in love, despite the time difference separating them, and at the end of the film they finally meet.

The main significance of this film is that it was remade by Warner Bros. in 2006 as *The Lake House*, which starred

Keanu Reeves and Sandra Bullock and is discussed later in this chapter.

Black Night (2001) is an American fantasy film directed by Gil Junger which starred Martin Lawrence. It was produced by Arnon Milchan, Darryl J. Quarles, Michael Green and Paul J. Schiff. The screenplay was by Darryl J. Quarles, Peter Gaulke and Gerry Swallow.

The plot concerns Jamal Walker (Martin Lawrence), a lazy employee at a theme park called *Medieval World*, who travels back to 1328 after finding a strange medallion in a moat. Jamal initially doesn't realise he has gone back in time, so he looks for Medieval World but finds instead an old building which he thinks is a rival theme park called *Castle World*. He meets King Leo (Kevin Conway), who believes him to be a messenger from Normandy, and Jamal is soon made head of security after preventing an assassination attempt. But he soon makes friends with various people and realises that he must overthrow the king and restore the Queen (Helen Carey) to the throne.

Jamal leads a revolt against the king and adopts the disguise of the 'Black Knight' to achieve this aim. After restoring the queen to the throne, he is knighted for his services but then finds himself back in Medieval World in the present day. His whole attitude to his work has changed, and he is determined to make the business better than the rival Castle World. He then meets a young woman called Nicole (Marsha Thomason) who looks just like a girl called Victoria (Thomason again) he had met in 1328. Before he can start a relationship with her, he falls back into the moat and finds himself in Ancient Rome.

The film opened on 21 November 2001, but it fared poorly at the box office and attracted mainly negative reviews.

Donnie Darko (2001) is an American science fiction film directed by Richard Kelly (who also wrote the script) and produced by Sean McKittrick, Nancy Juvonen and Adam Fields.

The story is about a teenager, Donald 'Donnie' Darko, who is troubled by disturbing visions. The film starts on 2nd October 1988 when Donnie is woken by 'Frank' (James Duval), a figure in a giant rabbit costume who tells him the world will end in 28 days. Donnie wakes up the next morning on the local golf course, and when he returns home he finds that his house has been demolished by a jet engine.

Donnie continues to have visions of Frank and is referred to a psychiatrist named Dr Thurman (Katharine Ross). Despite this intervention, Frank continues to influence Donnie's behaviour, causing him to flood his high school. He is forced to attend a lecture by motivational speaker Jim Cunningham (Patrick Swayze), but Frank persuades him to set Cunningham's house on fire and emergency workers find child pornography in the blazing ruins. Cunningham is arrested.

Donnie and his sister Elizabeth (Maggie Gyllenhaal) hold a Halloween party. But Donnie knows that Frank's prophesied end of the world is approaching, so he takes his new girlfriend Gretchen (Jena Malone) to see Roberta Sparrow. The pair get involved in a fight with two bullies as Sparrow is returning to her house, and Gretchen is then killed by a car which has swerved. The driver is Frank and Donnie shoots him in the eye and returns home, carrying Gretchen's body.

Donnie puts Gretchen's body into a car and drives to a nearby ridge as a time vortex forms over his house. An airliner cruises overhead and flies into the temporal anomaly, causing one of its jet engines to fall off. Donnie is pulled back to

2nd October and wakens in his bedroom as a jet engine falls on him, crushing him to death.

The film opened on 26th October 2001 but did not do well at the box office, making only $7.5 million against a budget of $4.5 million. One of the reasons for this failure was because it came out only a few weeks after the 9/11 terrorist attacks and the scenes of airliners crashing were deemed to be distressing to the general public.

Just Visiting (2001) is a French-American comedy film directed by Jean-Marie Gaubert and produced by Patrice Ledoux and Ricardo Mestres. The screenplay was by Jean-Marie Poire, Christian Claver and John Hughes – best-known for his wildly successful teen movies in the 1980s. The movie was an English language remake of the French film *Les Visiteurs* (discussed in an earlier chapter), and is about a medieval knight and his servant who travel to modern Chicago.

The film opens in England in the 12th century. Lord Thibault Malfete (Jean Reno) is about to marry Princess Rosalind (Christina Applegate). Unfortunately, Thibault kills his own bride after being given a hallucinatory potion by the Earl of Warwick. He is sentenced to death and asks his servant, Andre Le Pate (Christian Clavier), for help. Consequently, a wizard (Malcolm McDowell) gives him a potion which is meant to take him back to the moment before he killed his bride. But things go wrong, and he and Andre are instead transported to the 21st century.

The pair arrive in a Chicago museum and are arrested, but they are rescued by a museum employee Julia Malfete (Christina Applegate) who looks just like Princess Rosalind. (This is a common trope in time travel movies – the hero meets a person in the past or future who is the exact double of their lost

Just Visiting (2001): Gaumont/ Hollywood Pictures/Bruin Grip Services/Buena Vista Pictures

love.) Thibault realises that Julia must be a descendant of Princess Rosalind.

Thibault realises he must return to the past to put things right. Back in the 12th century the wizard has come to a similar conclusion and uses more of the potion to travel to the 21st century to help Thibault. Once there, he prepares a new potion to take the three of them back to the Middle Ages. There is a problem, however, because Andre does not want to go back due to the fact that he prefers life in the 21st century, and so he stays where he is.

The Wizard and Thibault travel back to the 12th century and successfully prevent the death of the Princess, while in 2001 Julia meets a man called Francois Le Combier (Alexis Loret) who knows about her family history. The film ends with Andre and his new girlfriend Angelique (Tara Reid) driving towards Las Vegas in a hot rod.

Unlike the original French version, the film was not a success, making just $35 million set against a budget of $16.2 million. Most reviews were negative.

Kate & Leopold (2001) was a romantic comedy which tells the story of a duke who travels from 1876 New York to the present day (2001) and falls in love with a woman. It was directed by James Mangold and produced by Cathy Konrad. The screenplay was by Steven Rogers and Mangold.

The film begins on 28th April 1876. Leopold, His Grace the Third Duke of Albany (Hugh Jackman) is a frustrated inventor who has built a working model of a new type of passenger lift. But his family disapproves of his activities.

One day Leopold meets the physicist Stuart Besser (Liev Schreiber), and the two men accidentally fall into a time portal which takes them to 2001. It transpires that Stuart is from the 21st century and is able to locate time portals. He explains that Leopold must stay in his apartment until the portal reopens in a week. Stuart then takes his dog for a walk and falls into a lift shaft. He is subsequently institutionalised for talking about his invention. It appears that Leopold's accidental journey to the 21st century has caused a temporal paradox affecting lifts, as he made his trip before he could patent his device. In this 'alternative' 2001, lifts don't exist!

Kate McKay (Meg Ryan), Stuart's ex-girlfriend, visits the apartment to retrieve the stylus for her Palm Pilot (remember them?) and meets Leopold. The two fall in love.

Stuart is eventually released from the psychiatric hospital and returns to his apartment, where he sends Leopold back in time. Later, Stuart looks through some photos he took on one of his time journeys and sees that Leopold and Kate are together at a ball. He shows them to Kate, who also twigs that she is meant to be with Leopold, so she travels to the time portal by the Brooklyn Bridge and goes back to 1876. She arrives just in time to interrupt an arranged marriage between Leopold and another woman. Kate and Leopold get married instead, and they discover that she is Stuart's great-great-great grandmother. The film was moderately successful, making $76

million against a budget of $48 million, and received favoura-
ble reviews.

Pokemon4Ever (2001) was a Japanese animated film which
was directed by Kunihiko Yuyama and produced by Yukako
Matsusako, Takemoto Mori and Choji Yoshikawa. It was one
of a number of cinema outings for the Pokemon franchise,
which is best known as a long-running TV series made by the
famous Toho Studios. This particular film qualifies as a time
travel movie as one of the characters, Celebi, is capable of
time travel. Despite being only 81 minutes long, it made over
$40 million at the box office.

Clockstoppers (2002) is an American science fiction film
directed by Jonathan Frakes who, as mentioned earlier, played
the role of Commander Riker in *Star Trek: The Next Generation* and its various movie spin-offs. The film was produced by
Julia Pistor and Gale Anne Hurd, who was a former wife of
James Cameron and worked with him on a number of films
including *Terminator* (1984) and *Aliens* (1986). The screenplay was by Rob Hedden, J. David Stem and Robert Weiss.

Clockstoppers has an interesting premise. The fictional
Quantum Tech (QT) Corporation has developed Hypertime,
a breakthrough which speeds up the user's molecules to the
point where everyone else appears frozen in time. Incidentally,
this is not a new idea, as a similar plot point occurs in *The
Time Travelers* (1964) and in an episode of classic *Star Trek,
Wink of An Eye*, *Star Trek: The Next Generation*'s sixth season episode *Timescape*, plus *Timelash*, a 1970 segment of the
TV series *UFO*.

Clockstoppers begins with the National Security Agency
(NSA) ending the Hypertime project. But QT's Chief Executive, Henry Gates (Michael Biehn), uses the technology to
extend the weekend, giving scientist Earl Dopler (French

Stewart) time to fix glitches in the technology. Dopler then undergoes rapid ageing.

Unfortunately Zak Gibbs (Jesse Bradford) acquires a prototype watch containing Hypertime technology. Gates finds out about this and sends henchmen after Zak, who tries to warn his father Dr George Gibbs (Robin Thomas) about the ulterior motives of the QT Corporation.

Zak is pursued and crashes a van into a river, damaging the watch, while his father is kidnapped by QT henchmen. He and his girlfriend, Francesca (Paula Garces), subsequently kidnap Dopler and force him to fix the watch. He also builds liquid nitrogen guns which freeze people back into normal time.

Zak and Francesca infiltrate QT but are thrown into a cell with Zak's father. Eventually they escape and defeat QT and Gates using the powers of the watch. Dopler attempts to reverse the effects of Hypertime using a machine, but ends up as a teenager. Zak and Francesca end up together but retain the watch, which still works.

The film opened on 29th March 2002 but only made $38.8 million at the box office against a budget of $26million, and received generally negative reviews.

2009: Lost Memories (2002) is a South Korean science fiction action film directed by Lee Si-myung and produced by Kim Yun-young and Seo Jun-won. The screenplay was by Lee Si-myung and Lee Sang-hak, based on a book by Bek Geo-il.

The film may be considered a crossover between a time travel movie and an alternative history film, as it is set in a universe in which the USA and Japan combined forces in 1936 to fight Nazi Germany and Korea was still occupied by Japan in 2009. This alternative reality came about because of the discovery of an ancient stone temple in Korea which allowed a

Japanese right-wing nationalist group, *Uyoku dantai*, to send an operative called Inoue back to 1909 to prevent the assassination of Resident-General Ito Hirodumi. As a result of this, Japan becomes allied to the USA, and the Second World War ends with the dropping of the atom bomb on Germany in 1945.

The plot of the film centres around the hero Sakamoto (Jang Dong-gun), who travels back to 1909 and kills Inoue, thus restoring the original timeline.

Returner (2002) is a Japanese science fiction film which was directed by Takashi Yamazaki, produced by Chikahiro Ando, Toru Horibe and Akifumi Takuma. The screenplay was by Kenya Hirata and Takashi Yamazaki.

The plot contains elements which will be familiar to anyone who has seen Western time travel movies. In 2084, aliens called Daggra have conquered the Earth. Milly (Anne Suzuki), a soldier from 2084, travels back to 2002 to kill the very first Daggra scout in the hope of preventing the invasion.

Milly becomes involved with a hitman called Miyamoto (Takeshi Kaneshiro), who is trying to kill a gangster called Mizoguchi (Goro Kishitani). They attempt to track down the alien spaceship, but it has been taken away to the National Institute of Space Sciences. Milly discovers that the alien is benign and the war was actually caused by evil humans. The real villain is Mizoguchi, who captures the alien and its ship.

Milly and Miyamoto battle Mizoguchi on an abandoned oil rig. The villain is shot, and a Daggra ship disguised as a Boeing 747 rescues the alien. As the future war will not now happen, Milly vanishes. Myamoto decides to give up his life of crime and disposes of his gun, but he is then shot by a thug. His life is saved by a metal plate which Milly (travelling from the future) had put in his coat earlier.

The film was released on 17th October 2003 and did well in Japan, making $10 million at the box office. It did not fare so well internationally, with many reviewers considering it to be highly derivative as it incorporated ideas from other time travel movies.

Time Changer (2002) is described as an 'independent science fiction Christian seriocomic film' (!), written and directed by Rich Christiano. It was produced by Christiano and Kevin Downes.

The film opens in 1890 as Bible professor Russell Carlisle (D. David Morin) chastises a boy for stealing marbles. Carlisle has just penned a new manuscript called *The Changing Times*, but colleague Dr Norris Anderson (Gavin MacLeod) objects to it. Anderson is concerned the book claims to teach good moral values without mentioning Christ and might therefore be harmful, so he sends Carlisle 100 years into the future using a time machine.

Carlisle is shocked at the decline in moral values in 1990. For example, half of all marriages end in divorce and blasphemous language is widespread. He tries to convince a laundromat worker, Eddie Martinez (Paul Rodriguez), that he should go to church and read the Bible. He also talks about the second coming of Christ before travelling back to 1890, where he tells Anderson that he intends to revise his book.

The movie ends with Anderson attempting and failing to send a Bible into the future. He concludes that the world will end before the mid-21st century. The film received a limited release and only made $1.5 million at the box office, against a production cost of $855,000.

Austin Powers in Goldmember (2002) is the third and (to date) final film in the Austin Powers series of spy spoofs which were largely parodies of the Bond films, although they incorporated influences from other movies. Like the previous entry, *Austin Powers: The Spy Who Shagged Me* (1999), the film incorporated time travel in its plot.

As before, the film was directed by Jay Roach, with a screenplay by Mike Myers and Michael McCullers. The producers were Jan Blenkin, John S. Lyons, Eric McLeod, Demi Moore and Mike Myers.

The film takes the concept of satire a stage further as it opens with a parody of the *Austin Powers* films themselves – a bio-pic called *Austinpussy*, supposedly directed by Steven Spielberg and starring Tom Cruise as Austin Powers and also featuring Gwyneth Paltrow, Kevin Spacey, Danny De Vito and John Travolta. The gag here is that Spielberg has always had an ambition to direct a Bond film, and it was this which led him to direct and co-create the *Raiders of the Lost Ark* series of films in which Indiana Jones was an 'archaelogical Bond'.

The film proper starts with Dr Evil (Mike Myers) travelling back to 1975 to bring back Johan van der Smut, aka 'Goldmember' (Myers again). Dr Evil wants to use Goldmember's tractor beam technology to divert a meteor and flood the Earth, but the plot is defeated by the British Secret Service and Dr Evil is imprisoned.

Powers' father, Nigel Powers (Michael Caine), is abducted and Austin travels to 1975 to try and rescue him. He meets his former lover, FBI agent Foxxy Cleopatra (Beyonce Knowles). Powers fails to rescue his father, and Goldmember takes him back to 2002. Dr Evil escapes from prison and hides in a new lair near Tokyo. Austin again unsuccessfully attempts to free his father, but Dr Evil and his son Scott (Seth Green) escape in a submarine.

Austin boards the submarine and is about to shoot Dr Evil, but then his father Nigel reveals that both Austin and Dr Evil are his sons who got split up after a car accident when they were young. Goldmember attempts to activate his tractor beam, but Austin and Dr Evil reverse its polarity (a nod to Jon Pertwee-era *Doctor Who*). Goldmember is arrested, but then reveals that the whole string of events was turned into a film by Steven Spielberg. Austin, Foxxy, Dr Evil, Mini-Me and Nigel are in the audience watching the film and – as they leave the theatre – Austin meets a slim version of Fat Bastard who reveals he has been on a low-carb diet. The film ends with Dr Evil's son Scott, now bald, declaring that he will get revenge on Austin.

The film was released on 26th July 2002 and was fairly successful, making nearly $300 million at the box office set against a budget of $63 million. There was a feeling, though, among many critics and cinemagoers that the joke was beginning to wear a bit thin, as the film repeated many ideas from the previous movie. A fourth *Austin Powers* film has been mooted since 2003, but has yet to enter production.

Timeline (2003) is an American science fiction adventure film directed by Richard Donner and starring Paul Walker, Frances

***Timeline* (2003)**: Paramount Pictures/Mutual Film Company/ Donners' Company/Cobalt Media Group/Artists Production Group

O'Connor, Gerard Butler, Billy Connolly, David Thewlis and Anna Friel. It was based on the novel by Michael Crichton (best-known for *Jurassic Park* and *Westworld*), and is about a team of archaeologists who travel back in time to rescue their professor from medieval France. It was produced by Lauren Shuler Donner, Jim Van Wyck and Richard Donner. The screenplay was by Jeff Maguire and George Nolfi.

The film begins with Professor Edward Johnson (Billy Connolly) involved in an archaeological study of the village of Castelegard near La Roque Castle in Dordogne, France. While excavating the site, the archaeology team find a sarcophagus containing a knight with an amputated ear who is holding the hand of his lady. Later, they find a pair of Johnson's bifocals and a note asking for help. Both appear to be over 600 years old.

The team contact the ITC Corporation (who sponsored the dig) and discover that they had accidentally created time travel technology which had resulted in Professor Johnson being trapped in 1357. A team is assembled to rescue him.

Unfortunately things soon go wrong after they arrive in 1357. A security man attached to the team accidentally sends a primed grenade back to 2003, where it explodes and wrecks the time transfer apparatus. The team are now trapped in the past, although Josh (Ethan Embry) and Steven (Matt Craven) start to repair the machine.

After a series of adventures in 1357, the team manage to return to the present. But ITC President Robert Doniger (David Thewlis) tries to sabotage the machine and is sent back to 1357, where he is killed on the battlefield. Marek (Gerard Butler) remains in 1357, as he has become infatuated with Lady Claire (Anna Friel). He is destined to be the knight with the lopped-off ear who the team find in 2003.

The film bombed at the box office, making just $43 million against a budget of $80 million. It also received predominantly negative reviews, with most critics commenting that the plot was hard to follow.

Harry Potter and the Prisoner of Azkaban (2004) was the third film adaptation based on the highly popular *Harry Potter* series of books by J.K. Rowling. It was directed by Alfonso Cuaron and produced by David Heyman, Chris Columbus and Mark Radcliffe. The screenplay was by Steve Kloves.

The film starred Daniel Radcliffe as Harry Potter, with Rupert Grint as Ron Weasley and Emma Watson as Hermione Granger. It was a sequel to *Harry Potter and the Chamber of Secrets*, and was followed by *Harry Potter and the Goblet of Fire*.

As is widely known, the *Harry Potter* series of films deals with the adventures of young wizard Harry Potter, who attends Hogwarts School with his friends and encounters various villains. This particular film only barely qualifies as a time travel movie, as it features a scene near the end where Harry and Hermione travel back in time using Hermione's Time Turner and watch themselves and Ron repeat that night's events. They then save Buckbeak from execution and rescue Sirius Black (Gary Oldman). A grateful Sirius then sends Harry a Firebolt broom which he takes for a ride.

Like all the *Harry Potter* films, *Prisoner of Azkaban* did very well at the box office and made almost $800 million set against a budget of $130 million. It was highly praised by critics.

Primer (2004) was a low-budget American science fiction film about the accidental discovery of time travel. It was written, produced and directed by Shane Carruth, who also composed the music and starred in the film.

The film opens with two engineers, Aaron (Shane Carruth) and Abe (David Sullivan), working on a new invention which will reduce an object's weight by electromagnetic means. But they discover that they have created a new type of field which can move objects backwards and forwards in time.

The two men use this ability to make money on the stock market, but fall out due to their differing personalities. Abe eventually concludes that time travel is dangerous and travels back four days to prevent the original experiment. The film ends with a future Aaron directing the construction of a warehouse-sized box which can travel in time.

The film only made $841,926 at the box office, but its budget was just $7,000 and so it made more than a hundred times its production cost – something that cannot be said about most blockbusters. It also won a Grand Jury Prize at the 2004 Sundance Film Festival, and has since developed a cult following.

The Butterfly Effect (2004) is an American supernatural psychological thriller film which was directed by Eric Bress and J. Mackye Gruber and produced by Anthony Rhulen, Chris Bender, Ashton Kutcher, J.C. Spink and A.J. Dix. It was written by Eric Bress and J. Mackye Gruber.

The plot concerns a college student named Evan Treborn (Ashton Kutcher), who can travel back in time simply by reading extracts from his personal journal which relate to that period. In this sense, the film's title – *The Butterfly Effect* – is a misnomer, since this phenomenon (deceptively small actions in the past having a big impact in the future) does not really appear in the movie.

The plot of the movie is fairly straightforward. Evan and his friends and siblings have suffered a number of traumas that have caused him to black out. Seven years later, as a young adult, Evan discovers that he can travel back in time to various traumatic events just by reading his journals which describe these incidents . This gives him the opportunity to ensure things happen differently.

Unfortunately his attempts to change the past have unexpected and unwelcome consequences for both him and his friends. For example, he experiences alternative futures in which he has lost both arms and is a prison inmate. Eventually, he concludes that his meddling with the past is causing problems for him and those close to him, and comes up with a solution. He time travels to the first day he met sister Kayleigh (Amy Smart) as a child and then insults her. As a result she goes to live with her mother in a different neighbourhood instead of staying with her abusive father, George (Eric Stoltz).

His mission complete, Evan burns all his journals. Eight years later he passes Kayleigh in the street. They recognise each other, but keep on walking.

The film was released on 23rd January 2004. Although it received mostly negative reviews from critics, it was quite successful, making $96.1 million at the box office set against a budget of just $13 million. It also received a Saturn Award in 2004 for Best Science Fiction Film.

As a result of its good box office performance, two straight-to-DVD sequels were made: *The Butterfly Effect 2* (2006) and *The Butterfly Effect 3: Revelations* (2009). These were poorly received and had little connection with the original film.

13 Going on 30 (2004) is an American romantic comedy fantasy film directed by Gary Winick and produced by Susan Arnold, Donna Arkoff Roth, Gina Matthews and Todd Garner. The screenplay was by Cathy Yuspa, Josh Goldsmith and Niels Mueller.

The film starred Jennifer Garner as Jenna Rink, a thirteen-year-old who travels from 1987 to 2004 and finds herself in the body of a thirty-year-old woman. In this respect it is a bit like *Peggy Sue Got Married* (q.v.), but with the journey in time being in the opposite direction.

The film opens in 1987. Jenna is shut in a closet during a party game and – in a moment of intense emotion – wishes she was thirty, just as some 'magic wishing dust' is raining down from the roof of a pink doll's house.

The next morning, Jenna wakes up in an apartment. It is now 2004, she is thirty years old, and a handsome hunk is in the shower. In her new world she works for a fashion magazine called *Poise,* but it is in trouble as it is continually being scooped by its rival, *Sparkle.* Jenna decides to track down her geeky friend Matty (Mark Ruffalo), who she knew in 1987 and is now a photographer.

Jenna can remember nothing of the past seventeen years, and still has the mental strategies of a thirteen-year-old. She gets back in touch with Matt, and they become an item. Despite Jenna's efforts, *Poise* magazine folds – largely because of competition from *Sparkle.* Eventually Matt and Jenna split up, and the photographer marries another woman. Just before the ceremony, Matt gives Jenna her old doll's house which still has some 'magic dust' on the roof.

Jenna then wishes she was back in 1987 and finds herself back in the closet. Matt then enters, the two kiss, and when they run out of the house together it is 2004 and they are a married couple. The movie ends with the pair moving into a pink house, which looks just like the dollhouse which started everything.

Fetching Cody (2005) is a low-budget Canadian science fiction film directed and written by David Ray and produced by Carolyn Allain and Christina Bulbrook. The film is set in Vancouver, and tells the story of Art Frankel (Jay Baruchel) who tries to save the life of his girlfriend Cody Wesson (Sarah Lind) after she takes a drugs overdose and ends up in hospital. Art finds a time machine and travels into the past in an attempt to save Cody. The film was panned by critics.

The Jacket (2005) is an American psychological horror film which was directed by John Maybury and produced by George Clooney, Peter Guber, Steven Soderbergh and March Rocco. The screenplay was by Massy Tadjedin and was inspired by a 1915 novel by Jack London. The music was by Brian Eno, who was part of the seventies band *Roxy Music* which was fronted by Brian Ferry.

The plot concerns an American serviceman, Jack Starks (Adrien Brody), who develops strange powers following a near-death experience during the 1991 Gulf War. The film opens with Jack returning to Vermont in 1992. After helping a young girl Jackie (Laura Marano) and her mother get their truck started, he accepts a lift from another motorist. Soon afterwards Jack – who has bouts of amnesia – is found lying by the roadside near a dead policeman. A gun is nearby. Jack is arrested and incarcerated in a mental institution.

Jack is then subjected to experimental treatments by Dr Thomas Becker (Kris Kristofferson). He is injected with drugs, put in a straitjacket, and placed in a mortuary drawer. This causes him to travel forward in time fifteen years, where he meets an older Jackie (now played by Keira Knightley) who has his dogtags. But she refuses to believe he is who he claims to be, as she knows he died on 1st January 1993.

Jack makes further journeys into the future. He learns that Jackie's mother died in a fire caused by her falling asleep with a cigarette in her hand, and tries to prevent this happening by giving her a letter. After he has been taken back to the hospital by Dr Beth Lorenson (Jennifer Jason Leigh), he slips on ice – banging his head – and asks to be allowed to make one more time journey. Jack returns to 2007 and finds that the letter made all the difference, as Jackie's mother is alive and well and Jackie herself is a nurse rather than a waitress.

The film was a flop, making just $21 million at the box office compared with a budget of $29 million, and received mainly negative reviews from critics.

A Sound of Thunder (2005) is a Czech-American science fiction film directed by Peter Hyams. It was produced by Moshe Diamant, Howard Baldwin and Karen Baldwin. The screenplay was by Thomas Dean Donnelly, Joshua Oppenheimer and Gregory Poirier, and was based on science fiction writer Ray Bradbury's novella with the same title.

The film begins in 2055. The Time Safari company is offering time journeys to the past to hunt dinosaurs. But Sonia Rand (Catherine McCormack), inventor of the TAMI time travel software, is critical of the company's activities as she fears they may alter the past.

Her fears prove correct. After one expedition goes wrong, there is an increase in temperature and humidity through the globe. 'Time waves' also hit Chicago, and there is an increase in the growth of vegetation. Team leader Travis Ryer (Edward Burns) goes back in time and prevents Christian Middleton (Corey Johnson) from stepping on a butterfly during a previous time expedition. It was this seemingly trivial event which caused the disruption of the timeline. The film ends with Ryer and Rand planning to close down Time Safari to ensure that the end of the world is prevented.

The film was released on 2nd September 2005 but bombed at the box office, making just $11.7 million against a budget of $80 million. It received predominantly negative reviews.

Camp Slaughter (2005) is an American horror film which can really be considered a variant of the popular 'slasher' genre as typified by John Carpenter's *Halloween* (1978). Indeed it is very similar to *Friday the Thirteenth* (1980) and its numerous sequels, albeit with added time travel elements.

The film was directed and produced by Alex Pucci and Peter Jacelone. The screenplay was by Draven Gonzales, from a story by Pucci.

The film has a plot which will be familiar to fans of this particular genre. A group of teenagers are enjoying a stay at Camp Hiawatha in the summer of 1981. Two of them sneak away to have sex and are killed by an unseen assailant. Twenty-four years later, four friends – Angela (Joanna Suhl), Mario (Matt Dallas), Jen (Anika McFall) and Vade (Eric McIntire) – are driving in the same area en-route for Boston when their vehicle breaks down after its electronics fail. They are forced to spend the night in the car.

The next day, some of the residents at Hiawatha Camp find the stranded teenagers and invite them to stay at the camp – which looks the same as it did in 1981. That night, the mysterious killer reappears and murders everyone except the four new arrivals. But the next morning everyone appears to be alive.

Daniel (Kyle Lupo) and Ivan (Jon Fleming) tell the four visitors that the camp is stuck in a time loop, with the grisly events of 1981 repeating themselves endlessly. They hope that the visitors may manage to break the cycle of killing. Unfortunately it soon transpires that Daniel and Ivan were actually the murderers, and they coerced Michelle (Bethany Taylor) and Ruben (Miles Davis) into assisting with the killing. They now hope the four travellers can take their places, allowing them to get out.

Vade and Mario are killed, but Jen and Angela murder Ivan and David. The girls escape to their car but find that Lou (Jim Marlowe) is attacking Michelle and Ruben. Lou breaks Michelle's neck, killing her, and then admits that he murdered the perpetrators of the original massacre minutes after it occurred. Ruben then fires an arrow into Angela's chest, but in turn is killed by Lou as Angela escapes in the car.

By 2008 Jen has become a successful writer. One day she receives an email from Daniel and Ivan, who say that they are looking forward to meeting her again soon. The film was released on 20th June 2005, but did poorly at the box office and was panned by critics.

The Lake House (2006) was an American time travel romance directed by Alejandro Agresti and produced by Doug Davison and Roy Le. The screenplay was by David Auburn and was based on the earlier South Korean film *Il Mare* (2000).

The film tells the story of an architect Alex Wyler (Keanu Reeves) and a doctor, Kate Forrester (Sandra Bullock) who live in the same house in different time period, but can send letters to one another using a mailbox outside the house, and subsequently fall in love.

The movie begins in 2006. Dr Kate Forrester is leaving her rented lake house in Madison, Wisconsin to move to Chicago, and leaves a note in the mailbox with her forwarding address. She also mentions that painted pawprint marks on the path were there when she arrived.

Back in 2004, Alex Wyler arrives at the house, and finds Kate's letter, which has somehow travelled back in time – though he doesn't know this. He restores the neglected house and a dog runs through some paint, causing the aforementioned pawprint marks.

Over the next few weeks the pair exchange letters through time using the mailbox and fall in love. Eventually, both characters realise that their letters are

***The Lake House* (2006):** Warner Bros./Village Roadshow Pictures/ Vertigo Entertainment

travelling through time, though how this happens is never explained. Alex and Kate eventually meet at a party in 2004, but unfortunately she doesn't know who he is as the exchange of letters between 2006 and 2004 has not yet happened in her timeline.

Alex and Kate continue with their correspondence and come up with a solution. Alex makes a reservation for the *Il Mare* restaurant in 2007, which is in both their futures. Kate makes the appointment, but Alex does not appear.

Kate is distraught but eventually discovers that Alex had died in a traffic accident on Valentine's Day 2006 while on his way to look for her and that is why he didn't turn up. Kate sends a letter to Alex, via the mailbox, which tells him not to look for her but simply to go the Lake House in two years' time.

On that chosen day in 2008, Kate goes to the Lake House and waits. She is afraid her plan has not worked, but then a green truck drives up and Alex steps out. At last the couple are reunited in a time in which they know each other. They kiss and walk towards the Lake House.

The Lake House was released on 16 June 2006 and was moderately successful, making $115 million at the box office against a budget of $40 million. It is one of a small number of 'time travel romances', with another being *Somewhere in Time* (1980).

Click (2006) is an American fantasy film directed by Frank Coraci, produced by Adam Sandler, Jack Giarraputo, Neal H. Moritz, Steve Koren and Mark O'Keefe and written by Steven Koren and Mark O'Keefe. It tells the story of Michael Newman (Adam Sandler), an architect who acquires a 'universal remote' which enables him to 'fast forward' through dull or uninteresting parts of his life.

The film opens with Michael buying a 'universal' remote control for his home from a man called Morty (Christopher Walken) in a department store. He soon finds that he can pause, rewind or fast forward events in his life. So when he has an argument with his wife Donna (Kate Beckinsale), he can fast forward to the point where the row is over.

When his teenage children want expensive bicycles, he fast forwards to a point in time when he has received promotion and is earning a higher salary. But there is a downside as the family dog, Sundance, has died and his marriage is in trouble. But the remote soon learns his preferences and moves him forwards in time in response to his casual wishes. Michael tries to destroy the remote, but it keeps reappearing.

Michael's boss, Ammer (David Hasselhoff), tells him he will be retiring and that Michael could eventually become

CEO of the company. The remote immediately sends Michael ten years into the future when he is now the CEO – but he is morbidly obese, and Donna has divorced him and married Bill (Sean Astin). Michael gets into an argument and is knocked over by the family dog, ending up in a coma for years. The remote reacts by sending him into the future when he has recovered and is no longer obese. His father, Ted (Henry Winkler), is now dead.

Morty appears again and reveals he is the Angel of Death. Michael goes several years into the future to his son's wedding, but then has a heart attack and apparently dies. He regains consciousness and discovers he has travelled back in time to the moment just before he first received the remote. He throws it away and it does not return. He has been given a second chance to put things right.

The film was released on 23rd June 2006 and was moderately successful, making $237.7 million against a budget of $82.5 million.

The Girl Who Leapt Through Time (2006) is a Japanese animated science fiction film which tells the story of a young woman who can jump through time to fix problems in her life using a walnut-shaped time travel device. It was directed by Mamoru Hodo and produced by Takafumi Watanabe and Yuichiro Saito. The screenplay was by Satoko Okudera and was based on the book *The Girl Who Leapt Through Time* by Yasutaka Tsutsui.

Déjà vu (2006) is an American science fiction thriller directed by the late Tony Scott (brother of Ridley Scott), whose best-known film was *Top Gun* (1986). The film was produced by Jerry Bruckheimer and written by Bill Marsilli and Terry Rossio.

The film begins with the ferry *Senator Alvin T. Stumpf* sinking in the Mississippi as a result of a terrorist bomb. 543 passengers (including many US Navy sailors) are killed.

Special Agent Doug Carlin (Denzel Washington) of the Bureau of Alcohol, Tobacco, Firearms and Explosives (ATF) is assigned to the case, and meets FBI Special Agent Paul Pryzwarra (Val Kilmer). One important clue is the burned body of Claire Kuchever (Paula Patton), which was dragged from the river before the explosion.

Working with Dr Alexander Denny (Adam Goldberg), the pair use a new technology called 'Snow White' which enables them to see into the past. They discover that the bomber had phoned Claire prior to the explosion. They also learn that Snow White can transmit inanimate objects to the past so Carlin sends a note to his past self, giving the location of the bomber prior to the terrorist incident. Unfortunately things go wrong, and his assistant – Larry Minuti (Matt Craven) – is killed by the terrorist, who then kidnaps Claire and steals her car.

In the present time, the bomber – Carroll Oerstadt (Jim Caviezel) – is arrested, but Doug is unhappy as he is sure he can use Snow White to travel back in time, save Claire and prevent the bombing. No-one is sure if human beings can survive the time transfer process, so Doug sends himself to a hospital emergency room where he is revived.

He races to the shack and prevents Claire's murder, but Oerstadt flees with the bomb. Eventually, all three of them end up on the ferry. Claire is captured, bound and gagged, and is placed in the bomb-carrying car. Doug shoots Oerstadt, but the only way he can prevent the atrocity is to drive the car off the ferry before it explodes. Claire escapes, but Doug is killed in the underwater explosion. She thinks Doug is dead, but then another (present day) Doug approaches her and consoles her.

The film was released on 22nd November 2006 and was moderately successful, making $180.6 million against a budget of $75 million.

Salvage (2006) was an American horror film which was written, directed and produced by Joshua and Jeffrey Crook. It had a budget of just $200,000.

The film opens as Claire (Lauren Currie Lewis) waits to be picked up by her boyfriend, as she has just finished her shift at a store. Her boyfriend's truck turns up, but it is being driven by someone else: a creepy guy called Duke (Chris Ferry). Duke takes her home, but makes a number of inappropriate sexual remarks during the journey before dropping her off. Later he turns up at her door again, claiming that she had dropped an earring. She refuses to let him, in so he drops the earring on the front door and leaves. Claire retrieves the earring, but Duke then breaks in through the back door and murders Claire.

However, Claire recovers consciousness and finds she has travelled back in time as it is now the morning of the day that just ended. This time Claire is driven home by her boyfriend Jimmy (Cody Darbe), but events are continually repeating themselves and she keeps being murdered before awakening at the convenience store. Eventually she realises that she, Duke and Jimmy are all dead. Desmond's soul has been occupying Claire's physical body, and she is reliving events over and over again as a punishment. The film ends with Claire awakening in the convenience store.

The film has an intriguing plot, but not necessarily an original one as it bears a close resemblance to the Amicus film *Tales From the Crypt* (1972) in which various people relate their horrific stories which end in their death. At the conclusion of the film it is revealed that they are all dead and they are actually in Hell.

Salvage only got a limited release, and was issued on DVD as *Gruesome*.

Premonition (2007) is an American supernatural film about a woman called Linda (Sandra Bullock) who experiences the events surrounding her husband's death in a non-chronological order and attempts to save him. The movie was directed by Mennan Yapo and produced by Ashok Amritaj, Jon Jashni, Adam Shankman, Jennifer Gibgot, Sunil Perkash and Nick Hamson. The screenplay was by Bill Kelly.

The film begins as Linda Hanson (Sandra Bullock) listens to an ansaphone message from her husband Jim (Julian McMahon). Sheriff Reilly (Marc MacAulay) then knocks on the door to tell Linda that her husband died in a car accident the previous day. The next day, she finds him sitting on the couch watching TV.

The following day Jim is again dead, and her daughter Bridgette (Courteney Taylor Burness) has scars on her face. Later, following Jim's funeral, Linda is incarcerated in a mental hospital. Her psychiatrist, Dr Roth (Peter Stormare), thinks she may have murdered Jim as she told him that he was dead the day before the accident.

But the next day Linda wakes up and finds Jim alive in the shower. She discovers that he is planning to have an affair with Claire (Amber Valetta), a stranger she saw at Jim's funeral. She concludes that Tuesday is her current day, Wednesday is the accident day and Saturday is the day of the funeral.

Linda tries to change the future. On the Wednesday she calls Jim on his mobile phone and persuades him to turn his car round – but this actually causes the car accident, and he dies. The movie ends with Linda discovering that she is pregnant.

The film premiered on 16th March 2007 and was moderately successful, making $84.1 million against a budget of $20 million. Many critics found the complex storyline very confusing, though.

Timecrimes (2007) was something of a rarity – a Spanish science fiction film, which was written and directed by Nacho Vigalondo and produced by Eduardo Cameros and Jorge Gomez.

The film starts in the Spanish countryside. Hector (Karra Elejalde) and his wife Clara (Candela Fernandez) are renovating their house when they spot a young woman in the forest near the house taking off her T-shirt and exposing her breasts. When Hector investigates and finds the woman lying on the ground, he is stabbed in the arm by a man who has pink bandages on his face.

He is rescued by a scientist (Nacho Vigalondo), who hides him in a machine. But when Hector leaves the device, he finds that he has gone back an hour in time. He sets off in a car and is run off the road by a van. This results in a head wound, which he covers with the bandage from his arm. The bandage turns pink through absorbing the blood.

Hector realises that he is stuck in a time loop with the bandaged stranger being himself at some point in the cycle. Unfortunately, even with the assistance of the scientist, Hector cannot alter what is due to happen and he ends up killing the woman as emergency vehicles arrive.

The film premiered on 20th September 2007 at the Fantastic Fest in the USA, where it won the award for Best Picture. Although it never achieved great commercial success, it has a cult following and an American version – to be directed by David Cronenberg – has been mooted for some time.

Star Trek (2009) was the first of a series of 'rebooted' *Star Trek* films featuring a new, younger cast. As will be recalled, the original *Star Trek* series (1966-68) was originally cancelled and was then resurrected as a series of high-budget movies starting with *Star Trek: The Motion Picture* in 1979. With the ageing of the original cast members, the movies gradually introduced the cast of the more recent TV series *Star Trek: The Next Generation*, and further films and spin-off TV series followed.

In the late 2000s a decision was made to go back to basics and remake the original *Star Trek* TV series as a number of movies with a new and much younger cast. This effectively set the new films in an alternate timeline compared to the original, avoiding continuity problems. For example a wheel-chair-bound character called Captain Christopher Pike appears in the new film. Is this the same Captain Pike who was featured in the 1965 Star Trek pilot *The Cage* and the spin-off 1966 two-parter *The Menagerie*? It is something which is never explained in the new film.

The first of these rebooted films was *Star Trek* in 2009, which starred Chris Pine as James T. Kirk, Zachary Quinto as Commander Spock and Simon Pegg as Engineering Officer Scott. The film was directed by J.J. Abrams, who also co-produced the film along with Daman Lindelof. The screenplay was by Roberto Orci and Alex Kurtzman.

The time travel element in the first of this rebooted film series involves both the villain Nero (Eric Bana) and an elderly Mr Spock (Leonard Nimoy), who both travel back in time 129 years. This results in a scene towards the end of the film in which the older Spock persuades his younger self to contin-ue serving in Starfleet.

The rebooted version of *Star Trek* was very successful, making $385.7 million set against a budget of $150 million, and led to a revived franchise which continues to this day.

Mr Nobody (2009) is a science fiction drama film which was a co-production between Belgium, Canada, France and Germany. It was directed and written by Jaco Van Dormael and produced by Phillipe Godeau. The multi-national cast included Jared Leto, Sarah Polley, Diane Kruger, Linh Dan Pham, Rhys Ifans, Narasha Little, Tonu Regbo and Juno Temple.

The film describes the story of Nemo Nobody (Jared Le-to), who has lived to the age of 118 and is now the last mortal man on Earth as the rest of humanity has achieved immortali-ty. As he looks back on his life, he realises that there were three critical points in his existence at ages nine, fifteen and thirty-four. If he made other decisions at these times in his life then things would have worked out differently.

The film shows how his life would have unfolded in an-other way if different decisions were made, and alternate timelines are presented.

The film had its world premiere at the 66th Venice Inter-national Film Festival, where it received the Golden Osella and Biografilm Lancia Award. It was released on 13th January 2010, and has since become a cult film.

The Time Traveler's Wife (2009) was directed by Robert Schwentke and produced by Nick Wechsler and Dede Gard-ner. The screenplay was by Bruce Joel Rubin, and was based on the best-selling book of the same name by Audrey Niff-enegger. The plot concerns Henry De Tamble (Eric Bana), who has the ability to travel in time as a result of a genetic disorder, and explores the effect this ability has on his relationship with Clare Abshire (Rachel McAdams) who would later become his wife.

The film opens in the early 1970s. Henry De Tamble survives a car accident which kills his mother by travelling back in time two weeks. Henry then finds he can make time jumps to various key points in his life, but cannot alter the future.

In 1991 Henry meets Clare in the library where he works. He has never met her before, but she has encountered his future self when she was a child and was told they would meet again. Henry makes many journeys to the past to meet Clare at different points in her childhood. One problem is that he arrives at his destination naked, so Clare has to have clothes ready (a nod to *The Terminator*).

Eventually the couple marry, but Henry's continuing time jumps put a strain on their relationship. They hope to have a baby, but Henry's genes cause the unborn foetuses to time travel. Henry has a vasectomy, but Clare still gets pregnant as a result of an encounter with an earlier version of her husband. This time the pregnancy is successful, and Henry travels forward to meet his daughter, Alba (Hailey McCann). She can also travel in time though, and has better control of the process, but informs Henry that he will die when she is five. Clare finds out eventually and is devastated by the news.

Later, Henry goes forward in time and is accidentally shot by Clare's father during a hunting trip. He goes back in time and dies in Clare's arms. Clare and Alba subsequently receive visits from a younger Henry, which he hopes will give them closure.

The film was moderately successful, making $101 million at the box office against a budget of $39 million. Reviews were generally positive, though some critics found the plot confusing.

Frequently Asked Questions About Time Travel (2009) is a British comic science fiction film directed by Gareth Carrivick and produced by Neil Peplow and Justin Anderson Smith, with a screenplay by Jamie Mathieson.

Rather unusually for a time travel movie, the action centres round a rather grubby pub and its even grottier toilets. The heroes are three scruffy young British men, the sort of people whom comedian Ben Elton would famously describe as 'blokey blokes'.

The film opens with Ray (Chris O' Dowd) being fired from his job as a guide in a theme park attraction called 'Star Ride'. With two of his friends, Pete (Dean Lennox Kelly) and Toby (Marc Wootton), he goes to his local pub after visiting the cinema.

The trio meet an American girl called Cassie (Anna Faris), who claims to have the ability to travel in time. Peter then goes to the toilet, but when he returns the pub is full of dead bodies. He goes back to the toilet and then flees, only to discover everything is back the way it was.

Over the next few hours, the trio encounter other versions of themselves from different time periods. Cassie eventually reappears in a glowing portal claiming that they only have fourteen hours to save the Earth. All three men enter the portal and leave. After the end credits have played, other later versions of Ray, Pete and Toby appear.

The film premiered on 24th April 2009 and received mixed reviews, with many finding the plot hard to follow.

A Christmas Carol (2009) is an American 3D computer-animated motion capture dark fantasy film written, co-produced and directed by Robert Zemeckis. This classic 1843

Charles Dickens story has been the subject of film adaptations in 1938, 1951, 1970, 1984, 1999 and 2004. There have also been countless variations and made-for-TV versions, including *The Muppet Christmas Carol* (1992).

The plot of *A Christmas Carol* is extremely well-known, so much so that the word 'Scrooge' is often used to describe a person with miserly tendencies. On Christmas Eve 1843, money lender Ebenezer Scrooge (Jim Carrey) reluctantly allows his employee Bob Cratchit (Gary Oldman) to have a day off so he can spend Christmas Day with his family.

Later that evening Scrooge is visited by the ghost of his deceased business partner Jacob Marley (Gary Oldman), who warns Scrooge that he must change his miserly ways or else be condemned to a life of misery in the afterlife.

Scrooge is subsequently visited by three ghosts – the Ghost of Christmas Past, the Ghost of Christmas Present and the Ghost of Christmas Yet to Come. As a result of these experiences, Scrooge realises he must change his ways. He also learns that Bob Cratchit has an ill son, Tiny Tim, who may not survive till next Christmas.

Scrooge is transformed by these experiences and becomes determined to make amends. He gives Cratchit's family a turkey dinner and also attends his nephew's Christmas meal. The next day he gives Cratchit a rise and becomes a second father to Tiny Tim. He has now become a compassionate, generous person.

The film cost a staggering $200 million to make but was only moderately successful, making over $325 million at the worldwide box office.

Land of the Lost (2009) was an American adventure comedy film directed by Brad Siberling and produced by Sid and Marty Krofft and Jimmy Miller. It was based on the 1974

American TV series of the same name by Sid and Marty Krofft, Allan Foshko and David Gerrold.

It starred Will Ferrell, Anna Friel and Danny McBride . Friel is actually English but can do a convincing American accent and has starred in a number of American films and TV series.

The film begins with palaeontologist Dr Rich Marshall (Will Ferrell) expounding on his theories about time warps with doctoral candidate Holly Cantrell (Anna Friel). Marshall is working on a tachyon amplifier which will enable journeys to be made through time. Along with gift shop owner Will Stanton (Danny McBride), the trio test the device and end up stranded in prehistoric times.

The three have a series of adventures in prehistoric times. They encounter various creatures including a race of lizard men called Sleestaks. They must recover the tachyon amplifier to return to the present, but it has been eaten by an Allosaurus and then stolen by a Pteranodon.

After various mishaps, Marshall and Holly make it back to present day Earth while Will chooses to stay behind. Marshall subsequently appears on the TV programme *Today* with a dinosaur egg Holly brought back to promote her new book *Matt Lauer Can Suck It*. The egg left behind on the *Today* set then hatches into a baby Sleestak.

The film premiered on 5 June 2009 but proved to be a box office disaster, making just $68.8 million against a budget of $100 million. It was also savaged by critics and received seven Golden Raspberry Award nominations including Worst Picture.

Triangle (2009) is a British-Australian psychological horror film which was written and directed by Christopher

Smith and produced by Jason Newmark, Julie Baines and Chris Brown.

The plot concerns a single mother named Jess (Melissa George) who goes on a boating trip with several friends. When they have to abandon the yacht, they board a derelict ocean liner and soon realise that someone is stalking them.

The film opens with Jess preparing to take her autistic son Tommy (Joshua McIvor) on a boat trip. Later, she goes on the voyage (on the yacht *Triangle*) without Tommy, but a strange, grey storm cloud appears filled with lightning bolts. (By the way, this strange cloud looks like the 'time storm' in 1980's *The Final Countdown*.) The boat soon capsizes and Jess's friend Heather (Emma Lung) is swept out to sea, while the other people on the trip cling on to the overturned boat.

Eventually the survivors board a passing ocean liner, the *Aeolus,* but all is not well. The ship appears to be of 1930s vintage, with an Art Deco interior and working steam engines. There is fresh food in the dining room but, when the friends go back later, it has rotted. Jess has a feeling of déjà vu and discovers the party is being stalked by a masked shooter intent on killing everyone.

As various strange events unfold, Jess realises that she is trapped in an endlessly repeating time loop in which she herself becomes the masked shooter. At different phases of the loop she is attacked by the shooter and then becomes the murderer. She can see herself walking around the ship and witnesses the arrival of the capsized yacht with the survivors clinging to it, including herself. This endlessly repeating loop results in all the characters having multiple iterations and, at one point, Jess finds about twenty different corpses which all appear to be Sally (Rachael Carpani). Jess concludes that the only way she can escape the ship is by killing everyone on board, including all the different versions of herself.

She succeeds in doing this, and finds herself lying on a beach (which she had dreamed about while on the yacht). Jess then makes her way to her house and sees another version of herself being abusive to her son. She kills this other Jess and puts her in the boot of her car. Then she drives to the marina with her son, but is involved in a car crash which kills him. In a distraught state, she takes a taxi to the harbour and boards the yacht. It is implied that the entire events of the film will now repeat themselves.

The film was made in Queensland, Australia, but is set in Florida. The 'Triangle' of the title (which is also the name of the yacht) is a subtle reference to the Bermuda Triangle, where ships often go missing. The liner *Aeolus* never existed as a real ship, but was created in various ways. The first shots of the ship were achieved with CGI. This gave the ship a 'ghost-like' appearance which was actually appropriate for the movie. A full size wooden mock-up of a large section the *Aeolus* was built on a spit of land which projected into the ocean, and a number of Art Deco interior sets such as the ballroom, theatre and corridors were constructed at Warner Bros. Studios in Queensland.

Triangle (2009): Icon Entertainment International/ Framestore/UK Film Council/Pacific Film and Television/Dan Films/Pictures in Paradise/Triangle Films

Lastly, some scenes (such as the engine and radio rooms) were filmed on board a WW2 vintage River-class frigate HMAS *Diamantina* at the Queensland Maritime Museum.

Interior shots of the liner in the film are very reminiscent of Stanley Kubrick's *The Shining* (1980), and the movie is open to various interpretations. Are the events which are depicted really happening, or is it all a dream? Is Jess going mad? Is she really dead and in some kind of purgatory?

It is a film which has become a cult classic, with many fans coming up with their own interpretations as to what is going on. In this respect, it can be compared with three acclaimed British TV series: *The Prisoner* (1967), *Life on Mars* (2006-07) and *Ashes to Ashes* (2008-10).

Unfortunately the film was a financial disaster, making just $1.6 million set against a budget of $12million. The movie was never released in the USA. Some critics enjoyed the film, though many found the plot hard to follow. However, as described above, it has since acquired a cult following on the Internet.

10
Out of Time
The 2010s

TIME travel has continued to be a popular subject for films in this current decade. *Action Replayy* [sic] (2010) is an Indian science fiction comedy film which is loosely based on *Back to the Future* (1985), although the director Vipul Shah – who also served as producer – has claimed it is an adaptation of a Gujarati play of the same name. The movie's screenplay was written by Suresh Nair and Aatish Kapadia.

The plot concerns Kishen (Akshay Kumar), who is unhappily married to Mala (Aishwarya Rai). Their son Bunty (Aditya Roy Kapoor) is reluctant to marry his girlfriend Tanya (Sudeepa Singh) because of his parents' dysfunctional relationship. Kishen and Mala argue and contemplate divorce. When Bunty learns of this, he goes to visit his friend – the inventor Anthony Gonsalves (Randhir Kapoor) – who has built a time machine. Bunty intends to go back in time to put things right.

He creates a plan to ensure that the younger Mala falls in love with Kishen. Things are complicated, as Kindan (Rannvijay Singh) is also interested in Mala. Thanks to Bunty's actions, his parents do fall in love but their parents disapprove as they believe in arranged marriages. The couple elope, and eventually Bunty get the parents to accept that they belong together. Bunty returns to the present using the time machine and marries Tanya.

The film premiered on 5th November 2010 but (unlike *Back to the Future*) was a box office disaster, making just 480 million rupees against a budget of 600 million rupees. It was also panned by critics.

Hot Tub Time Machine (2010) is an American comedy science fiction film directed by Steve Pink and produced by

***Hot Tub Time Machine* (2010):** Metro-Goldwyn-Mayer Pictures/United Artists/New Crime Productions/Lakeshore Entertainment

John Cusack, Grace Loh, John Morris and Matt Moore. The screenplay was by Josh Heald, Sean Anders and John Morris.

The film opens with three friends – Adam Yates (John Cusack), Nick Webber-Agnew (Craig Robinson) and Lou Dorchen (Rob Corddry) – having a short break at the Kodiak Valley Ski resort, where they are joined by Adam's nephew Jacob (Clark Duke). The four end up in a hot tub where they drunkenly douse its control panel with a strange energy drink called 'Chernobly'. This action has unforeseen consequences, as the quartet end up back in 1986 when they were much younger guests at the resort.

A hot tub repair man (Chevy Chase) arrives and warns them that they must live out the rest of their lives as before to avoid changing history, making exactly the same decisions and mistakes. This proves difficult, and they end up changing their own timelines. Meanwhile, the repairman tells Jacob that the Chernobly was the cause of the time jump.

Jacob, Nick and Adam retrieve the Chernobly and return to 2010 while Lou stays in 1986. When they arrive in 2010, Nick, Jacob and Adam find that Lou has changed history by setting up the very successful company, 'Lougle' (a pun on 'Google'), which has made him wealthy and given him a he-donistic lifestyle with his girlfriend Kelly (Collette Wolfe). Adam is now married to April (Lizzy Caplan), while Nick is an affluent music producer. The four are reunited at Lou's mansion.

The film premiered on 26th March 2010 and received mixed reviews. It performance at the box office ($64.6 million against a budget of $36 million) was deemed sufficient to warrant a 2015 sequel, *Hot Tub Time Machine 2*.

Repeaters (2010) is a Canadian thriller film directed by Carl Bessai and produced by Jason James, Carl Bessai, Richard de Klerk and Irene Nelson. The screenplay was by Anne Olsen. The film describes the experiences of three drug addicts who find themselves in a time loop. In this respect, the film is similar to *Groundhog Day* (1993).

The film begins with three addicts – Kyle (Dustin Milligan), Sonia (Amanda Crew) and Michael (Richard de Klerk) – attending a rehabilitation facility. Things are not going well, and their therapy is not working. Then a storm brews up and the trio are knocked unconscious.

When they wake up, they find it is the morning of that same day. They are stuck in an endlessly repeating time loop. Michael suggests they turn the situation to their advantage, committing various crimes and taking drugs, knowing that there will not be consequences as they will subsequently wake up at the start of the same day. Effectively the trio have become immortal as, even if they die, they will wake up with things the way they were.

Unfortunately Michael abuses his new powers and sexually assualts Michelle (Anja Savcic), leading to an argument with the other two time loopers. Kyle and Sonia subsequently make peace with their own families, which somehow results in the time loop ending for them. Regrettably Michael then becomes even more deranged, killing two people and taking Charlotte (Alexia Fast) hostage. He ends up committing suicide, but finds he is still stuck in a his own time loop, uncertain whether he can break out of it by making peace with his own family.

The film premiered at the Toronto International Film Festival on 13th September 2010 and only received a limited release. Reviews were mixed, with most critics correctly perceiving it as a more serious version of *Groundhog Day*.

Prince of Persia: The Sands of Time (2010) was a high-budget American action fantasy film directed by Mike Newell. It was produced by Jerry Bruckheimer with a screenplay by Boaz Yakin, Doug Miro and Carlo Bernard, based on a story by Jordan Mechner which had been used as the basis of a video game with the same title as the film.

The film is set in ancient Persia. Dastan (Jake Gyllenhaal/William Foster), a former street urchin, is adopted by King Sharaman (Ronald Pickup) and later becomes involved in a Persian army attack on the holy city of Alamut, during which Dastan acquires a sacred dagger.

Princess Tamina (Gemma Arterton) tries to steal the dagger from Dastan, who finds that it enables the wearer to travel in time. Tamina tells Dastan that she is the true guardian of the dagger, which was originally created by the gods. Tamina sacrifices herself and falls to her death to allow Dastan to fight Nizam (Ben Kingsley).

Dastan removes the dagger from a magic sandglass, and time immediately rewinds to the moment he first found the dagger. Nizam tries to kill Dastan but is killed by Tus (Richard Coyle). Dastan returns the dagger to Tamina, and the two get married.

The film premiered on 9th May 2010 and received generally favourable reviews. It was moderately successful, making $336.4 million set against a budget of $200 million. It remains the most successful film to be based on a video game.

Source Code (2011) is an American science fiction thriller directed by Duncan Jones. As is widely known, Jones is the son of the late pop star David Bowie. David Bowie was originally called David Jones, but had to change his name in the mid-sixties to avoid confusion with David ('Davy') Jones of The Monkees. The film was produced by Mark Gordon, Jordan Wynn and Phillipe Rousselet, and written by Ben Ripley.

The movie begins with US Army pilot Captain Colter Stevens (Jake Gylenhaal) waking up on a train heading for Chicago. He is disorientated, but can recall being involved in a mission in Afghanistan. People recognise him as a schoolteacher called Sean Fentress. Suddenly the train explodes.

Stevens regains consciousness inside what looks like an aircraft cockpit. US Air Force Captain Colleen Goodwin (Vera Farmiga) speaks to him by video link. He is inside the 'Source

Code', a machine which allows a subject to experience the last eight minutes of another person's life. He is engaged in a mission to find a train bomber.

Stevens goes back in time on a number of occasions, but cannot identify the bomber or disarm the device. He learns that he lost most of his body in Afghanistan and is in a coma with sensors attached. Only his mind really survives.

Stevens finally identifies the bomber as Derek Frost (Michael Arden), who is subsequently caught. He now wants to be allowed to die, but Rutledge (Jeffrey Wright) reneges on his previous promise to permit this and his mind is wiped so he can carry out further missions.

Stevens goes back to the train using the Source Code. He then deactivates the bomb, overpowers Frost and reports him to the authorities. Later, he starts a romance with his travelling companion Christina (Michelle Monaghan) and they kiss. Unfortunately at this point Goodwin disconnects his life support and Stevens dies, but in his alternate timeline he is still alive and with Christina. The couple complete their journey on the train and then stroll through Chicago to the Cloud Gate.

When the other version of Goodwin in the alternative timeline arrives at Nellis Air Force base she discovers an email from Stevens. It includes a coded message which confirms Stevens' identity and tells Goodwin that history has been changed and the Source Code must therefore work. He asks Goodwin to look after his alternative timeline body, which is still in a coma.

The film was very well received by critics and it was also a commercial success, making $147.3 million set against a budget of $32 million. A made-for-television sequel was scrapped in

2014 in favour of a second film, which is currently in development.

Midnight in Paris (2011) is a fantasy comedy film written and directed by Woody Allen and produced by Letty Aronson, Stephen Tenenbaum and Jaume Roures. It is Allen's second time travel movie, with the first being *Sleeper* (1973).

The film begins in 2010. Hollywood screenwriter Gil Pender (Owen Wilson) and his fiancée Inez (Rachel McAdams) are holidaying in Paris. Gil dreams of writing a novel about a man who works in a nostalgia shop.

One night Gil goes wine tasting and gets drunk. At exactly midnight, a 1920s car pulls up beside him, filled with people from that era. Gil gets in and discovers he has travelled back to that period. He attends a party and meets various celebrities from that era, including Ernest Hemingway who offers to show his novel manuscript to Gertrude Stein (Kathy Bates). As Gil leaves the building to collect his manuscript, he finds he has returned to 2010.

Gil repeats his time travel experience over the next three nights. Stein reads his manuscript. Gil finds himself attracted to Adriana (Marion Cotillard), who is Picasso's lover. When he returns to 2010 he finds her diary in an antique shop and discovers she was in love with him, so he buys her some earrings which he takes back to the 1920s. After he has given Adriana the earrings, the couple go for a walk and enter a horse-drawn carriage which takes them on another time journey – this time to the 19th century. Adriana elects to stay in 1890, while Gil returns to the 1920s.

After retrieving his manuscript and rewriting the first two chapters, he returns to 2010 and confronts Inez, who admits she slept with their friend Paul (Michael Sheen). The couple split up, but then Gil meets a woman called Gabrielle (Lea Seydoux) who shares his love of Paris in the rain.

The film premiered at the Cannes Film Festival on 11th May 2011 and was praised by critics as one of Woody Allen's best pictures. In 2012 the film won an Academy Award for Best Screenplay. It was also a financial success, making $151.1 million at the box office set against a budget of just $17 million.

O Homen do Futuro (The Man from the Future) is a 2011 Brazilian science fiction film directed, written and co-produced by Claudio Torres. The other co-producer was Tatiana Quintella.

The film starts in 2011. Scientist Joao 'Zero' is tormented by an incident twenty years earlier when his then-girlfriend Helena (Alinne Moraes) humiliated him. He builds a time machine and travels back to 1991 where he visits a party and sees his younger self having sex with Helena. Later, he tells his earlier self that he has come from the future to fix things.

Helena's humiliation of him in 1991 had been caused by her drinking drugged champagne provided by her ex, Ricardo (Gabriel Braga Nunes). After this, she had got back with Ricardo and moved to Spain.

The young Joao tells Helena not to drink the champagne. This causes the future Joao to disappear, and the younger version wakes up in an alternate 2011 in which he is rich, but not married. Things have not gone to plan. He has made money as a result of his knowledge of the future, but has been divorced four times.

Joao tries to put things right. He puts on a spacesuit and goes back to 1991. This time he (not Helena) drinks the drugged champagne. He then tells Helena to become a model and meet him in twenty years. The spaceman version of Joao then travels to 2011 and wrecks the time machine, preventing its further use.

Joao then meets Helena and they become a couple again. He is now very wealthy because he had told his colleague and sponsor Sandra (Maria Luiza Mendonca) to invest in Google when he travelled back to 1991. Sandra had re-invested the profits in Joao's company, making him very rich.

Safety Not Guaranteed (2012) is an American science fiction romantic comedy film directed, produced and written by Colin Trevorrow. The co-producers were Marc Turtletaub, Peter Saraf, Stephanie Langhoff and Derek Connolly.

The films begins with a journalist at *Seattle* magazine, Jeff Schwensen (Jake Johnson) discovering a newspaper classified ad in which a person seeks another individual to go back in time with him. Jeff's boss Bridget (Mary Lynn Rajskub) approves of the idea, and two people are assigned to the story – intern Darius Britt (Aubrey Plaza), and a biology student called Arnau (Karan Soni). Jeff has an ulterior motive for participating, as he wants to track down his long-lost love.

The duo find the person behind the ad is grocery store clerk Kenneth Calloway (Mark Duplass), and Darius gains his trust. She tells Kenneth she wants to go back in time to prevent her mother's death while he in turn wants to prevent an accident which killed his girlfriend, Belinda. Jeff tracks down his ex, Liz (Jenica Bergere), but she rejects him. The next morning, Bridget phones Jeff and tells him that Belinda (Kristen Bell) is still alive. The 'accident' that supposedly killed her happened as a result of Kenneth driving his car into the house where she lived with another man.

Darius attempts to confront Kenneth over his lies, but he then claims that Belinda is now alive because he altered the past through a successful time journey. He follows Kenneth out to a small boat on the lake where the time machine is housed. The pair activate the device and vanish. The film ends with a shot of them running through woods, followed by a filmed interview with Kenneth in which he explains why wanted a partner to accompany him on his time travels.

Despite being classed as an 'indie' film, *Safety Not Guaranteed* was well-received by critics. Made on a budget of just $750,000, the film made $4.4 million at the box office.

As the name suggests, *Men in Black 3* (2012) was the third in the series of popular *Men in Black* pictures. For those not in the know, the term 'Men in Black' is part of UFO mythology. People who have seen UFOs are supposedly visited by 'Men in Black' who warn them not to speak publicly about what they have witnessed.

This third MIB picture was directed by Barry Sonnenfeld and produced by Walter F. Parkes and Laurie MacDonald. The screenplay was by Etan Gohen, based on the book *The Men in Black* by Lowell Cunningham.

The film begins in 2012. Alien criminal Boris the Animal, a Boglodite, escapes from prison on the Moon and goes back in time to kill Agent K (Josh Brolin/Tommy Lee Jones) before he can shoot off his left arm and capture him in 1969. Boris succeeds in his mission and, in 2012, Agent J (Will Smith) is concerned at what has happened. Agent O (Emma Thompson/Alice Eve) deduces that the space-time continuum has been fractured. She also knows that K would have been responsible for the deployment of the 'Arc Net' defence system, which would have prevented a Boglodite invasion.

J travels back to 1969 to protect K. They acquire the Arc Net device and intend to attach it to the Apollo 11 rocket (which was launched in July 1969). As they are climbing the rocket's launch tower at Cape Canaveral, they are attacked by both the 1969 and 2012 incarnations of Boris. K manages to shoot off Boris's left arm and knocks him off the tower, while the 2012 Boris is incinerated by the rocket's blast.

Later, K kills Boris on a beach in 1969. J then returns to 2012, and the two partners are reconciled.

The film was hugely successful, making $624 million against a budget of $225 million, and was also well received by critics. A further sequel has been planned, but has not yet been made.

Looper (2012) is an American science fiction film directed and written by Rian Johnson. It was produced by Ram Bergman and James D. Stern.

The plot of the film is based on the idea that in 2074, criminal dispose of bodies by sending them back through time to 2044. They are then killed by a hitman known as a 'looper'. Payment is made via silver bars strapped to their victim. To prevent connections being made to criminal syndicates, a looper's final victim is their future self, and this time payment is made with gold bars.

The story centres on Joe Simmons (Joseph Gordon-Levitt), a 'looper' who is making a fortune from his activities and intends to retire to France. One day, as he is waiting for his next victim in a cornfield, he meets his future self (Bruce Willis). The young Joe is supposed to kill his older self, but he hesitates and his older version escapes.

The only way the young Joe can escape retribution from his boss, Abe (Jeff Daniels), is by killing his older self – a process known as 'closing the loop'. After a series of adventures, young Joe is unable to kill his older self and thus solves the problem by killing himself, thus ensuring that old Joe never exists.

BRUCE WILLIS   JOSEPH GORDON-LEVITT   EMILY BLUNT

HUNTED BY YOUR FUTURE. HAUNTED BY YOUR PAST.

WRITTEN AND DIRECTED BY RIAN JOHNSON

L O O P E R

SEPTEMBER 28

Looper (2012): Endgame Entertainment/DMG Entertainment/FilmDistrict/Ram Bergman Productions/TriStar Pictures

Despite its rather complicated plot, *Looper* performed well at the box office when it was released on 28th September 2012. It made $176.6 million set against a budget of just $30 million, and was warmly received by most critics.

Dimensions (2011) is a low-budget art house movie about time travel which attracted considerable acclaim. It was directed and co-produced by Sloane U'Ren, and written for the screen by Ant Neely who also served as co-producer.

The film tells the story of Stephen (Henry Lloyd-Hughes), who lives in Cambridge in the 1920s. One day he meets a Professor (Patrick Godfrey) who explains that his life would be very different if he was a one- or two-dimensional being. He then explains that – by utilising other dimensions – it may be possible to travel in time.

Sometime later, young Stephen, his cousin Conrad (Sean Heart) and his neighbour Victoria (Hannah Carson) are indulging in some horseplay next to a well. Conrad chucks Victoria's skipping rope down the well. Their nanny then arrives and takes the boys into the house, leaving Victoria to play outside on her own. After a while Victoria decides to climb down the well to retrieve the rope and promptly disappears.

From that point on, Stephen becomes obsessed with travelling back to the past, regardless of its effect on his mental health.

The film never received a widespread release as it was an 'indie' picture. It received its premiere at the Cambridge Film Festival on 21st September 2011. It was subsequently voted Best Film at the 37th Boston Science Fiction Film Festival in 2012 and received the Gort Award. The film also won Best Film at the London Independent Film Festival and Best Film at the Long Island International Film Expo. Sloane U'Ren was also voted Best Director at the same event.

Mine Games (2012) is an American time loop thriller film which was directed by Richard Gray. It was produced by Gray, Mike Gillespie and Christopher Lemole, and written by Gray, Michele Davis-Gray and Ross McQueen.

The film begins with a van arriving at a filling station. There are reports in a local newspaper that an unidentified girl has been found dead in the forest. The van contains seven people – Michael, Lyla, TJ, Claire, Rex, Rose and Guy – who are en-route to a cabin in the woods for a holiday.

The driver, Michael (Joseph Cross), swerves to avoid a waving figure and crashes, wrecking the van, so the group reach the cabin on foot. The group spend the night in the cabin, though Michael has nightmares. The next day the group explore an abandoned mine and lock Michael inside a cell as a prank. This makes him very anxious.

Michael then goes to the crashed van to retrieve his anti-psychotic medication and discovers blood on one wing. After returning to the cabin, the group decide to stay one more day, but Rose (Rebecca De Costa) – who is psychic – has visions of everyone suffering injury and death.

TJ (Alex Meraz) and Lex (Rafi Gavron) explore the mines and find three dead bodies. Two look like themselves, and the third is apparently Guy (Ethan Peck). TJ and Lex then find Claire (Julianna Guill) locked in a cell. She claims Michael was responsible. Hearing this, the group of friends decide to lock Michael in the cell for their own protection.

Michael subsequently escapes from the cell and attacks the others. He kills TJ and Lex, and locks Claire in a cell again. Rose dies from poisoning. Guy and Lyla flee to the main road and flag down a van, which swerves and hits Lyla. Guy realises it is their own van from the night before, and they are all stuck in a time loop.

Guy runs back to the cabin, but is killed by Michael who has realised what is happening. He gives his past self a key to the cell and tells him to burn his anti-psychotic medication. The van then arrives at the filling station and it appears that the cycle is going to restart, but Lyla is still alive and makes her way to the vehicle in the hope that she can break the cycle.

The film premiered at the Melbourne International Film Festival on 16th August 2012. It was not a box office success, being a low-budget 'indie' film. It was panned by critics, with some comparing it to the very similar Australian film *Triangle* (2009), which starred Melissa George.

Haunter (2013) is a Canadian supernatural horror film directed by Vincenzo Natali, produced by Steve Hoban and written by Brian King.

The plot of the film is relatively simple. Lisa Johnson (Abigail Breslin) is dead, but now realises that she still exists as a ghost. Her parents and brother are also deceased, but are unaware of their current spiritual existence and are still stuck in the same day in 1985 when they were murdered.

Lisa discovers that she can make contact with people in other timelines, but she is warned to stop her activities by a pale man. She ignores his threat and makes a psychic connection with Olivia (Eleanor Zichy), who is part of the family living in the house who will become future victims.

Lisa investigates and discovers that a previous resident, Edgar Mullins (Stephen McHattie), is possessing the fathers of all the families who will live in the house in order to ensure that further murders are carried out. Lisa sets out to thwart his plan. First of all, she allows her deceased relatives to realise that they are dead, allowing them to travel to the afterlife while she stays behind to deal with Edgar.

She contacts the spirits of Edgar's past victims, and they help her to defeat him. Mullins ends up being burnt in the furnace which he used to kill his victims. This changes the future, and Lisa wakes up in the physical world with her family alive. She realises that the time loop has been broken.

The film premiered at the South by Southwest film festival on 9th March 2013. It only received a limited cinema release before being issued on home video on 11th February 2014.

I'll Follow You Down (2013) is a Canadian thriller film written and directed by Richie Mehta. It was produced by Lee Kim. Outwith North America, it is known as *Continuum*.

The film begins in 2000. Gabe (Rufus Sewell) – who is a university professor – travels from Toronto to Princeton to attend a conference, but then goes missing. In 2012 his son Erol (Haley Joel Osment) speaks to his grandfather (Victor Garner), who suggests his father's disappearance may have been caused by a time travel experiment.

Erol investigates. As he is a maths genius, he builds a time machine with his grandfather and plans to return to 1946. His girlfriend, Grace (Susanna Fournier), has a miscarriage and his mother Marika (Gillian Anderson) commits suicide as a reaction to her husband's disappearance.

Erol realises he can go back in time and prevent these tragic events. He manages to go back to 1946 and finds his father working with Albert Einstein. But his father is reluctant to return to 2012, even when Erol explains the consequences of his action. Eventually Erol shoots himself in 1946, forcing his father to return to 2012 and put things right.

The film premiered at the Fantasia International Film Festival on 20th June 2014 and only received a limited cinema release.

The A.R.K. Report (2013) is a 32 minute action adventure science fiction film which was produced as a cinema feature with a view to it also being the pilot for a TV series. It was an Israeli-American co-production which was directed by Shmuel Hoffman, produced by Harry Moskoff and written by Asher Crispe, Harry Moskoff and Layla O' Shea.

The plot is similar to *Raiders of the Lost Ark* (1981). In the future, a young woman named Karmi (Katy Castaldi) is determined to prevent the ancient Ark of the Covenant from falling into the hands of criminals. She is approached by Roth (Pascal Yen-Pfister), who works for a secret Government agency. They are determined to find the Ark so they can use it to battle the evil Naarym children's army led by Teemah (Ayden Crispe).

In her quest to locate the Ark, Roth transports Karmi into the future, but – just when she has succeeded – Naarym army agents seize the artefact. Roth returns Karmi to her original time zone and gives her an ancient code book (the A.R.K report of the title) to help her find the relic. Her mission is to locate the Ark and return it to its proper place.

The film received a limited cinema release on 1st January 2013. It won the Gold Remi Award at the Worldfest International Film festival in Houston, Texas, in April 2013.

About Time (2013) is a romantic comedy-drama film about a young man who has an inherited ability to go back in time in order to change his past and bring about a better future. The film was written and directed by Richard Curtis, who is one of Britain's most experienced and respected comedy writers. Curtis originally found fame as one of the writers of the innovative BBC comedy series *Not the Nine O' Clock News* (1979-82), which also launched the careers of Mel Smith, Griff Rhys-Jones, Pamela Stephenson and Rowan Atkinson. One of Curtis's most famous sketches from the show involved a talking gorilla. By the nineties, Curtis had become a renowned writer of film screenplays, and his two most famous movies would be *Four Weddings and a Funeral* (1994) and *Love Actually* (2003).

About Time is a typical Richard Curtis film, as it combines real drama with gentle comedy. The story begins as Tim Lake (Dominic Gleeson) turns twenty-one. He is told by his father (Bill Nighy) that all males in the family have a special gift – they can travel back in time and space to a place they have been before. All they have to do is go into a dark place such as a cupboard, clench their fists and think of where they want to go. Tim decides to use this new-found ability to improve his love life.

He first tries to win over Charlotte (Margot Robbie), but fails because she is not really interested in him. Later, he moves to London and becomes a lawyer. One day he meets Mary (Rachel McAdams), a young American who works for a publishing house. They begin a romance which is enhanced by Tim's ability to go back and correct mistakes, such as saying the wrong thing.

He also helps a playwright, Harry (Tom Hollander), whose opening night is spoiled by an actor forgetting his lines. Tim corrects this through time travel, but in doing so he creates a new timeline in which he never met Mary. Fortunately he is able to meet her again at a party and he persuades her to leave early, thus preventing her from meeting another man who would otherwise become her boyfriend.

Mary and Tim marry and have a child, Posy. But there is a problem as Tim's sister, Kit-Kat (Lydia Wilson) has crashed her car while drunk. Her life is a mess because of her abusive boyfriend, Jimmy (Tom Hughes). But when Tim returns to the present, he finds that Posy has never been born and he has a son instead. He can only help Kit-Kat in the present, not the past. Eventually she settles down with an old friend of Tim's. Mary has a second child, another boy.

Tim's father reveals he has terminal cancer, while Mary becomes pregnant again. Tim goes back in time to visit his father, but he learns that he cannot do this once the baby is born because that would alter the timeline in such a way that his new child had never existed. Tim eventually concludes that the secret to happiness is to live each day just once.

The film was released in the UK on 4th September 2013 and was a critical and commercial success, making $87.1 million at the box office against a budget of just $12million.

11 A.M. (2013) is a South Korean science fiction film directed by Kim Hyun-seok and produced by Lee Jung-seob and Lee Han-seung. It was written for the screen by Lee Seung-hwan.

The plot is fairly simple. In the future, scientists invent a time machine which can transport objects 24 hours ahead in time, but it has never been tested on humans. Inventor Woo-seok decides to carry out a trial run. With his researcher Young-eun (Kim Ok-bin), he travels to the following day at 11.00 a.m. The two time travellers find their experimental facility in chaos, and other researchers have vanished. Using CCTV footage, they have to work out what happened and go back in time to prevent it. The film was released on 28th November 2013, but is largely unknown outside South Korea.

Mr Peabody & Sherman (2014) is an American computer-animated science fiction comedy film based on characters from the *Peabody's Improbable History* segments of the animated television series *The Rocky and Bullwinkle Show* (1959-64). It was directed by Rob Minkoff and produced by Alex Schwatz and Denise Nolan Cascino. The screenplay was by Craig Wright, based on *Peabody's Improbable History* by Ted Key.

The film tells the story of Mr Peabody, an anthropomorphic dog who has adopted a 7 year old human called Sherman who travels through time using a device called WABAC. Peabody is attending school, and realises that many so-called historical facts are untrue as he has visited these eras. During his travels he visits 18th Century France and Ancient Egypt. He also meets Leonardo Da Vinci in 1508 and goes back to the Trojan War in 1184 BC.

Unfortunately Peabody's travels cause a rip in the space-time continuum, but Sherman suggests they can fix the damage by travelling into the future. Eventually normality is restored and Sherman returns to school.

The film proved very successful, making $275 million set against a budget of $145 million, and resulted in a TV series – *The Mr Peabody & Sherman Show* – which premiered on Netflix on 9th October 2015.

X-Men: Days of Future Past (2014) is a superhero film based on the Marvel Comics' *X-Men* series. It is the seventh film in the series, and incorporates a time travel element as Wolverine (Hugh Jackman) travels back to 1973 to change history. It was directed by Bryan Singer, produced by Lauren Shuler Donner, Simon Kinberg and Hutch Parker, and had a screenplay by Simon Kinberg.

The film begins in 2023. Bishop (Omar Sy) is sent back in time by Kitty Pryde (Ellen Page) to warn other mutants that Sentinel robots are hunting them down. Wolverine (Hugh Jackman) is then sent back to 1973. He discovers that Erik Lensherr (Michael Fassbender) had been wrongly jailed for his role in the assassination of John F. Kennedy in 1963 and busts him out of jail. Later, Trask (Peter Dinklage) persuades President Richard Nixon to start the Sentinel programme.

In the future, the Sentinels attack the X-Men, while back in 1973 Xavier convinces Mystique to spare Traska after she saves President Nixon from Erik, thus altering history by ensuring the Sentinels are never made. Erik and Mystique leave, and Trask is jailed for trying to steal US military secrets. Wolverine wakes up in 2023 and finds all the other mutants are alive.

The film premiered on 10th May 2014 and was very successful, making $747.9 million at the box office against a budget of $200 million.

Edge of Tomorrow (2014) is an American science fiction film which was directed by Doug Liman. It was produced by Erwin Stoff, Tom Lassally, Jeffrey Silver, Gregory Jacobs and Jason Hoffs. The screenplay was by Christopher McQuarrie, Jez Butterworth and John-Henry Butterworth, and was based on the Japanese novel *All You Need is Kill* by Hiroshi Sakurazaka.

The film has an intriguing plot. In 2015 the Earth is under attack from an alien race called the Mimics, who start their assault on Europe through Germany. The United Defence Force (UDF) is created to fight the invaders. Major William Cage (Tom Cruise) – who is a Public Relations expert, not a fighting soldier – is demoted to Private, and forced to take part in a D-Day style assault on the French coast. The attack is a disaster and Cage is killed, but he finds himself back at the UDF base at Heathrow Airport and discovers he is in a time loop which enables him to improve his fighting skills.

He becomes acquainted with Sergeant Rita Vrataski (Emily Blunt), and learns that his ability to time loop has come about because he has been exposed to alien blood. The ordinary alien foot-soldiers are the Alpha but are controlled by the Omega, and Cage must kill this particular alien to win the war.

After a series of time loop adventures – during which he gradually enhances his soldiering skills – Cage is wounded and receives a blood transfusion, which makes him lose his ability to travel in time. Vrataski is killed, but Cage manages to kill the Omega with a belt of grenades. As Cage dies, he is again exposed to the Omega's blood, which restores his ability to time loop. He is taken back to his first meeting with General Brigham (Dominic Gleeson) at Heathrow. The alien menace has now been defeated, and he is reunited with Vrataski who is now alive again because of the time loop.

The film was released on 30th May 2014 and was a box office success, making $370.5 million set against a budget of $178 million. It received considerable critical acclaim and a sequel, *Live Die Repeat and Repeat*, is in development.

Predestination (2014) is an Australian science fiction thriller directed by the Spierig brothers, who also served as co-producers and screenwriters. The other producers were Tim McGahan and Paddy McDonald. The film was based on the 1959 novel *All You Zombies* by respected science fiction writer Robert A. Heinlein.

The film begins with a time travelling agent (Ethan Hawke) attempting to disarm a bomb placed by the 'Fizzle Bomber' in 1975. It explodes, and the agent travels to the future for reconstructive plastic surgery. He is then sent to 1970 New York where he meets a man called John (Sarah Snook) in a bar. She was born as 'Jane', but was subsequently discovered to be intersex when she fell pregnant and required a Caeserean section. As a result, surgeons discovered she had internalised male sex organs as well as external female sex organs. She now lived as 'John' and writes fiction under the pen name 'The Unmarried Mother'.

The time agent offers John a deal. He will take John back to 1963 and help them to get revenge on their former lover. Eventually the agent realises that John/Jane, their lover and the baby are all the same person, in what he terms a 'predestination paradox'. There are further plot complications, and eventually the time agent realises that the 'Fizzle Bomber' is his future self. He kills the criminal, and the film concludes in 1975 as the agent finally reveals that John, Jane, the 'Fizzle Bomber' and himself are all the same person but in different times.

The film was released in Australia on 28th August 2014. It performed poorly at the box office, making just $4.3 million. Although popular with science fiction fans, many critics found the plot hard to follow.

Premature (2014) is an American sex comedy film which features a time loop plot. It was directed by Dan Beers and produced by Aaron Ryder and Karen Lunder. The screenplay was by Beers and Mathew Harawitz.

Rob Crabbe (John Cama) is a typical American teenager who has wet dreams. One day his mother walks into his bedroom, sees his semen-stained sheets and tells him to wash them. Later that day he has an interview for admission to Georgetown University, during which one of the interviewers, Jack Roth (Alan Tudyk), bursts into tears because his wife died recently. He is having a bad day, and things aren't helped when his crotch is squirted by a water pistol and he is involved in a road traffic accident.

One of his classmates, Angela (Carlson Young), fancies him and – during a heavy petting session – he ejaculates and finds himself back in his bedroom as his mother walks in. He is caught in a time loop which is triggered by his own ejaculation. From that point on, Rob lives the same day over and over again and becomes more reckless. He drives a golf cart through the school, smokes pot and touches a teacher's breasts, but he is unable to break out of the time loop.

Eventually Rob realises that he really loves Gabrielle (Katie Findlay). The two become an item and have sex. Although Rob suffers from premature ejaculation when they sleep together, he is no longer stuck in a time loop.

The film was released on 2nd July 2014 and was panned by critics as it was perceived as a rip-off of *Groundhog Day* with added teenage sex. It made only \$5 million at the box office, although this was five times its budget.

Project Almanac (2015) is an American science fiction film directed by Dean Israelite. One of the three producers was Michael Bay, who is usually associated with blockbusters (he directed 2001's *Pearl Harbor*). On this occasion his two co-producers were Bradley Fuller and Andrew Form. The screenplay was written by Jason Harry Pagan and Andrew Deutschman, and concerns a group of high school students who build a time machine.

The plot begins in 2014 as David Raskin (Jonny Weston) enrols at Massachusetts Institute of Technology. He can't afford the fees, so he looks through his late inventor father Ben's belongings in search of something which may help him get a scholarship. He finds a video camera containing a recording of his seventh birthday party, and sees the reflection of his seventeen-year-old self in the recording.

David and his friends search the basement and find plans for a time machine called Project Almanac. They build a working apparatus from the blueprints and travel back in time. Unfortunately their time experiments have unintended consequences, including a plane crash, and Adam (Allen Evangelista) ending up in hospital after being run over.

David makes repeated trips to the past to try and put events right, but things keep going wrong and he ends up accidentally erasing his girlfriend Jessie (Sofia Black-D'Elia) from existence. He decides the only answer is to go back in time and stop the machine being built. Unfortunately the apparatus is short of hydrogen and, when he returns to the present, he is chased by police who suspect him of murdering Jessie. As the police are closing in on him, he obtains some hydrogen and goes back to his seventh birthday where he meets his father.

David destroys the machine and the blueprints, erasing himself from existence. Unfortunately the video camera containing the footage survives and is found by David and Christina (Virginia Gardner) in an alternative future timeline. Later, at their school, David approaches Jessie and suggests building the time machine, implying that the whole series of events is going to start again.

The film was released on 30th January 2015 and made $33.2 million at the box office against a budget of $12 million. It received mainly negative reviews.

Hot Tub Time Machine 2 (2015) was a sequel to the 2010 film *Hot Tub Time Machine* and featured all of the original cast, except for John Cusack who only makes a cameo appearance. The film was directed by Steve Pink, produced by Andrew Panay and written by Josh Heald.

The film is set in 2015. Lou Dorchen (Rob Corddry) is a billionaire while Nick Webber (Craig Robinson) is a famous singer. When Lou is shot at a party, his son Jacob (Clark Duke) and Nick take him to the hot tub time machine in the hope they can send him back in time and locate the killer. Unfortunately they all end up ten years in the future in an alternate timeline.

Lou suspects that Gary Winkle (Jason D. Jones), his archenemy, is the killer. Jacob gets drunk at Gary's club and tries to kill himself by jumping off a high building. Lou stops him. The son of their friend Adam Yates, Adam Junior (Adam Scott), acquires some nitrotrinadium – the ingredient which makes time travel possible – and journeys into the past. Multiple Lous have now been created, and one of them kills the 2015 version of Lou. As the closing credits roll, the group use the time machine to change history.

The film was released on 20th February 2015 but was not a success, making just $13.1 million set against a budget of $18 million. Critics were withering in their reception of the movie.

Synchronicity (2015) is an American science fiction film written and directed by Jacob Gentry and produced by Christopher Alender and Alexander Motlagh.

The film begins with physicist Jim Beale (Chad McKnight) working with two colleagues – Chuck (A.J. Bowen) and Matt (Scott Poythress) – to build a time machine. The device works by creating wormholes and requires isotopes provided by KMC, a company owned by Klaus Meisner (Michael Ironside).

The process is dangerous and the first test is inconclusive, although Beale receives a Dahlia flower from the wormhole. More isotopes are needed to complete the tests, but Meisner wants a greater share of ownership. Beale starts a relationship with Abby Ross (Brianne Davis), but she is passing on information to Meisner.

When Beale learns this, he is upset and jumps into the wormhole. He goes back to the time of the first test, but has ended up in a parallel timeline. His alternative universe equivalent is called Jim Prime. Eventually Beale withers away and dies, and only Prime is left. He meets Abby, who reveals she is writing a novel about a physicist called 'John Bain' who died in a laboratory explosion.

Synchronicity (2015): Soapbox Films/POP Films

Synchronicity premiered at the Fantasia International Film Festival on 22nd July 2015. It only had a limited cinema release before being made available on video-on-demand and Apple iTunes in January 2016.

Indru Netru Naalai (2015) is an Indian science fiction comedy film which was written and directed by R. Ravikumar. It was produced by C.V. Kumar and K.E. Gnanavel Rana.

The film begins in 2065 as a scientist (Arya) sends a proto-type time machine back to 2015. It fails to return. The device ends up in the hands of Parthasarathy (K.T. Karthik), but he receives an electric shock which leaves him comatose and the apparatus is stolen by Elango (Vishnu Vishnal) and Arumu-gam (Karunakaran). The duo use the machine to help Ar-umugan's astrology business by going back in time to find lost objects. Elando also uses the device to make money on the stock market.

Elango and Arumugan become involved with gangster Ku-zhandaivelu (P. Ravi Shankar) who shoots the machine, dam-aging it. Parthasarathy manages to fix the apparatus, and Elango marries Anu (Miya) while the machine returns to 2065.

The film is little-known outside India, but received positive reviews from critics.

ARQ (2016) is an American-Canadian 'time loop' film di-rected and written by Tony Elliott. It was produced by John Finemorea, Kyle Franke, Mason Novick and Nick Spicer.

The film begins with Renton (Robbie Arnell) waking up beside his former lover Hannah (Rachael Taylor). Three men, led by Father (Gray Powell), burst into the room. Renton breaks his neck and then wakes up, finding that he has gone back in time a few minutes. The intruders appear again and tie the two of them to chairs.

The pair work their way loose as the gang eat next door. Renton reveals he has built a perpetual motion machine, the ARQ, while working for Torus. Renton tries to escape, but when he wakes up again he urges Hannah to kill the gang with cyanide gas. But Hanna is actually a gang member and betrays him. Gang member Sonny (Shaun Benson) shoots him.

The time loop repeats itself with different people being killed each time. Renton realises the ARQ is causing the time loops and the cycle will repeat endlessly. Finally, a robot appears and kills them, and Hannah wakes up once more. It is implied that the loop will continue indefinitely.

The film had its premiere at the Toronto International Film Festival on 9th September 2016. It received favourable reviews from critics, who praised what had been achieved on a limited budget of about $2 million.

Happy Death Day (2017) is an American 'time loop slasher film' which was directed by Christopher Landon, produced by Jason Blum and written by Scott Lobdell. It tells the story of a college student who is killed on her birthday, enters a time loop, and vows to find her killer and prevent her own murder.

The film begins with university student Theresa 'Tree' Gelbman waking up on her birthday in the dorm room of her classmate Carter Davis (Israel Broussard). Her life is complicated, as she is having an affair with a married professor named Gregory Butler (Charles Aitken). That night she is murdered by a killer wearing a baby mask, but wakes up again the next morning in Carter's bed.

Tree realises she is in a time loop and that she can avoid getting murdered. But the killer simply follows her to a party and kills her again. On the next loop she barricades herself into her room, but the killer is already there and slays her.

Over many loop cycles Tree tries to identify her killer. She and Carter suspect John Tombs (Rob Mello), a known serial killer who is supposedly being held in a mental hospital. Tree rushes to the hospital to warn staff of his imminent escape. Tombs murders Carter, and Tree is about to kill Tombs when she realises that if she ends the loop there, Carter will remain dead. Thus she hangs herself.

On the next cycle of the loop, Tree tracks down Tombs and kills him. When she wakes up the next day, she discovers that Lori (Ruby Modine) was really behind the murders. She was also having an affair with Butler, and had attempted to kill Tree with a poisoned cupcake. Lori had also framed Tombs for the murders. Tree shoves the poisoned cupcake into her mouth and kicks her out the window. She dies. The next morning, when Tree awakens, she finds she has broken out of the time loop.

The film was released on 13th October 2017 and was well-received by critics, even though it was acknowledged that it was really a cross between *Groundhog Day* and *Scream* (1997). It was also very successful. Although it was made on a budget of just $4.8 million, it made $122.6 million at the box office. As a result, a sequel – *Happy Death Day 2U* – was scheduled for release in February 2019.

The most recent time travel movie at the time of writing is *A Wrinkle in Time* (2018), which was produced by Walt Disney Pictures and Whitaker Entertainment and tells the story of a young girl who sets out on a quest to find her missing father with the help of three astral travellers. The movie was directed by Ava Du Vernay and was produced by Jim Whitaker and Catherine Hand. The screenplay was by Jennifer Lee and Jeff Stockwell, and was based on *A Wrinkle in Time* by Madeleine L'Engle.

The film opens with thirteen-year-old Meg Murry (Storm Reid) trying to come to terms with the death of her father Alex (Chris Pine). Both Meg and her mother Kate (Gugu Mbatha-Raw) believe he had been teleported to another world.

They subsequently meet Mrs Whatsit (Reece Witherspoon) – who claims Alex had discovered a type of time travel called tesseract – and two other 'astral travellers' called Mrs Who (Mindy Kaling) and Mrs Which (Oprah Winfrey). They all travel to the planet of Uriel using tesseract, and then make a jump to another planet where the Happy Medium (Zach Galifinakis) lives.

The Happy Medium reveals that Alex is trapped on a planet called Camazotz. This is also the homeworld of the IT, which represent all negative tendencies found on Earth. The three astral travellers want to return to Earth, but Meg redirects everyone to Camazotz. The travellers cannot stay on Camazotz, but give Meg special powers to assist her. After a series of adventures Meg returns to Earth, having freed her father.

The film premiered on 26th February 2018 but subsequently bombed at the box office, making only $132 million against a budget of $130 million. The marketing budget for the film was $150 million, so this was a serious loss. Reviews were mixed, with many critics slating the poor CGI and many plot holes.

Time travel films continue to fascinate audiences, and given their perennial popularity it seems unlikely that their appeal will wane in the years ahead. Movies in this genre have produced some of the most memorable science fiction features of the last few decades, and the captivating concepts behind changing the decisions of our past or interacting with the future remain as engaging now as they have always been. But as to the ways in which the past and present of this category of film will inform its future... well, only time will tell!

About the Author

Image by kind permission of Bo'ness Motor Museum.

Dr Colin M. Barron was born in Greenock, Scotland in 1956, and was educated at Greenock Academy (1961-74) and Glasgow University (1974-79) where he graduated in Medicine (M.B. Ch.B.) in 1979. He worked for the next five years in hospital medicine, eventually becoming a Registrar in Ophthalmology at Gartnavel General Hospital and Glasgow Eye Infirmary.

In December 1984 he left the National Health Service to set up Ashlea Nursing Home in Callander, which he established with his first wife Sandra and ran until 1999. He was the chairman of the Scottish branch of the British Federation of Care Home Proprietors (BFCHP) from 1985 to 1991, and then a founding member and chairman of the Scottish Association of Care Home Owners (SACHO) from 1991 to 1999.

Colin has a special interest in writing – his first non-fiction book *Running Your Own Private Residential and Nursing Home* was published by Jessica Kingsley Publishers in 1990. He has also written around 150 articles for various publications including *This Caring Business*, *The Glasgow Herald*, *Caring Times*, *Care Weekly*, *The British Medical Journal*, *The Hypnotherapist*, *The Thought Field* and many others. He was a regular columnist for *This Caring Business* between 1991 and 1999.

Colin has always had a special interest in hypnosis and alternative medicine. In 1999 he completed a one-year Diploma course in hypnotherapy and neuro-linguistic programming with the British Society of Clinical and Medical Ericksonian Hypnosis (BSCMEH), an organisation created by Stephen Brooks who was the first person in the UK to teach Ericksonian Hypnosis. He has also trained with the British Society of Medical and Dental Hypnosis (BSMDH) and with Valerie Austin, who is a top Harley Street hypnotherapist. Colin is also a licensed NLP practitioner. In 1992 he was made a Fellow of the Royal Society of Health (FRSH). He is a former member of various societies including the British Society of Medical and Dental Hypnosis - Scotland (BSMDH), the British Thought Field Therapy Association (BTFTA), the Association for Thought Field Therapy (ATFT), the British Complementary Medicine Association (BCMA), and the Hypnotherapy Association.

Colin has been using TFT since early in 2000, and in November 2001 he became the first British person to qualify as a Voice Technology TFT practitioner. He used to work from home in Dunblane and at the Glasgow Nuffield Hospital.

Colin has also had 40 years of experience in public speaking, and did some training with the John May School of Public Speaking in London in January 1990.

In May 2011 his wife Vivien, then 55, collapsed at home due to a massive stroke. Colin then became his wife's carer but continued to see a few hypnotherapy and TFT clients. In late July 2015 Colin suffered a very severe heart attack and was rushed to hospital. Investigation showed that he had suffered a rare and very serious complication of myocardial infarction known as a ventricular septal defect (VSD) - effectively a large hole between the two main pumping chambers of the heart.

Colin had open heart surgery to repair the defect in August 2015, but this first operation was unsuccessful and a second procedure had to be carried out three months later. On 30th November he was finally discharged home after spending four months in hospital.

As a result of his wife's care needs and his own health problems Colin closed down his hypnotherapy and TFT business in April 2016 to concentrate on writing books and looking after his wife.

Colin's books for Extremis Publishing include *The Craft of Public Speaking* (2016), *Planes on Film: Ten Favourite Aviation Films* (2016), *Dying Harder: Action Movies of the 1980s* (2017), *Battles on Screen: World War II Action Movies* (2017), and *Victories at Sea: In Films and TV* (2018).

His interests include walking, cycling, military history, aviation, plastic modelling, and reading.

For more details about Colin and his work, please visit his website at: **www.colinbarron.co.uk**

Battles on Screen
World War II Action Movies

By Colin M. Barron

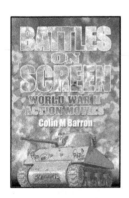

The Second World War was one of the defining historical events of the Twentieth Century. This global conflict was responsible for enormous trials and great heroism, and the horrors and gallantry that it inspired has formed the basis of some of the most striking movies ever committed to celluloid.

From the author of *Planes on Film*, *Battles on Screen* offers both an analysis and celebration of cinema's engagement with World War II, discussing the actors, the locations, the vehicles and the production teams responsible for bringing these epics to life. Reaching across the decades, the impact and effectiveness of many classic war films are examined in detail, complete with full listings of their cast and crew.

Ranging from the real–life figures and historical events which lay behind many of these features to the behind-the-scenes challenges which confronted the film crews at the time of their production, *Battles on Screen* contains facts, statistics and critical commentary to satisfy even the most stalwart fan of the war movie genre.

Planes on Film
Ten Favourite Aviation Films

By Colin M. Barron

One of the most durable genres in cinema, the aviation film has captivated audiences for decades with tales of heroism, bravery and overcoming seemingly insurmountable odds. Some of these movies have become national icons, achieving critical and commercial success when first released in cinemas and still attracting new audiences today.

In *Planes on Film: Ten Favourite Aviation Films*, Colin M. Barron reveals many little-known facts about the making of several aviation epics. Every movie is discussed in comprehensive detail, including a thorough analysis of the action and a complete listing of all the aircraft involved. With information about where the various planes were obtained from and their current location, the book also explores the subject of aviation films which were proposed but ultimately never saw the light of day.

With illustrations and meticulous factual commentary, *Planes on Film* is a book which will appeal to aviation enthusiasts, military historians and anyone who has an interest in cinema. Written by an author with a lifelong passion for aircraft and their depiction on the silver screen, *Planes on Film* presents a lively and thought-provoking discourse on a carefully-chosen selection of movies which have been drawn from right across the history of this fascinating cinematic genre.

Dying Harder
Action Movies of the 1980s

By Colin M. Barron

The 1980s were a golden age for action movies, with the genre proving popular at the box-office as never before. Across the world, stars such as Sylvester Stallone, Arnold Schwarzenegger and Bruce Willis were becoming household names as a result of their appearances in some of the best-known films of the decade.

But what were the stories which lay behind the making of these movies? Why were the eighties to bear witness to so many truly iconic action features? And who were the people who brought these legends of action cinema to life?

In *Dying Harder: Action Movies of the 1980s*, Colin M. Barron considers some of the most unforgettable movies of the decade, exploring the reasons behind their success and assessing the extent of their enduring acclaim amongst audiences which continues into the present day.

The Craft of Public Speaking

By Colin M. Barron

Public speaking is one of the most important skills in personal and professional life. Yet too often this key ability is neglected, leading to presentations which are dull, uninspired and poorly delivered.

The Craft of Public Speaking examines some of the crucial aptitudes which are fundamental to delivering an effective presentation for listeners. These include preparation, structure and rehearsal, in addition to some of the more overlooked aspects of oration such as the use of visual aids, adding humour, and dressing for success. As well as discussing how to deliver effective live addresses in public settings, the book also covers interview techniques for TV and radio along with how to organise seminars and conferences.

Dr Colin M. Barron has delivered hundreds of lectures and presentations to audiences during a long career, giving speeches on a wide variety of different subjects over many years. In *The Craft of Public Speaking*, he shares the essential knowledge that you will need to become a truly successful public speaker.

Also Available from Extremis Publishing

Victories at Sea
In Films and TV

By Colin M. Barron

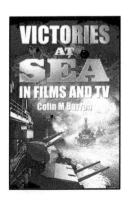

Naval battles have inspired countless films and television dramas over the years, recounting the bravery and tragedy that have unfolded over centuries of conflict on the high seas. From the author of *Planes on Film* and *Battles on Screen*, this book examines some of the most exciting features that have dealt with naval warfare, exploring the ways in which they have achieved critical success and enduring popularity with audiences.

Victories at Sea considers the many different aspects of warfare on (and below) the waves as they have been depicted on screen, discussing such topics as amphibious operations, carrier warfare, underwater sabotage, and Cold War strategies. Covering films ranging from vintage World War II classics to modern seaborne thrillers, the book investigates the real-life stories which lay behind the production of these features as well as how they eventually came to be received at the box-office.

From blockbuster Hollywood epics to must-see television series, *Victories at Sea* is a comprehensive guide to the greats of the genre, combining a forensic eye for detail with meticulous analysis of the features under discussion. With discussion of low-budget dramas and high-octane action movies alike, this examination of naval warfare on the big and small screens relates all of the exhilaration and gallantry that have made these films such lasting favourites amongst cinema and TV aficionados.

Also Available from Extremis Publishing

A Righteously Awesome Eighties Christmas
Festive Cinema of the 1980s

By Thomas A. Christie

The cinema of the festive season has blazed a trail through the world of film-making for more than a century, ranging from silent movies to the latest CGI features. From the author of *The Christmas Movie Book*, this new text explores the different narrative themes which emerged in the genre over the course of the 1980s, considering the developments which have helped to make the Christmas films of that decade amongst the most fascinating and engaging motion pictures in the history of festive movie production.

Released against the backdrop of a turbulent and rapidly-changing world, the Christmas films of the 1980s celebrated traditions and challenged assumptions in equal measure. With warm nostalgia colliding with aggressive modernity as never before, the eighties saw the movies of the holiday season being deconstructed and reconfigured to remain relevant in an age of cynicism and innovation.

Whether exploring comedy, drama, horror or fantasy, Christmas cinema has an unparalleled capacity to attract and inspire audiences. With a discussion ranging from the best-known titles to some of the most obscure, *A Righteously Awesome Eighties Christmas* examines the ways in which the Christmas motion pictures of the 1980s fit into the wider context of this captivating and ever-evolving genre.

Contested Mindscapes

**Exploring Approaches to
Dementia in Modern
Popular Culture**

By Thomas A. Christie

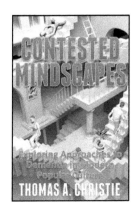

Dementia is a mental health condition which affects an estimated 50 million people worldwide. Yet it has, until recently, been an unfairly neglected subject in popular culture.

Contested Mindscapes considers the ways in which the arts have engaged with dementia over the past twenty years, looking at particular examples drawn from the disciplines of film and television, popular music, performance art, and interactive entertainment.

Examining a variety of creative approaches ranging from the thought-provoking to the controversial, *Contested Mindscapes* carefully contemplates the many ways in which the humanities and entertainment industries have engaged with dementia, exploring how the wide-ranging implications of this complex condition have been communicated through a variety of artistic nodes.

For details of new and forthcoming books
from Extremis Publishing,
please visit our official website at:

www.extremispublishing.com

or follow us on social media at:

www.facebook.com/extremispublishing

www.linkedin.com/company/extremis-publishing-ltd-/

Lightning Source UK Ltd.
Milton Keynes UK
UKHW021351071220
374769UK00016B/1488